TEACHER RESEARCH AND SCHOOL IMPROVEMENT

TEACHER RESEARCH AND SCHOOL IMPROVEMENT
Opening doors from the inside

Edited by **Rob Halsall**

OPEN UNIVERSITY PRESS
Buckingham · Philadelphia

Open University Press
Celtic Court
22 Ballmoor
Buckingham
MK18 1XW

and
1900 Frost Road, Suite 101
Bristol, PA 19007, USA

First Published 1998

A catalogue record of this book is available from the British Library

ISBN   0 335 19952 6 (pb)   0 335 19953 4 (hb)

Library of Congress Cataloging-in-Publication Data
Teacher research and school improvement : opening doors from the
   inside / edited by Rob Halsall.
        p.   cm.
   Includes bibliographical references and index.
   ISBN 0-335-19953-4 (hardcover). — ISBN 0-335-19952-6 (pbk.)
   1. School improvement programs—United States—Case studies.
   2. Action research in education—United States—Case studies.
   I. Halsall, Rob.
   LB2822.82. T43   1997
   371.2′00973—dc21   97-23229
                                                                  CIP

Typeset by Graphicraft Typesetters Ltd, Hong Kong
Printed in Great Britain by St Edmundsbury Press Ltd,
Bury St Edmunds, Suffolk

Contents

List of contributors

Michael Bassey is Emeritus Professor of Education, Nottingham Trent University and part-time Research Fellow, Didsbury School of Education at the Manchester Metropolitan University (MMU).

Kevin Brain is Research worker at Manchester Victoria University, formerly Research Assistant, Didsbury School of Education, MMU.

Karen Carter is Senior Lecturer in Education Management, Didsbury School of Education, MMU.

Mike Cockett is Research Fellow, Didsbury School of Education, MMU. Formerly Manchester LEA Inspector, TVEI coordinator and LAP project co-ordinator.

Mary Connery is a member of Manchester Education – Business Partnership, formerly careers teacher and truancy project coordinator in a Manchester high school.

Patricia Donald, Susan Gosling and Jean Hamilton are all primary school teachers involved in the Scottish Central Region's teacher research network.

Jan Green is Senior Lecturer in Sciences Education, Didsbury School of Education, MMU.

Rob Halsall is Principal Lecturer, Didsbury School of Education, MMU.

Karen Hanks is Head of the Humanities Faculty in a Tameside high school.

Jill Richford is Special Needs coordinator, Wright Robinson High School, Manchester.

Rosemary Rodger is Senior Lecturer in Early Years Education, Didsbury School of Education, MMU.

Ian Stronach is Research Professor of Education, MMU.

Tim Whitwell is Learning Support teacher, Wright Robinson High School, Manchester.

Preface

It is possible to observe in several countries throughout the world a theme of teachers being agents of change through their engagement in research activity. In the UK this dates back to the 1960s and 1970s, to the work of Lawrence Stenhouse and his colleagues on the Humanities Curriculum Project, and then John Elliott and his colleagues on the Ford Teaching Project. The theme has never been lost sight of since those years but it demands an even greater visibility today.

The fact is that in many parts of the world, the teaching profession and educationalists generally have been under attack for a decade and more. The charge has been levelled that schools have failed to meet nations' needs and expectations. This has been accompanied by narrow prescriptions from policy makers on what should be taught, increasing pressure on how the curriculum should be taught, schemes for school self-evaluation, teacher appraisal, school development planning, league tables of performance, and tighter prescriptions concerning the focus of the inservice education of teachers. These reflect a school effectiveness and improvement agenda dominated by a mechanistic performance management approach which, in large part, has sidelined the teachers themselves.

However, Hopkins, in the UK (1993), suggests that some of the imposed initiatives can actually combine to form an infrastructure at the school level to support the management of change. Moreover, both he and Berlin, in the US (1990), suggest that at the intersection of many of these developments lies the potential for a teacher-as-researcher model which can represent 'a direct response to the social, political and cultural moment' (Berlin 1990: 9). This book argues that there is a need for teachers themselves to become more directly involved as contributors to effectiveness and improvement work, and presents a particular case for, and examples of, the role of teacher research in this. It is offered, then, as a contribution to the debate on why the model of teacher-as-researcher is a necessary response to the 'moment', and how it can be employed as a powerful strategy in efforts to improve schools for the benefit of our children.

A note on our choice of words

Although the context and theme of the book have an international dimension, it is rooted in the UK experience in particular. Our choice of words reflects this. The following list is intended to be helpful in orienting the reader to that choice:

Our choice	*Alternatives*
students, children	pupils
head	headteacher, principal
local education authority	district, school board
governing body	school (advisory) council
primary school	elementary school
secondary education	high school education
teacher appraisal	teacher evaluation
senior management team, senior managers	school administrators

Part I

The case for teacher
research as a strategy
for school improvement

1

School effectiveness and school improvement: meanings and traditions

Karen Carter

At a time when school effectiveness and school improvement are considered to be 'flavour of the month' there is a case to be made for addressing teachers' perspectives of these terms and their understanding and interpretation of the findings which have emanated from both school effectiveness research (SER) and school improvement research (SIR). The rationale for taking such an approach is based upon a strong commitment to the need to acknowledge teachers themselves as taking centre stage as key players in the current debate which surrounds SER and SIR and the possible future of the two traditions. In exploring the multiplicity and accessibility of the meanings of the terms 'effectiveness' and 'improvement', attention will, therefore, be given not just to the established meanings put forward by the academic research community, but to other possible interpretations of the terms from the standpoint of the practising classroom teacher. I will consider the ways in which teachers are currently making sense of SER and SIR outcomes, and the impact their interpretations might have upon their willingness to engage in any committed sense to what might be perceived to be an externally imposed agenda for school, teacher and student development. The issue of teacher ownership of school effectiveness concerns and school improvement strategies is presented as a key point within this discussion.

The approach adopted throughout this chapter, therefore, places an emphasis upon a belief that 'Educators, themselves, are the fundamental backbone of school improvement' (Stoll 1996: 53). In exploring this theme there are a number of constraining factors, however, which necessarily have to be accounted for and these relate to the key issues of the acceptability and adaptability of SIR and SER. The discussion which follows considers the problems associated with each of these, on the basis that they represent potential barriers to the active involvement of teachers themselves in school effectiveness and improvement work. The chapter then raises questions about the future of SER and SIR and some possibilities are considered, especially in terms of how they might become more accepted by teachers. Here, the possibility of a merger between the two traditions is considered. Attention is also given to the potential of school-based action research projects in providing one doorway to the future of school effectiveness and improvement. Indeed, as Stoll (1996) suggests, it is teachers who have brought together ideas from both traditions: 'they have taken the pieces of research from both traditions that have made most sense to them and, albeit unknowingly, have linked the two areas through their improvement efforts' (p. 51).

School effectiveness and improvement: the multiplicity and accessibility of meanings

School effectiveness

The effective schools movement has been described as being concerned with 'a concerted attempt in several countries to rediscover ways of creating really excellent schools' (Beare *et al.* 1989: 1). This concern has its roots not only in the professional orientation and commitment of the teaching profession, but in the political climate which has influenced school development over the last decade. Alongside the push for excellence has been an emerging need to address the effectiveness of schools. In considering these two elements together, it would seem that the identification of factors which make schools effective has the potential to provide a starting point for moves towards the creation of excellence in our schools. It is this link with the external demand to strive for excellence, quality and high standards in school management and organization which has provided, at least in part, the rationale for a heightened interest in research into effective schooling.

The element which is missing in this process of moving from the identification of effectiveness to the achievement of excellence, however, is a consideration of the way in which this excellence is achieved. It is the work on school improvement which has attempted to address this area, focusing upon various approaches to development and change in schools. In this way the school effectiveness research and study of school improvement could be described as complementary. The former has a role in identifying the targets for effectiveness while the latter provides insights into the route one might take to achieve them. Such a definition is, however, rather simplistic and does not sufficiently capture the complexity of meanings associated with the SER and SIR traditions. For this reason it is necessary to consider the meanings of school effectiveness and school improvement a little more closely.

In the case of school effectiveness this is a difficult task. Effectiveness has always been an elusive term; one that requires clarification before we can understand the significance of what is meant by effective schools. Stoll and Fink (1996) offer Levine and Lezotte's (1990) definition of effectiveness as, 'the production of a desired result or outcome', while Beare *et al.* (1989) point to Chester Barnard's definition, which they claim remains as robust today as when he invoked it in the 1930s. 'An action is effective if it accomplishes its specific objective aim' (Barnard 1938: 20). In this way:

'To effect' means 'to bring about, to accomplish'; thus to be effective, an action or an institution or an individual must bring something about, must accomplish something. Indeed the term implies that the action is deliberate. You are effective if you set yourself a target and hit it. Definition of a target is a prior requirement before it is possible to be effective.

(Beare *et al.* 1989: 11)

Therein lies one of the problematics of school effectiveness. As Stoll and Fink suggest, in the process of being effective, in the setting of targets, the production of outcomes, the accomplishment of aims – the question is, by whom are these targets, results or outcomes desired?

To arrive at a definition of a school as effective, people are forced to choose between competing values. What educators perceive as important outcomes of schooling may not coincide with views of pupils, parents, governors, the local community, government or the media. It is also feasible that any or all of the above groups may have differing perceptions of effectiveness, and that individuals within any of these groups may not agree with each other on a definition.

(Stoll and Fink 1996: 27)

In short, effectiveness is not a neutral term. In this respect it is possible to identify the problem of the multiplicity of the meanings of school effectiveness and to point to this as significant, particularly in coming to appreciate the task facing teachers as they attempt to make sense of, and come to terms with, the various meanings of school effectiveness as defined by various groups. In this context school effectiveness researchers might be considered to be just one of many groups.

The impact of SER upon teachers can be viewed, then, as part of what Skelton *et al.* (1991) describe as 'a background of heightened awareness of the problems of education from the general public and a range of expectations from many sectors of society which are sometimes confused, often contradictory and occasionally just unrealistic' (p. 8). Tsoukas (1994) goes further, suggesting that not only do teachers currently have to contend with these varying expectations, but that society keeps changing its mind about what the purposes of education should be, and about the way in which teachers might realize these purposes. If the school effectiveness movement is taken by teachers to be part of this ambiguous context of changing priorities in education, it could be viewed as presenting merely another example of forces external to the school changing its mind about what education should be about and how it should be delivered.

With varying statements, varying interpretations and varying demands coming from an array of interested bodies, it is not surprising that there is confusion about what the real intentions of education are, or should be. As one teacher said, 'looking into the fog, we call it'. This presents difficulties for those involved in SER as they attempt to make the findings of their work accessible to the teaching profession, in that they can expect hostility or indifference from those who feel that it presents yet another set of expectations about the nature and purpose of their work. It is also important to acknowledge the lack of ownership which the teaching profession might feel, as the task of defining what is effective about their schools is undertaken by such a variety of groups, particularly those who are viewed to represent an outsider perspective of the school.

Sammons *et al.* (1994) suggest that the body of research emanating from the effective schools movement 'was borne out of a quest for more robust evidence to illuminate a complex area and to reveal a more accurate picture of the many factors in schools which determine standards amongst pupils' (p. 1). Within this definition the key issue is whether or not teachers perceive this quest as being their own. The argument advanced here is that this is not the case, and that practising teachers do not see moves towards school effectiveness, or the research associated with it, as being fundamentally concerned with their professional commitment to provide high quality education or improve provision. Rather, many teachers are more likely to view the quest as being concerned with yet another strand of the complex web of measures intended to increase both school and teacher accountability. In short, teachers' perceptions of school effectiveness could be seen to reflect an understanding of the term as being associated with the need to 'prove rather than improve quality' (Rogers and Badham 1992).

All of this has clear implications for exploring teachers' perceptions of school effectiveness in terms of their point of contact with the concept and the movement itself. The contention here is that, as a result of the emergence of the term 'effectiveness' within the context of the package of performance management measures, teachers are more likely to associate the school effectiveness movement with government imperatives concerning the accountability of schools, rather than to appreciate that its roots lie in a substantial body of educational research which originated in response to a widely held view in the 1960s and 1970s that schools had comparatively little influence upon student achievement (e.g. Coleman *et al.* 1966, Jenks 1972). So, while the new body of research in the area of effective schooling has largely focused upon whether and how schools make a difference, the likelihood is that teachers do not see the work in this way. It is more likely that they perceive it as part of a large scale, government-backed initiative to discredit their performance with the intention of attempting to prove that, in fact, their work makes little difference.

It is not surprising, then, that teachers may feel that it is not they who have ownership over this quest for increased knowledge of the factors of school effectiveness but, rather, that the quest is for others external to the school who are concerned with imposing still further accountability demands. This is further highlighted when the findings of SER and SIR appear to have been used by policy makers to tell schools how to improve, for such an approach according to Brown *et al.* (1995):

> fails to address the issue of how the findings are to be integrated into the thinking and practice of those who are seen as needing to improve. The involvement and commitment of teachers, with a sense of ownership and responsibility for decision making, is an essential element for innovation. In those circumstances, it cannot be assumed that teachers will be ready to accept findings as an agenda handed down from on high.
>
> (p. 9)

School improvement

In turning to definitions of school improvement it is evident that SIR has not suffered from the problem of multiplicity of meanings in the way in which school effectiveness has. However, subtly different issues are raised for teachers as they attempt to interpret SIR. Unlike the case of school effectiveness there appears to be broad agreement of what school improvement is and the much quoted definition provided by the OECD-sponsored International School Improvement project (ISIP) is testament to this: 'a systematic, sustained effort aimed at change in learning conditions and other related internal conditions in one or more schools, with the ultimate aim of accomplishing educational goals more effectively' (Van Velzen *et al.* 1985: 48). The work of the ISIP 'served to popularize a school improvement approach to educational change' (Hargreaves and Hopkins 1993: 234) and as such the analysis provided by Stoll and Fink (1996) is useful in exploring the meanings behind this broadly accepted definition. They suggest that it emphasizes several important dimensions: the necessity for careful planning, management and continuity even in the face of difficulties, and the need for a focus on teaching and learning as well as upon supporting organizational conditions. Additionally, the intricate relationship between school improvement and change is signalled, and while improvement occurs within schools, their location within a larger educational system is indicated. 'The range of school improvement goals includes those related to pupils, teachers and school organization. School improvement's ultimate aim, however, is to enhance pupil progress, achievement and development. This is the bottom line' (pp. 42–3). In short, there is a dual emphasis on student outcomes and change management capacity.

So while school improvement can be described as 'the strategies by which the findings of research can be used to bring about change' (Glover 1995: 3), it is important to acknowledge the nature of school improvement studies as 'more action oriented than the effective schools research', embodying the long term goal of moving towards the vision of a 'problem solving' or 'thinking' school (Hargreaves and Hopkins 1993: 234). SIR can be seen to have all the potential which SER demonstrates in addressing the issue of quality in education, but the framework for addressing the quality issue is more explicitly framed within a concern to account for change. The dual focus on addressing the processes of achieving and on strategies for coping with change, might be considered to be a more attractive proposition for practising teachers, in that, of late, their everyday concerns have necessarily been located within an environment of continuing change reflected in many aspects of their working lives. The provision of an approach which encourages problem solving and thinking at the local level of the school or the classroom would, then, seem to have much to offer teachers as they tackle the task of school improvement.

Fundamental to the school improvement paradigm is the emphasis placed upon notions of the school as the centre of change, where it is recognized that ultimately school improvement comes from within and cannot be externally mandated. As Hargreaves and Hopkins (1993) suggest, it 'implies a very different way of thinking about change than the ubiquitous 'top down' approach so popular with policy makers' (p. 234). However, while there is a heavy emphasis upon the internal context of the school, the external environment is not ignored: in fact, school development is viewed to be 'the process through which schools adapt external changes to internal purpose' (Hopkins 1996: 33). The crucial point here is that while policy can be externally mandated, change cannot; improvement, it is argued, comes from the internal process of implementation, not from the mere imposition of innovation from outside of the school. Thus, SIR does not deny the influence of the external environment but places school improvement efforts within this context, with a strong emphasis upon internal organizational features and teacher interpretation:

> Although policies set directions and provide a framework, they do not and cannot determine student outcomes. It is implementation, rather than the decision to adopt a new policy that determines student achievement. It is also the case that the most effective school improvement strategies seem to be internal rather than external to the school ... What is needed is 'implementation-friendly' policy that is concerned with the process as well as the substance of change at the teacher and school level.
>
> (Hopkins 1996: 41)

Therein lies one of the strengths of the school improvement approach, when considered from the point of view of the practising teacher. For, unlike SER which many teachers associate with the imposition of 'top-down' policy, SIR places teachers and their schools at the centre, providing a means by which 'bottom-up' strategies might be used to achieve educational improvement. Indeed, as Stoll and Fink point out, it was as a result of the 'lack of teacher commitment to government-initiated top down reforms which led to a new improvement paradigm in the 1980s that celebrated a "bottom up" approach through the use of practitioner rather than exclusively external knowledge' (1996: 43). Although the more recent focus of SIR has been to address both the processes and outcomes of improvement efforts, the commitment to the involvement of teachers as key players in informing 'bottom-up' strategies has been maintained, and while such strategies might be developed in response to externally imposed change, the way in which they are implemented and the way in which improvement is achieved still lies very firmly with the teacher. Teachers' interpretations of the meaning of SIR are, therefore, perhaps more likely to elicit a more favourable response than that suggested as being associated with SER.

The issue of ownership is also worthy of consideration here, as a significant factor in teachers' responses to the SIR outcomes and their willingness to engage with school improvement concepts. The notion of teacher ownership of school improvement efforts has remained central to the guidelines and models offered by school improvers. As Reynolds (1992: 18) describes, the school improvement paradigm in Britain probably began with the teacher-researcher movement, moving on to encompass school self-evaluation and review, and later looking at the review process in relation to an improvement policy. Now, SIR has been criticized on this front for its celebration of practitioner knowledge 'whether it is itself a valid improvement strategy or not' (Reynolds 1992: 18), where such a reliance upon internally generated knowledge 'may condemn practitioners to ignorance or even, at best, lead to a futile reinvention of the wheel in each change attempt' (Reynolds and Packer 1992: 183). SIR does, however, provide the scope for teachers to offer their own definitions and interpretations of what makes an effective school and to incorporate these values and judgements into targets for improvement. On this premise alone, it is more likely to engage teachers with issues of effectiveness and improvement than what might be perceived to be the externally imposed notions provided by SER.

Furthermore, if one is to account truly for the changing and ambiguous, if not unique, context of each school, then perhaps reinvention of the wheel can actually be viewed as a developmental process. While we would want to draw out broad lessons or guidelines from both SER and SIR, there is much to be said for the active engagement of teachers in seeking their own truth. Providing this quest is undertaken with an eye to the outside environment of the school, and encompasses a consideration of the experiences of others in their improvement efforts, then it is likely that in real terms teachers will be much more willing to grapple with school improvement concepts and the findings from SIR in that, at least, they share a common philosophy which acknowledges the power of practitioner knowledge and not just its limitations. On this basis, the very premise upon which SIR is based is more akin to the philosophical and practical concerns of teachers as educators and, if SIR is also viewed to be useful in enabling teachers to cope in times of rapid externally imposed change, then all the better. The possibility of such active interpretation and application of SIR findings is in the first place, however, dependent upon the accessibility of the research to teachers (a theme to which we shall return in Chapter 4).

It is important here, however, in assessing the way in which teachers are currently deriving meaning from school effectiveness and improvement, to account for two further contextual factors which have had an impact upon teachers' willingness to engage with SER in particular: the acceptability and adaptability of school effectiveness. It is to these concerns I now turn, in an effort to acknowledge, not just the multiplicity of meanings which school effectiveness might have, but the multiplicity of interpretations which teachers might apply, as they attempt to make sense of the drive towards effectiveness in their schools.

The acceptability of effectiveness and the emergence of managerialism in schools

Denny (1992) outlines the emergence of interest in school effectiveness as part of a move towards the adoption of a 'performance management' approach in schools. He points to statements by the government in 1979 which highlighted a view that the public sector could be improved and re-defined through the introduction of private sector management techniques and explicitly commercial objectives. However, because the public sector role was still expected to perform a 'social function', performance was to be judged in terms of 'economy', 'efficiency' and 'effectiveness'. These, he claims have become familiar terms throughout the public sector and he suggests that when taken together with a fourth factor, equity, they 'could act as our main criteria for assessing organisational performance' (p. 3). In similar vein, Beare *et al.* (1989) see effectiveness, efficiency, equity and excellence, as 'the four Es' of school management. They go further in suggesting that the impact of these performance management concepts upon schools has been to imply a change in the role and function of schools and, by implication, teachers. The teaching profession, it would seem, should no longer be exclusively concerned with the basics of teaching and learning, but with the effective management and performance of its teachers and its schools.

From the 3Rs to the 4Es: the changing role of teachers

In considering the impact of recent educational reform upon the teacher's role, it is possible to identify the direct influence of the 'E' factors upon the everyday working lives of teachers and to support the suggestion that an attempt has been made by government to augment the 3Rs with the 'Es' as central concepts in school management and organization. Recent developments concerned with this new age of managerialism in schools have encouraged a paradigm shift in teachers' conception of their role. A shift in attitudes has been necessary in order to embrace the newly defined elements of the teacher's role as being more centrally concerned with whole school rather than classroom level issues. This movement is one which some teachers feel less than happy about and many feel explicitly uncomfortable with, on the basis that it seems to be far removed from notions of improving practice at classroom level. This point is highlighted in the findings of Webb's (1994) research which looks at the changing roles of teachers in primary schools:

> The work of primary teachers has changed dramatically in recent years. Many of the changes have been in relation to responsibilities outside, and often only indirectly related to, the classroom. On the one hand, these have contributed to teachers' professional development; on the other hand, they have dissipated their energies, reducing the time and effort available for focusing on pupil learning.
>
> (p. vi)

An increasing number of teachers have begun to ask the question, 'Why can't I just be a class teacher?' As one teacher recently said when asked if she had discussed her management responsibilities and career aspirations in an appraisal interview, 'Oh no, I don't want to do any of that management lark – I just want to be a normal person.' Such a perspective is illustrative of a deep-seated concern among teachers that an increased emphasis upon their responsibilities for whole school management dissipates their effectiveness in the classroom. In this way teachers have come to question their priorities as they have had to deal with a certain amount of role ambiguity and, in some cases, role overload.

Teachers, then, have been expected to accept an addition to their teaching responsibilities and this has placed their role very firmly within the context of a new and enhanced management dimension. Consequently, there has been an established need for teachers to change their previously held assumptions, in order that they can begin to view their role within a wider managerial perspective. Inevitably, this has meant more explicit exposure to whole school concerns associated with effectiveness, efficiency, economy, equity and excellence, and a shift towards a new management paradigm which centrally encompasses the notion of classroom teachers as managers.

It is as part of an acceptance of this paradigm that teachers are most likely to have come across notions of school effectiveness, perceiving it to be part of this thrust towards managerialism. A particular issue is identified by Denny (1992):

> Whilst the prime objective of the Education Reform Act 1988 (ERA) is to improve the quality of education . . . One of the major assumptions embedded in [it] is that many of the same basic management processes such as planning, organising, activating, monitoring and controlling are universal. However, there are some features which deserve careful consideration and scrutiny before private sector management techniques and structures are adopted by schools. In particular the emphasis placed on outputs.
>
> (pp. 6–7)

As Everard (1988) highlighted, just prior to the Education Reform Act, 'there remains in the teaching profession a sizeable body of opinion voicing concern about the possible infiltration of education by commercial values and alien management practices' (p. 187). This is an important contextual factor in the emergence of the effective schools movement, as it could be argued that it is the perception of teachers that the increasing demands for the measurement of school effectiveness have emerged as part of this movement towards the imposed adoption of school management approaches and systems more familiar to, and more readily accepted by, the private sector.

Their concern about this can be particularly great if their view is that the emergence of a school management culture is based on principles of economy, with measures of effectiveness identified as the tool for establishing 'value for money' or 'value added', in a manner more akin to the measurement of productivity in an industrial setting. Beare *et al.* (1989) warn of the dangers of this for the school effectiveness movement itself stating that, 'School effectiveness concerns have grown up alongside concerns about productivity, efficiency and accountability . . . in consequence it could easily become another "cult of efficiency" movement based upon economic rather than educational imperatives' (p. 16). Menter *et al.* (1995) take this further in pursuing an 'economizing of education' theme. In their research with primary headteachers on the role of marketization and managerialism in teachers' work, they suggest the establishment of a market economy in education has had a significant impact in enhancing teacher accountability and in changing perceptions about the role of teachers from that of professional to that of service provider:

> The initial phase of our project alerted us to the significance of marketization in changing relationships, particularly in reducing professional autonomy and authority. The highly regulated market relationships

embodied in recent and current policy ... disempower professionals, redefining them as service providers accountable to government agencies, funding bodies and consumers.

(p. 2)

In view of this, it is easy to see how teachers' interpretations of effectiveness may reflect an understanding of SER as being based upon just such economic imperatives, and significantly reinforced by the framework of accountability provided by the ERA among other reforms. Rogers and Badham (1992) contend that 'accountability is a central thread running through most of the changes enshrined in the 1988 ERA'. In the light of this, they suggest that school-based evaluation is more likely to take root because schools have to provide information in some detail to parents, governors and the local education authority (LEA). With the advent of the parents charter this has been brought very much to the forefront of teacher concerns, placing even greater responsibility on schools to address the E factors of school management. Denny (1992) continues this theme, highlighting the increasingly strident demands being made by the public and politicians for teachers to address the 'E factors' in order that they are able to:

- provide better information about how education is organized;
- provide better information about the outcomes of education;
- measure 'value added' and understand the context in which that occurs effectively;
- improve skills to interpret data;
- understand efficiency and productivity (p. 20).

Effectiveness and the changing pattern of school management

It would appear that the emergence of political interest in school effectiveness lies very firmly within the pattern of changing demands made of schools over the last decade. It is within this context that teachers have come to understand and interpret the meaning of school effectiveness as being closely associated with notions of external accountability. The current political climate to which the education system is exposed would, therefore, seem to reinforce the 'E' factors as central to the life and development of schools in both operational and organizational terms. Undoubtedly such terms as 'efficiency' and 'effectiveness' have come to dominate many areas of school management, delivery and accountability, this being significantly reinforced by a plethora of school management initiatives which have emerged since ERA. Among these, Ofsted inspection, delegation of budgets, school development planning, teacher appraisal and National Curriculum assessment and testing can all be identified as having, at least in some part, a concern for one if not all of the E factors at the core of its rationale. Indeed, many of the changes facing schools, which emerged in their initial stages in the 1980s, embrace a broad range of activity associated with this emphasis on 'managerialism'. This is evident in casting even a cursory glance over the documented lists of changes which have faced schools and presented in Figure 1.1. It is interesting to observe these in terms of their focus on at

---

List 1
- introducing local management (LMS)
- opting out
- developing a whole school policy
- bringing computers and information into school administration
- introducing a formal system of staff appraisal and development
- building closer links with the community
- improving the quality of school management or leadership
- setting and implementing educational objectives for the school

Source: Everard and Morris (1990: 230–1)

List 2
- the implementation of the National Curriculum
- open enrolment and its implications
- teacher appraisal
- school development planning
- establish priorities
- allow for the appropriate involvement of others in the life of the school
- the local management of schools
- evaluation and assessment
- effective staff development
- provide a direction to the school
- provide mechanisms for reviewing progress

Source: Skelton et al. (1991: 8–9)

List 3
- teacher appraisal
- falling rolls
- ageing teacher force
- prolonged industrial action by teachers
- low teacher morale
- introduction of the National Curriculum
- increase in governor powers
- contracting education system
- reduced teacher mobility
- closure of teacher training courses/colleges
- imposition of new conditions of service
- sometimes hostile press
- requirements of the Education Reform Act

Source: Hewton and West (1992: 116–17)

Figure 1.1 Documented examples of changes requiring response from schools

least one of the E factors, a focus which has emanated largely from the legislative reform of the 1980s.

Furthermore, a performance and accountability view of education, which many teachers would associate with notions of school effectiveness, does little according to Day *et al.* (1990) to support teacher development. If, indeed, school effectiveness is viewed to be part of the 'judgmental climate' which Day *et al.* describe, it is possible to recognize the reason why teachers may feel less than comfortable with the philosophy underpinning the effective schools movement and question why they should be pushed towards school improvement by those external to the school:

> Professional development is severely hampered by this performance view of teaching. If professional competence and expertise are to be extended there needs to be a climate in which the intensely practical aspects of classroom work are seen as an essential part of any curriculum-development activity. This will not be achieved if teachers, like the pupils they work with day by day, constantly see themselves as being judged and graded. A judgmental climate is not an easy one in which to talk freely about 'how' and 'why' you teach as you do, or indeed to identify areas where you may need help and guidance.
>
> (pp. 37–8)

Many teachers remain steadfast in their distaste of the general premise that the application of management practice, theories and precepts from industry and commerce are in any way appropriate to the management of schools. In short, effectiveness can be understood by teachers to be part of this imposed philosophy and this, as we have seen, presents a potential barrier to teacher engagement with SER findings. Academics have a rather difficult job on their hands, therefore, in overcoming such hostility and in communicating the fact that the origins of the study of school effectiveness lie, not in government reform, but in a substantial body of educational research.

Effectiveness and its measurement: the case for adaptability

A key aspect of the emerging picture presented here concerning teacher perceptions of school effectiveness, is a view of effectiveness as one of a number of initiatives associated with the demand for the measurement of performance and standards in schools. This is illustrated at an organization level by demands for the introduction of performance tables of examination results, the publication of attendance records and enhanced public access to school inspection reports; and at an individual level by developments such as the introduction of teacher appraisal, accompanying rumours about the imposition of performance related pay, and the grading of lessons (of teachers) by school inspectors.

In taking appraisal as one area within this individual dimension, Fletcher's (1993) analysis of 'appraisal as neither a deadly disease nor a panacea' raises a number of issues which can be applied to a consideration of school effectiveness from the measurement perspective. In discussing the merits of performance appraisal, Fletcher refers to the work of Deming (1986) who identified performance appraisal as 'one of the seven deadly diseases of current management'. He suggests that Deming's arguments on this point are in line with his own belief that the traditional assessment-oriented approach to appraisal, with its emphasis on comparing people and links with pay, fails to deliver on almost every count. Trying to persist with traditional appraisal approaches in these circumstances is, according to Fletcher, doomed to failure, although he argues that to judge all appraisal schemes to be 'deadly' would be a mistake:

> It [the traditional assessment-oriented approach] might well be regarded as a deadly disease, but it does not mean that other approaches to appraisal are equally lethal. Performance appraisal centred on performance improvement and development . . . is likely to be more successful. There is, of course, still a need to assess within the framework of such an approach, but it is not assessment done for its own sake, or as a primary purpose, it is simply a means to an end . . . Performance appraisal does not have to be a deadly disease, but neither is it likely to be a panacea.
>
> (pp. 144–7)

Measuring effectiveness: process and outcome issues

The quote above is interesting and relevant, because the effectiveness movement can be viewed as having at the centre of its concern an approach to the measurement of school performance not dissimilar to the traditional assessment-oriented approach which, in terms of appraisal at least, has been discredited. It could be argued, therefore, that for school effectiveness theories to have any real or successful impact upon teachers they need to be presented as part of a framework for improvement rather than assessment. This is particularly the case when SER seems to suggest that the effectiveness of schools and, by implication, the effectiveness of teachers, should be judged in terms of an assessment of only those aspects of 'product quality' which can be quantified. As Hewton and West (1992) point out, there are inherent dangers in adopting such an outcomes-based approach, not least of which is a lack of attention given to the value that teachers place upon the processes of education which require adaptability rather than control:

Such simplistic measures run the danger of reinforcing a view in which those features of schools which are most easily measured become the most important. There is a strong view within the profession that improvement is about enhancing the quality of learning experiences and valuing the less easily measured, but critically important processes of education rather than the products of schooling. The processes of education are not the same as industrial or commercial processes.

(pp. 7–8)

School effectiveness developments are in many teachers' eyes associated with moves towards measurement in productivity terms. Their concern is that the human product of the educational process, the children's development, is somewhat more difficult to measure quantifiably than an industrial product. Additional concerns relate to the notion of their students being conceived of as 'products' in the first place. An inescapable fact remains, however, that the study of school effectiveness requires the measurement of the performance of schools and that measures of the products of schooling are more easily established and quantifiable than measures of process. What is ignored are those indicators of effectiveness which are process-based and which require an acknowledgement of the importance of adaptability within the school environment. Perhaps the challenge for education over the next decade is to address how the processes of education can be effectively assessed alongside the product-type measures, thereby accounting for both ongoing and end-point performance. As Denny (1992) argues:

> In many cases the real task is to provide a learning environment which is able to sustain a meaningful and purposeful set of relationships for pupils with and between staff providing the service. So, one is also concerned with monitoring the quality of these relationships rather than solely identifying some discrete outcome. Clearly it is important that certain values should be attached to the very process by which education is delivered, as well as the outputs and outcomes ... process and criteria are both important and will be widely applied in most face-to-face activities if effective learning is to take place.
>
> (p. 4)

Postmodernism: issues for SER

If we consider these issues within an analysis of the postmodern context in which our schools exist (pursued at some length by Cockett in Chapter 3) the perceptions of teachers regarding the focus of school effectiveness as being more concerned with outcomes than processes is brought into particularly sharp relief. The association between school effectiveness approaches and concepts of performance measurement place it firmly within a 'rational' consideration of schools as organizations. Such a rational approach is increasingly seen as inappropriate in that it does not adequately address the need for schools to demonstrate increased adaptability, openness, interpretation and reflective action, all seen as necessary for organizational survival within the ambiguous climate of the postmodern world. From a postmodern perspective, therefore, focusing only upon outcomes can be seen to have severe limitations which may impede the ability of schools and their teachers to respond adequately in a rapidly changing world beset by uncertainty. By attempting to control the rational elements of the organization (such as bureaucratic systems and systems of performance assessment) in a way which does not account for the influence of the non-rational human elements, schools would seem to have little chance of success in dealing with the instability and constant change which characterizes society today. In this respect, the association of SER with the measurement of the explicitly rational elements of school performance does little to endear teachers, in that its concern for them and their students as the human elements in this process, is often obscured behind the measurement facade. As Burrell (1994) suggests, these rational elements 'are mechanical devices to shore up organisations . . . they are scaffolding for the facade of order but mask much uncertainty' (p. x).

In considering how effectively schools have been able to make the transition, from a modern to a postmodern phase of organizational existence, one must ask whether developments in school effectiveness actually help or hinder this process, particularly in terms of providing the necessary scope for organizational and professional adaptability. In many respects, the struggle currently facing schools as they attempt to make this transition reflects the distinction made by Tsoukas (1994) between social engineering and reflective action perspectives in the study of organizations. The two perspectives suggest a tension between a view of organizations as concerned with 'objectivity, detachment and control versus openness, ambiguity and interpretation; mechanisms versus self organisation' (Burrell 1994: ix). If an objective, detached, controlling and mechanistic emphasis can be associated with a modernist perspective, then an open, ambiguous, interpretive and self-organizing emphasis can be recognized as being associated with a postmodernist view of organizations. An important consideration here, is the extent to which schools have been able to cope with, and respond to, the increasingly ambiguous nature of their internal and external environment, described as characteristic of the postmodern world. If we accept Burrell's argument, the kind of mechanistic or bureaucratic devices, often associated with the measurement of school effectiveness, will only provide part of this picture. Rosenholtz (1989) and Barth (1990) support this in their critique of school effectiveness models which are driven by mechanistic approaches to the measurement of schools against lists of effectiveness characteristics, test scores or performance indicators. They comment upon the limitations of the 'list logic' often associated with school effectiveness:

The list logic has begotten a list sweepstake to see whose is the best list. Advocates argue that their description of a desirable school, their catalogue of the desirable characteristics of school people, and their prescribed methods for attaining these ends rest on the firmest grounds ... In short, the list logic of educational change seems simple, straightforward and compelling. Its only flaw is that it does not seem to work very well.

(Barth, quoted in Glover 1995: 17)

This perspective is further illustrated in considering the role of league tables as one such indicator of a mechanistic detached perspective, which for many teachers is seen to be very firmly embodied within school effectiveness approaches. As Tsoukas (1994) points out, the problem with such a rationally driven approach to management and the measurement of performance is that it does not account for the fact that the education system is in a state of oscillation. So while the external climate of schools may demonstrate all the characteristics of a postmodern environment, such as oscillation, the adoption of internal management devices for measuring performance are clearly modernist and, what is more, become distracting from the real task:

A system in oscillation cannot be managed effectively, it is never quite right: it sways between extreme positions. What is even more important is that such a social system leads eventually to the management of problematic 'solutions' (e.g. managing league tables) instead of the management of the original problems which the system was set up to deal with. Pushing the logic of the social engineering image to the extreme, management becomes tantamount to keeping up appearances and fighting shadows: managing via league tables leads to managing the league tables themselves!

(pp. 7–8)

In considering this perspective we are presented with a clear mismatch between the acknowledged need for schools to be responsive to the postmodern context in which they operate, and the external imposition of a mechanistic approach to the measurement of effectiveness, more characteristic of modernist thinking. If SER is perceived to be associated with the reinforcement of this kind of approach, then it could be seen to be contributing to a process of legitimizing the use of such mechanistic devices in the way which Raab (1991) describes: 'Government's hope must be that the implementation of the systems and ethos of management will take root sufficiently to legitimise new mechanisms and routines and to make them appear to be self imposed, or collaboratively adopted, from top to toe' (p. 16).

The work of Menter et al. (1995) explores further the externally imposed philosophy of education as a market commodity. Their work on the interdependence of marketization and managerialism in schools emphasizes the way in which schools have faced the imposition of a modernist approach to the management of their organizations. They argue that marketization of education has not been accompanied by the elimination of mechanisms of centralist control (which one would expect in postmodern organizations) but by their reformulation and relocation:

> The efficient operation of the market is secured through the combination of legislative controls (juridification) and internal, institutional mechanisms, notably performance indicators and inspections, which ostensibly provide consumers with a basis for selection but more importantly provide powerful managerial imperatives. Marketization thus greatly enhances the significance of management.
>
> (p. 2)

Closely associated with an analysis of these perspectives and the need for schools to make the transition from a modern (social engineering) to a postmodern (reflective action) state, is the influence of the pattern of centralization and decentralization of power which has emerged within the education service as a whole over the last decade. This issue has two important dimensions concerned with the contrast between a modern and postmodern view of what Boje and Dennehy (1993) refer to as the organizing and controlling elements of the organization. In 'modernist organizing there is centralization of decisions, policies and objectives, [whereas in] postmodern organizing teams of equals are skilled to do their own planning, organizing and controlling' (p. 106). If we apply these descriptors to schools it appears that they have experienced over the last decade a rather confusing combination of both approaches to organization. Schools have found themselves subject to high levels of centralized policy making from central government, while simultaneously experiencing new levels of autonomy and independence as a result of the decentralization of certain aspects of policy and practice associated with school management (e.g. school governance, financial management, human resource management). Similarly, schools have been subject to the type of externally driven control associated with a modernist approach, where 'all sorts of controls are legally mandated', while at the same time, at school level (and particularly in primary schools) in many respects 'control is de-differentiated and de-centred so there is not as much gap between leaders and workers' (Boje and Dennehy 1993: 278). This presents an additional tension, as it would appear that schools are stuck in a kind of limbo between modernism and postmodernism.

In short, it would appear that schools need to be responding to a postmodern world in a way which is reflected in the management and organization of their institutions and yet the interventionist action of government seems to mitigate against this. It would seem, therefore, that in attempting to explore these two distinct approaches to understanding organizations, there is an apparent dilemma which faces those concerned with the management of schools. This dilemma is concerned with the need for schools to come to terms with the philosophy of managerialism and measurement imposed on schools via the external environment which reinforces a modernist, social engineering perspective, while at the same time trying to move forward in the adoption of a postmodern approach to organization and management based on reflective action, in order that their very survival in a postmodern world is ensured. School effectiveness concerns alone will do little to enable teachers to make the transition to postmodernism. Indeed, by their very nature they reinforce the characteristics of modernism, being concerned more with control than with the kind of adaptability that is necessarily required by schools within the current context of educational change.

Merging traditions: the way ahead?

So what of the future for school effectiveness and improvement? In the light of the issues raised concerning the acceptability and adaptability of the two approaches, it seems appropriate to consider the future of SER and SIR and the possibilities they offer in providing a way ahead towards the active involvement of teachers in the task of improving their schools. This is important because, beyond the constraint of teachers' perceptions of SER and SIR, the two fields of research *do* have important contributions to make, in informing the action which schools might take in tackling the current effectiveness agenda and in coping with the organizational and individual change this requires.

Towards acceptability and adaptability

While I have suggested that a school improvement approach appears more acceptable to teachers and more appropriate in the way in which it addresses the importance of adaptability, it is difficult to envisage a way forward which does not necessitate teacher involvement in the effectiveness agenda whether it is perceived to be externally imposed or not. SER cannot, therefore, be ignored in that understandings of what is meant by school effectiveness are likely to dominate any future work which would bring together the effectiveness and improvement movements. As Sammons *et al.* (1994: 1) point out, 'awareness of the findings of school effectiveness research is a necessary (although not sufficient) condition for school improvement'. What is perhaps required, then, is a transfer of knowledge and skills from SER to SIR in the way envisaged by Barber:

> Now attention at school level is shifting from these characteristics of effective schools to the strategies required to achieve effectiveness; in

other words to school improvement ... This area may be less well researched but in practical terms it is surely more important. It has become necessary to transfer the energy, knowledge and skills of school effectiveness research to the study of school improvement.

(1995: 11)

There is much to be said for such a transfer of energy, particularly if this were to take account of the less rational and more adaptive approaches necessitated by the implementation of change within the current educational climate, and if the concern for the measurement of demonstrable effectiveness were to be tempered with a concern to tackle underlying problems rather than merely the measurement of outcomes. Furthermore, if integration were to occur and school effectiveness initiatives were seen to have improvement rather than measurement as their primary purpose, then such initiatives are likely to be more successful at an operational level in schools, in that they are likely to be more readily embraced by teachers. As Fletcher (1993) suggests in considering the orientation of appraisal, the adoption of such an approach does not remove 'the need for assessment', it is simply to shift the focus of such activity towards that which is more readily acceptable to those charged with the responsibility of implementation. In this way school effectiveness concerns will simply become a means to an end, and that end will be school improvement. This is to place an emphasis upon the professional integrity of the teaching profession.

I would also argue that the future must lie in an increasing emphasis upon SIR as a potential tool for developing a reflective action approach. The success of school improvement developments in this context would be dependent upon its ability to resist a dominating concern for the use of rational methods, giving greater emphasis to an open, adaptive, interpretive, and self-organizing approach to the analysis, organization and management of schools. This, in combination with a shift towards a stronger focus on classroom-based research and a greater concern for teaching and learning would point the way to a future for school improvement less influenced by managerialist principles and more informed by the engagement of the less rational elements of school organizations: 'the hearts and minds' of its teachers. Now, nothing more fully engages the thoughts and minds of teachers than their students; 'change has to be meaningful, and teachers derive most meaning from work with pupils in the classroom' (Lortie 1975). In this context Barber's (1995) thoughts about the possible future direction of SIR emphasize classroom level concerns. 'One prediction would be that there will be a welcome renewal of emphasis upon classroom practice ... in other words the next debate may well be about teaching effectiveness and improvement' (p. 11). If this proves to be correct, bringing school effectiveness and school improvement work together through a more explicit focus on teaching and learning at classroom level may provide teachers with one doorway to improvement which is more acceptable to them. This doorway would be opened by the reorientation of school effectiveness and improvement research, with an emphasis upon practice and strategy at classroom level as well as upon whole school effectiveness factors or strategies for improvement, though the relevance of these to the classroom needs to be much clearer than it often has been. Such a doorway may prove appealing to those teachers who have, up until the present time, been rather resistant to accepting notions of effectiveness and, even, improvement on the grounds that they emphasize managerial rather than professional priorities.

There are a series of important issues here in considering the merger of the two traditions, particularly in the context of the active involvement of teachers in interpreting SER and SIR findings at school level. By way of illustration I offer my own recent experiences of working with teachers, as one of a team of tutors involved in school based action research, as part of the North West Consortium for the Study of Effectiveness in Urban Schools (NWCSEUS[1]). In this example the initial choice of the focus for investigation was clearly concerned with the implementation of a performance management approach to curriculum coordination, a focus explicitly associated with the managerialist perspective alluded to earlier. It became quite clear, however, from discussions with senior teachers, who were to lead project developments within the school, that while they saw opportunities for their own professional development within an investigation of their management role, their major concern was to address their practice and that of their colleagues at a classroom level.

While the ultimate aim of the project was to provide lessons for whole school improvement, the immediate concerns of teachers in the early stages of project development reflected the need to see immediate outcomes for students and for fellow staff. This was identified as a significant motivating factor in encouraging staff participation in the project. It must be acknowledged, however, that the impetus for this research project was to some extent created by an external agenda (in this case a recent Ofsted inspection) and was initially based upon an investigation of one of the factors of school effectiveness established through research: monitoring progress. In the light of this, and in view of the arguments presented previously regarding the acceptability of SER and SIR to teachers, it has proved essential in engaging in the process of facilitating project action, that the participating teachers were given the opportunity to explore the research focus within the context of their own concerns as practitioners. This approach has enabled the teachers to account for the specific context of their school and more particularly their classrooms within their own research. Furthermore, it has provided a basis upon which they have been able to consider issues of school effectiveness which they have identified as being relevant and helpful in striving towards improvement in their practice.

A significant outcome of this process of refining the project focus was that the adoption of an action research framework resulted in an emphasis upon how classroom teachers 'make sense of their educational world' and upon 'which variables are most salient in their thinking' (Brown *et al.* 1995: 9). In the light of the discussion presented here, it is clear that such an approach, which is explicitly fostered by the action research process, avoids the assumptions described by Elliott (1996: 208) as being associated with SER, that is, 'that the achievements in "effective classrooms" would be even better if they were more nested within an effective system of managerial control'. The acceptability to teachers of school effectiveness findings based upon such assumptions about managerialism is clearly limited. What is perhaps more acceptable, however, is a recognition of these findings as constituting 'an important resource for helping teachers to reflect about the relationship between factors in the organisational context and the teaching-learning process' (Elliott 1996: 219). This represents a more acceptable basis on which to conduct school effectiveness and improvement research, in that it places the teachers at the centre of the reflective process, giving them access to the research findings of others, while providing the freedom to interpret and explore, from a practitioner perspective, personal understandings of the significance of these findings, within their own classrooms and schools.

From this example, it would appear that while assessment, measurement and accountability are accepted as indicative of the current climate in which schools must operate, as concepts they still engender a lot of hostility, whereas notions of improvement or development at least seem to be more akin to the professional orientation of teachers. We must be wary, however, that in attempting to make school effectiveness seem less of a deadly disease to teachers, neither do we present its integration with school improvement as a panacea. As Elliott (1996) suggests, although it might be argued that SIR is more akin to practitioners' views of education as an adaptive, educative process as opposed to a view of it as a controlling managerial system (which he associates with SER) it is important to recognize that much of this work focuses upon whole school issues for improvement, not always obviously linked to classroom concerns. A merger of the two traditions which emphasizes much more a focus on teaching, learning and the classroom, then, might be seen to provide one means by which the practical concerns of teachers might be addressed. This would result in a more balanced consideration of both outcomes and processes, to a view of measurement as a means to an improvement end, thereby accounting for the impact of external reform but with a licence for internal interpretation and adaptation through the use of a developmental framework for improvement. This is, however, a demanding task and not one which is likely to happen overnight, even if the motivation for such a merger was based upon the extended interaction of practising teachers with the findings of SER and SIR.

Towards a caring culture: learning from each other

Although the task of merger may appear daunting, it is perhaps important in order that teachers are able to establish a clearer sense of the relationship between what makes a school effective and the way in which such effectiveness might be achieved. As Reynolds suggests 'the two disciplines of school effectiveness and school improvement need each other intellectually . . . both communities and bodies of knowledge, have much to learn from each other' (1992: 19). So just as teachers are urged to learn from the research and to learn from their partners in higher education who undertake it, so the researchers must learn from each other also. For as Reynolds continues, 'For school effectiveness researchers, school improvement programmes are the ultimate empirical test of whether effective school variables are causal . . . [while] For school improvement practitioners, school effectiveness research can provide an increasingly sensitive description of good practice' (p. 19).

So, while there are some significant differences between SER and SIR approaches, 'the two research traditions complement each other, and shortcomings of each approach can be counterbalanced by the strengths of the other' (Stoll 1996: 55). Furthermore, there are signs that the two paradigms are moving towards each other in addressing their differences. As Stoll points out, 'some researchers are moving towards a broader definition of effectiveness to encompass process and teacher outcomes . . . interestingly at the same time, the definition of school improvement is moving closer to those of school effectiveness in its more recent acknowledgement of outcomes' (p. 52). Each paradigm then, has positive contributions to make, though it remains important to acknowledge that there are important differences:

> There are differences of perspective and purpose to be mediated, understood and overcome. There are, in other words, some more fundamental barriers to linking the knowledge of 'what works' from the two paradigms with their respective understanding of 'effectiveness' and 'improvement'. What has been perceived as a simple matter of integrating two knowledge bases turns out not to be as simple as first supposed . . . A good deal of ground-clearing will be required before progress can be further made.
>
> (Gray *et al*. 1996: 171)

Reynolds (1992) points to the fact that these differences have historically formed a barrier to the take up of SER in relation to school improvement programmes. He suggests that this limitation probably exists as a result of the fact that, 'the school improvement knowledge base (popular with practitioners) has virtually diametrically opposed intellectual characteristics' to its school effectiveness counterpart (p. 18). This in itself highlights a further problem, for if the future of effectiveness and improvement work is to be based on a process of bringing together SER and SIR, then this would demand a process of reconciling the value systems which underpin each field of research. It would seem, therefore, that although such a union has the potential to provide a means by which the acceptability and adaptability of the research findings might well be enhanced from a practitioner perspective, Elliott would have us believe that such a conjoining may prove 'unlikely to materialize' on the grounds that, 'The majority of . . . critics of SER are school improvement researchers operating with a completely different vision or "theory" of education' (p. 201).

It would appear, therefore, that the prospect of merger has both its supporters and its critics, and the reality of a future for SER and SIR as a unified force at present seems a long way off. As Hopkins (1996) suggests, it will be necessary for SIR to address three sets of issues (methodology, policy and practice) in order that it may 'enter a full and mutually supportive partnership with school effectiveness; assuming of course that those working in that tradition do likewise' (p. 48). Thus it would seem, as Hopkins suggests, that the prospect of merger will remain at the level of aspiration unless such discussion and conceptual work is done. This view is underlined by Gray *et al.* (1996) who suggest 'that suspension of historic disciplinary disagreements and a willingness to merge historically determined disciplinary beliefs are both essential for the effectiveness and improvement communities in the remainder of the 1990s' (p. 18).

In drawing upon my own experiences of working with teachers on school-based improvement projects, I would want to reinforce Stoll's assertion that, 'If practitioners can see and make links between school effectiveness and school improvement, surely it is time for researchers studying the two areas to do the same and to work with schools to develop a deeper and more meaningful understanding of the research and its implications for practice' (Stoll 1996: 52). There is a need to move beyond the rhetoric of effectiveness and improvement towards the reality of involving teachers as key players in a process of striving for excellence. This cannot be achieved by simple exhortation of the virtues of such work. It needs to encompass, as Fletcher suggests in the case of appraisal, a more explicit recognition of teachers as individuals, and as such requires stronger emphasis to be placed upon the management of the relationship between the rational and non-rational elements of schools as postmodern organizations:

> Better performance does not come from simply setting goals, giving a small amount of extra financial reward and exhorting people to go for improved quality and customer care. It comes from a better and more even relationship, or contract, between organisations and individuals, one that recognises individual differences in needs and capacities, and which accepts that, beyond certain levels, asking more of people is actually counter-productive. So alongside the performance management

culture and the learning organisation, we have to put something else
– the caring organisation.

(p. 148)

In this respect, the future success of school effectiveness and improvement research in having any real impact at school level may in some part
prove to be reliant upon how widely it is perceived to be making a contribution to the development of the kind of adaptive, learning and caring cultures
described by Fletcher. As Stoll and Fink (1996) conclude, this should perhaps be considered to be 'the final ingredient' which underlies the bringing together of concepts from both school effectiveness and improvement:

> caring requires expectations of quality work from all children . . .
> Caring teachers expect all pupils to do well; they do what it takes to
> the best of their abilities to help each pupil achieve. The same prin-
> ciples of caring that engage pupils in their learning apply equally to
> caring for teachers, for parents, for important ideas, or for organisa-
> tions like schools.

(p. 192)

In acknowledging the place which teachers deserve on the school effectiveness and improvement stage, we are faced with the task not just of caring
for them, but with the need to empower them, in order that they may, in
partnership with us (their researcher colleagues in higher education) make
a real contribution to the school effectiveness and improvement debate.
Facilitating such involvement must be recognized, therefore, as the most
important challenge in finding a way ahead for school effectiveness and
improvement research in the future.

Note

1 NWCSEUS is a partnership of schools, colleges, LEAs and universities working
together on school-based action research. Current membership includes Liverpool, Manchester and Salford LEAs, primary, secondary and special schools and
colleges in these authorities, together with Manchester Victoria University and
the Manchester Metropolitan University.

2

School improvement: an overview of key findings and messages

Rob Halsall

As Carter suggests in the preceding chapter, the school effectiveness paradigm cannot be ignored because 'understandings of what is meant by school effectiveness are likely to dominate any future work which would bring together the effectiveness and improvement movements'. Additionally, the findings of effectiveness research do have the potential to be used as data to feed into debates concerning school improvement. However, it is clear from her chapter that it is the improvement paradigm, with its concerns to do with the processes of achieving effectiveness and with managing change, that demands greater attention. As Stoll (1996) notes, in relation to the Effective Schools Project in Ontario, while this began as an attempt to bring the results of school effectiveness research into schooling practices, it soon became clear that what was most important to the effective implementation of the project was:

> the adoption at school and system level of organizational and planning arrangements from the school improvement literature . . . 'top-down' mandates to schools to address the characteristics of effectiveness failed because they did not engender ownership and commitment, nor did they pay attention to the process and impact of change of those who worked through it.
>
> (p. 58)

The purpose of this chapter, then, is to overview the main findings of, and messages from, those who have been at the 'leading edge' in working within the school improvement paradigm.

The importance of culture

What is culture?

One of the most consistent messages from the school improvement literature is that school culture has a powerful impact on any change effort. Indeed, the notion which is reinforced time and again is that the crucial change is not to do with this or that innovation or development priority, but with changing the culture of an institution. It is this that enables and supports the effective planning and management of change. 'Unless we address the issue of school culture . . . there is little chance that school improvement will be achieved' (Hopkins *et al.* 1994: 85).

Now, culture is difficult to define. Essentially, it is the set of assumptions, beliefs and values that predominate in an organization, and which operate in an unconscious or semi-unconscious way. These are not as intangible as they might first seem. They are often reflected in behavioural regularities, for example, how teachers interact with one another and with students, and how students interact with one another. It is also possible to identify values that are espoused through staff room conversations and institutional mission statements. Equally, one can identify guiding philosophies, for example those underlying approaches to teaching and learning, such as student-centredness. Finally, aspects of culture can be gleaned from the climate or ethos of a school. While this is difficult to 'see', there is little doubt that people, especially those with experience of several organizations, can often – and quickly – get a sense of it.

Cultures for school improvement

Equally consistent as the general message concerning the influence of culture on change efforts is that to do with the relationship between a collaborative culture and the likelihood of those efforts being successful. Chief among the characteristics of collaborative cultures are:

- Teachers working with and for each other on a range of tasks such as curriculum planning and design, resources preparation, action research, paired teaching and the observation of each others' teaching and mentoring. There is a cooperative, rather than individualistic or competitive, set of relationships.
- Voluntarism: collaboration arises from teachers' views regarding its value to themselves and to the students. This is in stark contrast to the contrived collegiality, described by Hargreaves (1994), which is compulsory, bureaucratically administered and geared to mandates of the government or

headteacher which the staff do not endorse – redolent of too many school development plans, for instance.

- A collective commitment to the school's vision, values, purposes and development priorities.
- Leadership roles for, and involvement in planning by, more rather than fewer teachers, and a shared understanding and endorsement of the responsibilities and obligations of different role-holders.

This set of characteristics of collaborative cultures closely mirror two of the cultural norms that Stoll and Fink (1996) identify as underpinning successful school improvement efforts. The first concerns the existence of shared goals, pursuit of a common vision and a shared sense of direction. The second is collegiality: mutual assistance, joint work and sharing – the sense of 'we're all working on it together'. Others either clearly contribute to the development and maintenance of a collaborative culture, or are more likely to arise out of it than they are from one that is less so:

- A belief that everyone can and should make a difference to student progress, development and achievements and that 'it's the responsibility of us all'.
- A belief in the notion that improvement is always possible, that it is a process and an always shifting end.
- A belief that teachers are learners and that maximization of student learning is dependent on this.
- A belief that everyone, both teachers and students, has something to offer and, consequently, a sense of mutual respect.
- Openness: a willingness and ability to speak one's mind and to listen to others, with a view to being constructively critical and a readiness to handle disagreements.
- A willingness to take risks, to try something different, in the knowledge that if it does not quite work out there will be an acknowledgement of the intent and of the effort made, and an absence of unconstructive criticism.
- A readiness to celebrate peoples' efforts and successes, both those of teachers and students, manifested in such things as verbal and written praise and the celebration of (student) achievement evenings.

Such cultural norms and collaborative cultures do not simply emerge from nowhere. Although ultimately they depend on the proclivities of staff themselves, they are facilitated by senior managers through the deliberate creation of structures that support the work of teachers and through the identification of tasks that teachers can collaborate on and take leadership roles in. Indeed, Hopkins *et al.* (1994) suggest that 'knowing how to bring about cultural change will become an increasingly important topic for school managers' (p. 108). This is pursued later in this chapter.

Expressions of school culture

One of the most interesting outcomes of the literature has been the identification and portrayal of different types of school in terms of how their culture is 'expressed'. Hopkins *et al.* offer four which are rooted in their notion of school improvement as a journey. Stoll and Fink's (1996) five-fold typology is based on a matrix of effective – ineffective and improving – declining schools.

Both typologies identify moving schools which possess many of the cultural norms described earlier. They feature most elements of a collaborative culture, have achieved an appropriate balance between development and maintenance activity, and continually adapt calmly but surely to changing internal and external environments. These schools know what they want to achieve and have the skills, systems and willingness to succeed. Stoll and Fink see these schools as both effective and improving. In stark contrast are those that Hopkins *et al.* refer to as stuck, Stoll and Fink as sinking and Reynolds (1996) as failing. They exhibit a sense of powerlessness on the part of staff, low expectations all around and an individualistic mode of working, within which teaching is an isolated activity. Indeed, many of the relationships are actually dysfunctional. Change is seen as either unnecessary or as being the responsibility of senior managers alone. In contrast with the norm that 'everyone can make a difference', there tends to be externalization of blame: lack of student progress and achievement is laid at the door of others, for example the students themselves, their home background or the local community. These are Stoll and Fink's ineffective and declining schools and, as they contend, are often found in lower socioeconomic status (SES) areas which have relatively few demanding parents and plenty of targets for blame.

Both sets of authors have also drawn portraits of schools which are living on past achievements, promenading or cruising schools. These are the schools which seem to be effective: their raw test and examination results are good, but the value added by them is not particularly impressive and they are not as effective for all their students as one would hope. However, because the overall raw results place them relatively well in league tables and please many parents, they are reluctant to change: 'Why fix it if it ain't broke?' is the overriding mentality. These are the schools that Stoll and Fink describe as 'the good schools if this were 1965'. One danger they face is that more and more moving schools will 'overtake' them.

The fourth expression of culture penned by Hopkins *et al.* relates to the wandering school. This has, in one sense, too much innovation. There are too many disparate targets, reflecting a lack of clear vision and destination. Indeed, there is often a lack of agreement about the main purposes of the school and, often, the pursuit of different aims by individuals and groups. 'Balkanization', rather than collaboration, is the order of the day. One result is that much of the change that does occur is not deep-seated. Another is that development takes place at the expense of, rather than in tandem with, maintenance of what is already sound practice. Stoll and Fink's strolling and struggling schools are separate categories but both share elements of the wandering school. The strolling school is willing to change and is moving to some kind of improvement, but at a fairly slow rate. It, too, has ill-defined and sometimes conflicting aims that do not help in the efforts to improve. Struggling schools also wish to implement change and make the effort. However, while there might be more in the way of a shared vision, the skills necessary to manage the change process are lacking and much work is needed on the internal conditions of the school.

The sorts of descriptions provided by such typologies can usefully be considered by schools as part of their audit or self-reflection processes when considering their future priorities. The fact of the matter is that although certain 'broad brush stroke' suggestions regarding school improvement strategies can be useful to most schools – and some of these are signalled later in this chapter – the existence of different expressions of culture means that there can be no blueprint for how to improve. Different schools require different strategies for different priorities. Thus, it would seem to make sense that while a promenading or cruising school could do with attending more to development, rather than maintenance, activity, wandering or strolling schools need to consider the opposite. They also need to achieve greater clarity and a clearer focus regarding their priorities and to attend to the integration of some of these. And all of these types of school, together with struggling schools, would almost certainly benefit from staff development activity concerning the skills and processes of school development planning. As for stuck schools, the culture and situation is such that the first steps toward improvement might need to include what Reynolds (1996) refers to as quasi-therapeutic programmes for staff, and to make a particular point of celebrating, and learning from what successes there are in 'pockets' of the school. However, it might be the case that relatively little can actually be achieved solely from within: a significant degree of external support and, even, direction could be necessary.

Finally, it does need to be recognized that it can be unhelpful to over-generalize about the culture of an organization. First, no typology can capture the nuances of the differences between schools. Secondly, although it might be possible to perceive of culture as a school-level phenomenon, there are also subcultures and different levels and forms of both effectiveness and improvement within schools. This, of course, is one reason why schools can be pulled in different directions and why there might be barriers to the development of whole school collegiality. It also means that different strategies might be needed for different elements and activities. In short, not only is it simplistic to think about an improvement blueprint which is appropriate for all schools, but it is likely that a varied menu of specific strategies and actions are required within any one institution.

The importance of structures

Structure and culture

If, then, culture is such an important factor in school improvement, how can it be changed? It is unlikely that it can be changed directly. Rather, one needs to work on changing organizational structures in order to begin shifting the culture. This shift, in turn, enables the new structures to work more effectively and this then serves to sustain the changed culture. As a result, efforts to impact on teaching and learning will be less likely to founder. A good deal of attention has been paid to the relationship between structure and culture by Hopkins and his colleagues, especially in connection with their involvement in the Improving the Quality of Education for All (IQEA) project. Hopkins (1996) points out that culture is often revealed through an organization's structures, especially those that bear on how teachers work together and define their professional relationships. 'It is through the new relationships and the content and style of talk arising from structural changes that the culture begins to shift' (p. 37).

Their work in the IQEA project has led Hopkins and his colleagues to identify the importance of what they call management arrangements, which they classify into:

- Frameworks that provide the structures which guide actions and within which action occurs. They include the school's aims, policies, decision making and consultative systems, and implementation strategies.
- Shared understanding and clarification of different roles within the school, and of whom is responsible for what.
- Ways of working.

In the context of these, a set of internal conditions has been identified which seem to underpin the work of the more successful IQEA schools.

Internal conditions

Hopkins (1996) lists the internal conditions as:

- attention to the potential benefits of enquiry and reflection;
- a commitment to collaborative planning;
- a commitment to staff development;
- the involvement of staff, students and the community in school policies and decisions;
- effective coordination strategies;
- effective leadership, but not just by the head; the leadership function is spread throughout the school.

These are considered in greater depth later in this chapter, along with other factors conducive to school improvement, but for now, the key point is that it is the existence of these internal conditions that can promote the sort of collaborative, involving and learning culture which has been proposed as being most supportive of successful and lasting school improvement efforts. 'If they are not promising, altering or dealing with them should become part of the design of the improvement programme' (Louis and Miles 1992: 189). It is these modifications that will represent some of the priorities within school development plans to do with 'root' innovations, with 'branch' innovations aimed at more directly impacting on student outcomes stemming from these. 'Unless a school is prepared to make tangible changes in conditions in order to support staff in working towards the priorities [to do with outcomes], little progress can be anticipated' (Hopkins *et al.* 1994: 204). In short, attending to the internal conditions strengthens the school's capacity to manage the sorts of change it desires for its students. Some of the key elements identified within the IQEA project have been the use of organizational structures such as senior management teams and school-wide task groups, active involvement of the headteacher in development projects, the appointment of school improvement coordinators and appropriate training of these, for example in how to organize and use whole staff training more effectively.

However, it should be noted that different sorts of structures might be needed for different purposes. In particular, and as described earlier in discussing the differing needs of, say, promenading and wandering schools, due attention needs to be paid to the distinction between schools' development and maintenance activities. Different, though complementary, structures and management arrangements are likely to be needed to undertake these. 'The most successful schools are deliberately creating contrasting but mutually supportive structural arrangements to cope with the twin pressures of development and maintenance ... structures that attempt to do both usually do neither satisfactorily' (Hopkins 1996: 38). Clearly, though, it is development and change which is at the heart of school improvement. So far we have identified the crucial importance of considering the role of cultures and structures in this. We now turn our attention to other key factors, most of which can be seen as arising out of the discussion of the culture-structure dimension of schooling.

A focus on teachers and students, teaching and learning

School improvement is ultimately about the enhancement of student progress, development and achievements, so it is not surprising that most commentators have identified the central importance of addressing issues concerning the quality of learning and teacher development. 'Successful schools are successful in so far as they facilitate the learning of both students and teachers' (Hopkins *et al.* 1994: 60). What are the conditions for effective classroom teaching which will support student learning, and for effective teacher development?

Effective teaching and effective teachers

Extensive research has been undertaken on the themes of effective teaching and effective teachers. There is not the space in this chapter to review this, though readers will find a useful, succinct discussion in Sammons *et al.* (1995). My focus is on the various sets of 'guidelines' or 'conditions' that have been produced concerning effective teaching and learning, which have been informed by the research. The first is that adopted by the Office for Standards in Education (Ofsted) in its Framework for the Inspection of Schools in England and Wales (Figure 2.1).

The second set of guidelines emanates from the extension of the IQEA project's focus on school-level conditions for school improvement to classroom conditions (Figure 2.2).

Clearly, there is considerable overlap between these two sets of guidelines. What is interesting, though, are the differences between them, which can possibly be located in the differences between the social engineering and reflective action perspectives which Carter associates with the school effectiveness and improvement paradigms respectively. Certainly, the emphases in Hopkins's contribution on the quality of relationships and on reflection on one's own practice are notably absent from Ofsted's framework.

Judgements (about the quality of teaching) should be based on the extent to which teachers:

• have a secure knowledge and understanding of the subjects or areas they teach;

• set high expectations so as to challenge pupils and deepen their knowledge and understanding;

• plan effectively;

• employ methods and organizational strategies which match curricular objectives and the needs of all pupils;

• manage pupils well and achieve high standards of discipline;

• use time and resources effectively;

• assess pupils' work thoroughly and constructively, and use assessments to inform teaching;

• use homework effectively to reinforce and/or extend what is learned in school.

Figure 2.1 The quality of teaching I
Source: Ofsted (1995)

- *Authentic relationships* – being the quality, openness and congruence of relationships existing in the classroom.

- *Rules and boundaries* – being the pattern of expectations set by the teacher and school for student performance and behaviour.

- *Teacher's repertoire* – being the range of teaching styles and models available to a teacher which can be used at different times and with different students depending on the nature of the outcomes desired, and the curriculum context.

- *Reflection on teaching* – being the capacity of the individual teacher to reflect on their own practice and to put to the test of practice specifications of teaching from other sources.

- *Resources and preparation* – being the access of teachers to a range of pertinent teaching materials and the ability to plan and differentiate these materials for a range of students.

- *Pedagogic partnerships* – being the ability of teachers to form professional relationships within the classroom that focus on the study and improvement of the practice of teaching.

Figure 2.2   The quality of teaching II
Source: Hopkins (1995)

Teacher development

If effective teachers and effective teaching are key factors in the enhancement of student outcomes, then teacher development must be central to school improvement efforts. I would suggest that there are three broad focus areas to consider in relation to teacher development:

- content and pedagogy relevant to particular initiatives being pursued;
- more generic skills, attitudes and attributes that can impact on classroom performance, irrespective of the nature of any particular initiative;
- understanding of the change process itself: 'In school improvement efforts, a key capacity that differentiates more and less successful schools is understanding of the change process'. (Stoll and Fink 1996: 45)

However, research concerning the effect of teacher development initiatives on improved teaching and learning suggests that the impact has been disappointing. 'We have a picture of in-service initiatives that are poorly conceptualized, insensitive to the concerns of individual participants, and . . . make little effort to help participants relate their learning experiences to their usual workplace conditions' (Hopkins *et al.* 1994: 61). Too much teacher development has been in aid of the search for quick fix solutions to the variety of external imperatives that have bedeviled schools in recent years. This does not sit well with the notion of a thoughtful, coherent teacher development strategy. What is needed is a developmental approach which, though it cannot ignore immediate needs, should not be constrained by them. Rather, we need to identify skills and qualities that, at the end of the day, represent attributes that will enable staff to respond effectively to whatever imperatives arise. Here lies the importance of the second and third focus areas for teacher development outlined above.

Moore (1988) suggests a number of guidelines for facilitating teacher development. Of these, I would prioritize the following:

- a collaborative approach to diagnosing needs and to designing, implementing and evaluating teacher development activities;
- using teachers' own experiences as the chief starting point for learning activities;
- encouraging and enabling staff to define their own learning objectives;
- developing the skills of critical, reflective thinking about classroom practice, school level issues and factors, and about the process of change;
- integrating learning with action: the adoption of a problem posing and problem solving perspective.

The second and last of these in particular relate closely to another useful pointer, deriving from Joyce's (1992) distinction between the workshop and the workplace. While activity in the former context can promote enhanced understandings and provide opportunities to 'practice' skills, these need to be transferred to the workplace if they are to have any practical impact. Moreover, staff will need to be supported in this transfer process. Here, Hopkins *et al.* argue that successful schools build infrastructures for teacher development within their day-to-day arrangements. For example, teacher development is an integral part of school development plans, it takes place on a regular basis, it includes a focus on teaching and learning as well as on school-level issues, and it rests on the availability of workplace-based activities such as peer observation, regular discussion and reviews of practice, and on mentoring arrangements. In relation to the last of these, there is now in the UK an increasing number of schools that can build upon their expertise in the mentoring of student teachers, that has arisen out of the reforms which have given a greater role to schools in initial teacher training. To put it bluntly, a school might be very supportive of its teachers by way, for example, of sending them on courses and conferences, or by inviting visiting speakers. But what do they then do to ensure that such experiences are used and built upon?

This leads us to what is, perhaps, the most crucial 'guideline'. There is a need to integrate the development needs of the school itself and of its teachers as individuals: to interrelate school and teacher development in mutually supportive ways. Schools cannot develop unless their teachers also develop but, at the same time, as a result of the changed educational scene it is inescapable that much teacher development has to be linked to that of colleagues and to whole school priorities. However, it is only in conditions where collaborative cultures pertain, and where staff have contributed to the establishment of priorities, that teachers will feel that such linkage really does benefit themselves as individuals. Some of the most promising school improvement initiatives have attempted to embrace this integrated teacher-school development guideline as a key feature of their work. For example, in Toronto's Learning Consortium (Fullan *et al.* 1990), teachers worked to improve their knowledge of the curriculum, child development and learning styles, of classroom management, and of instructional skills and strategies. Simultaneously, schools worked on improving shared purpose, on establishing collegial norms and a norm of continuous improvement and on structures, for example organizational arrangements, policies (including those to do with staff development), role clarification and ways of working (including mentoring practice). Central to all of this was the concept of teachers as learners.

Inquiry and reflection

Much of the preceding section is about the need for schools to be learning organizations, and it comes as no surprise that another consistent message from the literature is that successful school improvement is associated with inquiry and reflection at both individual and institutional levels. Such activity is seen as increasingly important in the context of an education system which is becoming ever more complex at all levels. This is partly because in such circumstances more and more decisions have to be made, and they are increasingly difficult to take. The most appropriate, or 'best', decisions are usually those informed by sufficient and relevant information, and by careful analysis of this – though other factors, such as the school's aims and values and available resources, must also be taken into account.

Inquiry covers a variety of activities. Here, I touch briefly on monitoring, evaluation and research. Regarding the first of these, Fitz-Gibbon (1996) argues that:

> If schools evolve . . . they do so in response to information about their students, their potential students, external requirements and internal information about resources . . . Self-organizing units can only respond effectively if they have the necessary information . . . the system needs the capacity to act in multiple self-organizing, adequately informed, local units, i.e. the capacity to act on the basis of feedback . . . Monitoring systems . . . provide a constant flow of feedback. Thus monitoring systems fit in with the model of a school as an evolving complex system.
> (pp. 83–4)

Indeed, Fitz-Gibbon suggests that 'the setting up of systems of monitoring with feedback is the most vital task of the next decade' (p. 87). To this, though, we must add the role of evaluation. The distinction here is that while monitoring is about the routine collection of data on a wide front – which helps in meeting many regular information needs quickly – evaluation is to do with data collection for the purpose of making judgements about a specific problem or activity. Evaluation (and here I mean, in particular, self-evaluation) can support both teacher and school development by informing staff, and others, as to whether they have, in fact, made a difference, for whom they have made a difference, and in what ways they have. It can also provide insights into what has contributed to, or impeded, success and the reasons for this, thus providing the basis for reflective activity and for the next stage of action.

More generally, there is the role of research to consider. First, there is research undertaken by teachers themselves, usually for the purpose of helping them to understand and refine their own practice. Secondly, there is their study of, and response to, the research of others. In both cases there are important issues to do with consciousness of, and accessibility to, research findings, and with the development of a range of research skills, for example regarding both the undertaking of research activity and the critical understanding of findings. Here, the role of LEA-schools-university consortia can be significant, as can that of other bodies such as the Teacher Training Agency (TTA) which has, as part of its mission, the development of 'Teaching as a Research Based Profession'.

Now, I do not intend to further elaborate on monitoring and evaluation in this chapter, nor indeed on the broader issues of teacher research and the study and use of research by teachers. These are matters that are at the heart of this book; it would be repetitive to say more in this chapter where the aim is to simply 'flag' them as key issues arising out of the more general school improvement literature. What I will stress here, though, is something which serves to underline the variety of case studies of teacher research presented as Part 2 of this book. There is a parallel with what has been argued in relation to teacher and school development. Inquiry and reflection are activities that are necessary for, and pertinent to, all levels of the system: across schools, whole school activities and reviews, individual departments and individual classrooms. Also, in line with school improvement being about both enhancing the school's capacity for managing change and enhancing student outcomes, inquiry and reflection must be directed towards both of these concerns.

The process of change

Much of what has been written so far in this book suggests that change is not an event but, rather, a long-term process. What is needed is an orientation towards ongoing development: movement is always necessary, it is only its extent and direction that varies. Moreover, schools cannot be seen simply as the focus of change, but also as being at the centre of change.

Change as everyone's business

Top-down measures on their own will not prove effective because they ignore the process of how reforms and innovations are actually put into practice. It is the implementation and institutionalization of change that determine what outcomes there will be. As Hopkins *et al.* (1994) argue, 'Although policies set directions and provide a framework, they do not and cannot determine outcomes' (p. 18). Additionally, they refer to McLaughlin's analysis of the Rand Change Agent Study in the US:

> it is exceedingly difficult for policy to change practice ... the nature, amount, and pace of change at the local level was a product of local factors that were largely beyond the control of higher-level policy makers.
>
> (McLaughlin 1990: 12)

Successful, sustained change, then, can only come about through those who are responsible for its implementation and it is because of this, of course, that so much importance needs to be attached to the acquisition of new knowledge and skills on the part of teachers, and to impacting on their attitudes, beliefs and values.

Evolutionary planning

As Carter points out in Chapter 1, and as Cockett explores in Chapter 3, change is also messy and unpredictable. Because both internal and external environments are always subject to change, tightly specified and fixed organizational plans are not appropriate; the need is for an evolutionary plan (which fits with Hopkins's metaphor of school improvement as a journey). Although there needs to be a clear general destination, based on an initial image or vision of what sort of future is desired, the strategies for arriving there are formulated in the knowledge that they will need to be constantly reviewed and refined as new, and often unexpected, events arise.

Louis and Miles (1992) point out that detailed planning has usually been regarded as an activity that precedes action: it comes before implementation, an essential feature of the 'rational' change model. However, they suggest that it might be more appropriate to act first. This might be in order, for example, to create a sense of excitement, to create the energy for change or to help defuse scepticism, and thence to provide a more solid foundation for planning efforts. 'Effective action ... often stimulates an interest in planning rather than vice-versa' (p. 204). Additionally, 'action first' can help to stimulate the thinking that effective planning requires: often, 'planning cannot be carried out very effectively until people already find themselves in a learning mode' (p. 202). That learning, Louis and Miles suggest, comes about when we take action, gather information about it and its effects, and then reflect on it in the light of an emerging sense of what it is precisely that we wish to achieve. In similar vein, Hopkins and his colleagues (e.g. Hargreaves and Hopkins 1991, Hopkins *et al.* 1994) have warned against approaches to school development planning which encourage schools to view the elements of planning in a linear fashion. Although delineating different stages can be helpful in raising understanding of the planning process, a linear model rarely works in practice. In fact, it can be counter-productive as necessary responses to new opportunities and threats can be missed.

Louis and Miles also warn against another feature often associated with 'rational' change. Following detailed analysis of five case study schools involved in school improvement efforts, they conclude that the more narrow and specific the goals, the more likely it was that a school would run into problems in creating an environment for change. Broader and vaguer goals actually allowed much more action across the school that generated support for change. In turn, a much clearer vision emerged as different actions became linked, successful and owned by staff.

An adaptive model of change

While the messiness of change demands an evolutionary approach, the uniqueness of institutions, the power of culture and the importance of ownership of change all call for an adaptive perspective to be taken, 'sensitive to the situation of the individual school . . . and demonstrating a concern for developing a capacity for change within the school situation' (Hopkins *et al.* 1994: 29). Louis and Miles (1992) characterize the adaptive model of change thus:

- *Vision-driven*: schools do not simply react to crises or external imperatives, but have a clear sense of what sort of future they want. Consequently, they have their own priorities, and when external demands arise these are tailored to, and interpreted in the light of, the school's vision.
- *Guided by judgement, not rules*: teachers are seen as autonomous, or at least semi-autonomous, professionals who possess problem-posing and problem-solving skills. Schools progress by drawing on teachers' own judgements about what is appropriate; 'teaching is viewed as a highly skilled craft rather than as predictable technology that can be predetermined and managed via rules' (p. 24).
- *Self-accountability*: a sense of responsibility and accountability are owned by members of an organization rather than simply imposed from outside; 'learning and improvement of performance will occur only from serious peer and group assessments of how well their own judgements are working' (p. 24).

- *Team-focused*: organizations need to operate on the basis of teams rather than hierarchies, with membership drawn from across different 'levels' and roles, and based on interest and expertise rather than position. Teams are not necessarily permanent groups but established in the light of, and organized around, changing needs and problems.
- *Flexibility*: although specialization is important, it is necessary for people to be versatile and able to carry out different functions and activities, with the authority to carry out tasks being based on ability rather than on position.

Clearly, such a model of change implies a particular view of leadership, more widespread leadership, new ways of working together and the sort of climate for constant learning and teacher development that has been highlighted earlier. More generally, it lays stress on the notion of an involving and empowering organization.

The involving and empowering organization

Central to the adaptive model of change is a view of teachers as decision makers. Much of the literature focuses on the key role that teachers have to play in school improvement and, of course, the need for this is a major theme in Chapter 1. It is imperative, then, to develop their will to make school improvement work and to enable them to achieve their potential as key players on the school improvement stage: 'it is the task of all educationalists . . . to serve the teachers; for only teachers are in a position to create good teaching' (Stenhouse 1984: 69). Central to this is the whole business of teacher development that was explored earlier, but here, I focus on involving staff in vision building, planning and leadership.

Vision building and planning

I mean by vision an expression of a desired future which encapsulates the over-arching purposes of an organization. A key message is that 'followers are not sold a vision, but know they have helped create it' (Louis and Miles 1992: 236). In considering the case studies in the National Commission on Education's study of how schools in disadvantaged areas can become effective, Maden and Hillman (1996) indicate a variety of ways in which visions originate. They include particular histories of long-standing aims, for example a community school ideal; responses to dramatic threats, for example the threat of closure; responses to particular local circumstances, for example racism or unemployment; and personnel changes, especially the appointment of a new headteacher. They comment that the change process often

originates with the headteacher, engaging in the identification and analysis of critical issues, and defining out of this key priorities. However, they
also observe from the case study schools how these had been reshaped and
given substance by the staff at large. This had led to the gradual emergence
of an often redefined and clearer vision through a participatory process
involving, for example, the use of working groups and reflection on early
actions taken.

It is not the case that all members of staff have to be directly involved in
the participatory processes. However, where they are not, it is also essential
to ensure that the resulting vision and priorities are communicated to all
teachers and support staff, and understood and approved by as many people
as possible, resulting in a unity of purpose: a *shared* vision. The importance
of this cannot be overstated. It 'provides both a sense of higher purpose
beyond the everyday routines of school life, and ballast against the turbulent waves of excessive change [and can] be used as a guide for exercising a
multitude of judgements during the course of day-to-day working life' (Maden
and Hillman 1996: 317). It also helps to give shape to staff attitudes, to create
a driving force for change, and to provide a sense of values and criteria for
choosing both development and maintenance priorities.

Similarly, a critical mass of staff needs to be actively involved in the planning process, and as many as possible need to be made aware of the outcomes of this and how these relate to the vision. They also need to understand
the implications for future practice. Without such knowledge, understanding
and, of course, support for the decisions taken, there is likely to be a gap
between planning and implementation. This underlines what an increasing
number of writers have commented on in relation to school development
plans: it is not so much the plan itself that is the key to successful development, but the planning process. It is this which has the potential to spread
ownership of, and commitment to, the plan and to maximize the chances
of implementation 'taking off'.

Sharing and extending leadership

There is a wealth of material concerning the key role of headteachers in the
development of more successful schools. Here, there is a specific focus on
the kinds of approach they might adopt to leadership. Thus:

- Transactional leadership is actually more about management than leadership. While there is a concern for identifying goals and producing
  development plans, the emphasis tends to be on maintenance rather than
  change, in the design of operational systems for carrying out the plans,
  and on ensuring that productive work ensues. What we have, in essence,
  is a series of top-down transactions within a given, unchanging cultural
  context. The purposes of the organization might or might not be clear,

but either way the approach is not conducive to successful management of change in an era of instability and unpredictability.

- Transformational leadership, on the other hand, is more about making new things happen in the light of vision building and as a response to changing circumstances. There is recognition of a need, if change is to occur, to stimulate and inspire people, and to empower them. Both of these conditions are met in part by encouraging teachers to take on, and supporting them in, leadership roles of their own; and more generally by transforming their feelings, attitudes and beliefs. At the heart of this, then, is the leader's role in transforming the culture of a school. 'Transformational leaders not only manage the structure: they purposefully impact the culture to achieve school development' (Stoll and Fink 1996: 106). Indeed, returning to the culture-structure dimension of schooling discussed earlier, structures are seen as important because they can influence the culture and because of their potential to empower rather than control.
- Invitational leadership is in one sense complementary to, or a way into, transformational activity. It has been discussed at some length by Stoll and Fink (1996). They refer to Purkey and Novak's (1990) metaphor of invitation and disinvitation to describe positive and negative interactions which shape people's self-concepts and self-images which, in turn, affect how they behave. As organizational change rests on promoting change in people then efforts to alter their self-perceptions are necessary. One way of approaching this is to communicate invitational messages to staff, predicated on transparently high expectations of them, respect for them and trust in their capacities.

In short, it is attention to transformational activity and the communication of positive, invitational messages that enable cultures and self-beliefs to shift in ways supportive of school improvement efforts, through the involvement and empowerment of staff both generally and, more specifically, in leadership roles themselves. It is in this sense that the most important role of the organizational leader is to spread leadership. It is not surprising that Maden and Hillman (1996) observe that all of the headteachers in the National Commission's study were:

- accessible to staff;
- willing to build the expertise of others to undertake leadership roles, and shared leadership responsibilities wherever possible;
- adept at building effective teams;
- attentive to working on school structures and to ways in which staff could work together in order to encourage collegiality.

To close this section, and indeed to presage the next, Maden and Hillman capture well the importance of leadership both 'from the top' and across the school:

it is clear . . . that the will-power of one strong leader . . . or even of a determined management team, is important but not in itself enough. Improvement is achieved by the whole school: by the teachers, but also by the pupils; by all the staff, not only the teachers; and by the parents and the wider community.

(1996: 362)

Partnerships

The last part of the quote above is a reminder that, so far, I have focused almost exclusively on the role of teachers and headteachers in school improvement. However, just as school leaders need to share ownership and responsibility with teachers, so they must all share these with students, parents and others. 'It does seem that some schools are able to create positive relationships with their wider community that help to create a supportive climate for learning' (Hopkins *et al.* 1994: 126). This section, then, examines the role of the wider school community and the role of partnerships between schools and other bodies.

The wider school community

Students
There is a particular need to work with students in school improvement efforts because they are major participants in the change process, not simply 'end users'. Some of the more powerful ways in which they have been involved have included:

- Encouraging them to take greater control over their own work. This does not imply unlimited responsibility for a long list of tasks, but it does call for greater variety in teaching strategies and learning environments, including more use of active and experiential learning strategies and the development of skills that are required for more autonomous learning.
- Listening, and responding, to students' views. One of the greatest barriers to change is their feeling that teachers do not listen to students' opinions and, indeed, are not interested in them as people. This does little for their self-esteem and is unlikely to encourage them to respond positively to demands made on them. Stoll and Fink (1996) reported the results of a questionnaire administered to secondary students in the Halton district of Ontario. Only half of them believed that teachers listened when they had an opinion about school-related issues, and one-quarter felt that teachers were not interested in them as people.
- Giving students responsibility (leadership roles) in the life of the school. Forms of responsibility noted by Maden and Hillman (1996) in the

National Commission's case study schools include helping younger children, for example through paired reading schemes; non-elitist prefect systems; involvement in school councils and the formulation of whole school policies, for example in behaviour or bullying; and involvement in the production of materials, for example induction booklets for new entrants.

Parents
Since the 1950s, educational sociologists have repeatedly demonstrated that parental attitudes have a significant impact on student attitudes and achievement. The establishment of parent–school partnerships is one way forward in affecting these, as well as in providing a broader base for the recruitment of 'critical friends'. The following abridged version of Epstein's (1995) framework for school–family partnerships usefully points to the variety of activities which can be undertaken in the furtherance of school improvement efforts:

- *Parenting*: helping to create an environment in homes that is supportive of learning, for example by schools providing advice on how parents can support their children's homework tasks and habits or, even, by providing parenting skills training. An excellent example of this approach to parent–school partnership is the Summer Home Learning Packets project in Baltimore, USA (Epstein *et al.* 1996). Another is the IMPACT mathematics home learning project in the UK which, tellingly, found that the factor which influences the choice of parents to participate is not social class but the enthusiasm of the teacher (Merttens 1996).
- *Communicating*: ensuring that there is a free flow of information to and from parents. This includes parents being sufficiently informed about the school itself, its policies and practices, and about their children's progress. Here, Maden and Hillman (1996) point to examples of different practices such as newsletters, regular progress reports and the use of schoolwork and homework diaries.
- *Volunteering*: obtaining parental assistance in the school. This pertains to the classroom, for example generally as 'teachers' helpers' or more specifically in reading with, and listening to, children read. Such activity is often an important element of family literacy projects. It also embraces activities such as fund raising and organizing social events, helping to supervise school trips, running the school bookshop and a host of other possibilities, again well documented by the National Commission's case study schools.
- *Decision-making*: for example, through including parents in vision building and the establishment of school priorities. Thus, Hopkins *et al.* (1994) describe an example of one school that wanted to stand back from itself in order to appraise its strengths and weaknesses. Parents were invited to

join the 'appraisal team' and to comment on the framework for appraisal. Together with staff and governor representatives, they were then involved in identifying a range of issues, in evaluating different areas of school life and in identifying targets for further evaluation.

Of course, the development of a strong family-school partnership cannot be achieved overnight. Time is needed to build mutual trust and respect, to convince parents that there is indeed a genuine welcome on offer, and to define new roles and relationships. Also, it is often the case that teachers need to develop the skills that will enable them to work effectively with parents. However, as Chrispeels argues, the 'efforts that schools are undertaking to restructure the school learning environment offer rich opportunities to rethink and restructure home-school-community partnerships' (1996 p. 318).

Governing bodies
Especially since the 1988 Education Reform Act which invested them with greater powers, the role of school governors in school improvement has to be considered. Barber *et al.* (1995) identify three major roles for governing bodies:

- *To provide a strategic view*: by producing a strategy for improvement, by setting and reviewing the framework within which the headteacher and staff run the school, and by focusing on the key issues of raising standards of achievement, establishing high expectations and promoting effective teaching and learning.
- *To act as critical friend*: by providing support, advice and information for the headteacher and staff, by taking responsibility for monitoring the school's effectiveness, and by promoting the interest of the school and its students.
- *To ensure accountability*: by not rubber-stamping every decision of the headteacher, but by discussing and questioning proposals (while respecting the professional roles of headteacher and staff), and by answering to parents and the community on the school's overall performance.

This implies a partnership in which governors take a very active role, especially in school development planning and in monitoring and evaluation, and with a judicious blend of support and challenge. At the same time, they acknowledge and respect the professionalism of the headteacher and the staff; for example, they recognize clear role boundaries which preclude them from interference in the day-to-day management of the school. However, it is clear that this picture does not always exist. In examining the division of responsibility between the head and the governors in 21 schools, Shearn *et al.* (1993) identify different sorts of partnership:

- Head has major role with governors' approval: they are happy to delegate just about everything to the head in whom they have total trust.

- Head takes major role by default: the governors are apathetic and do not try to become involved.
- Head has major role by out-manoeuvring governors: here, there is manipulation by the head who lets governors think that they are well informed but actually feeds unimportant things to them, and gives them only minimal opportunity to make decisions.
- Conflict, with areas of responsibility contested: there is tension in the relationship between the head and governors, significant disagreements and jockeying for control of some aspects of school activity, including the day-to-day management of the school.
- Responsibility shared with agreement about how this should be done: a positive relationship built on mutual trust and respect, and considerable openness, with both parties clear about the boundaries of their own responsibility but happy to let the other in on discussions about issues in their area.

Clearly, it is only the last of these forms of partnership that is likely to adequately and productively fulfil the roles identified by Barber *et al.* (1995). It seems there is much still to be done if the potential involved by way of the powers invested in governing bodies is to be realized.

Other bodies

Decentralization of the education system in the UK and elsewhere has led to a number of benefits for schools and their students, but it has threatened the existence or effectiveness of networking across schools and, thus, a much-needed sharing of knowledge and ideas. Certainly, one of the effects of decentralization in the UK has been a reduction in LEA powers and resources, but in many cases this has stimulated an even greater desire on their part to engage with schools, especially in relation to their school improvement efforts. In this context, there remains for them an important role in such matters as support in development planning, teacher development, monitoring, networking and, indeed, the building of an overarching vision. My own view is that one impact of the revised relationship between many schools and LEAs has been to more clearly promote the notion of critical friendship on the part of the latter. (By a critical friend, I mean a person or group who is trusted, who understands the school's context and purposes, who wishes it to be successful and who, because of these things, can be constructively critical.)

There are currently many examples of this LEA-as-critical friend in action. One account is provided by Hargreaves (1990): the Inner London Education Authority's (ILEA) Inspectors Based in Schools Scheme of the late 1980s. The ILEA Inspectorate negotiated access to schools and explained the purpose of the scheme. They observed school life and lessons, and interviewed staff, students and parents. A diagnostic report on each school was then presented to staff as a series of discussion documents, and discussed with them. Finally, the inspectors stayed in the school for several more weeks, contributing to development planning.

There are also school improvement partnerships that embrace not just LEAs and 'their' schools but other critical friends too: higher education institutions (HEIs). Reference has already been made to Ontario's Learning Consortium. Here, I focus on just one example of a UK partnership: the North West Consortium for the Study of Effectiveness in Urban Schools (NWCSEUS), referred to in Chapter 1. There are two reasons for choosing this. First, it is an initiative with which several of the contributors to this book are involved, including myself. Secondly, the particular approach it adopts to school improvement closely relates to the main theme of the book; indeed, two of the case studies in Part 2 of the book arise out of its activities. However, there have been several multi-party initiatives that have been a powerful force, and generated significant lessons, for school improvement. Two of these have been drawn on extensively in writing this chapter: the IQEA and the Halton Effective Schools projects (e.g. Hopkins *et al.* 1994, and Stoll and Fink 1996 respectively). Others include the Teacher–Student Interaction and Quality of Learning project (e.g. Elliott and Ebbutt 1986), the Schools Make a Difference project (Myers 1996), and the Lewisham School Improvement project (Stoll and Thomson 1996).

The North West Consortium for the Study of Effectiveness in Urban Schools (NWCSEUS)
This Consortium was set up in 1994 by Manchester and Salford LEAs, Didsbury School of Education at The Manchester Metropolitan University and Manchester Victoria University. Its main aims are to support school improvement through action-based research and development projects in schools, and to generate a culture of practitioner research as one basis for improving practice and informing the process of change. In this sense it has some things in common with other teacher development and school improvement projects, such as the Australian Innovative Links between Schools and Universities Project for Teacher Professional Development (Sachs 1996), and much of the work undertaken by John Elliott and David Hopkins and their colleagues.

Those partner schools which undertake action-based research with the support of the Consortium receive up to five days of consultancy free of charge from LEA and/or university personnel. This normally covers advice on planning the project, advice on selecting the evaluation methods and tools, and help with the analysis and evaluation of data. However, the precise form of the consultancy role is negotiable; it has also included, for example, help in formulating change strategies and the provision, or arrangement, of inservice activities. The Consortium also has a project officer who coordinates all activity, and provides support for individual projects, for example by way of a literature search facility. There is also a concern to disseminate and share information. Thus, free copies of a Consortium newsletter and of the London Institute of Education's School Improvement Network News are provided for all schools in the LEAs, and there is an annual programme of conferences and workshops (including those on research training), some of which are without charge and some charged at cost.

There are three routes to active involvement in a Consortium project:

- *School-based projects*, where the focus relates to issues identified for the whole school or a major department or a development area within the school. The assumption is that the school has a development plan which includes a set of more or less urgent priorities for development, each of which has its own action plan (or an action plan which has been developed following an Ofsted Inspection). There is an expectation that the NWCSEUS project will normally arise out of issues identified in one or more of these action plans.
- *Cluster-based projects*, where a group of schools, united through an existing partnership or in pursuit of a common theme, agree to undertake a collaborative project or to develop and share their individual experiences of action research with a common focus.
- *Teacher-based projects* where an individual teacher, or small group of teachers, decide to research a focus area specific to their own interests or needs.

The initial steps of the process normally look like this:

- Idea for action-based research project originates from school/cluster group/individual teacher.
- Preliminary discussion with an LEA Link Inspector/Advisor helps to focus the idea.
- A school or cluster project team is identified.
- Proposal proforma acquired from and, when completed, submitted to the Consortium project officer.
- Project officer submits proposal to a sub-group of the NWCSEUS steering committee who discuss it and possibly suggest forms of appropriate support, including consultancy from other LEA advisors or from university staff – who might then become a member/s of the project team.

Currently, there is a wide range of schools with active projects. Examples include improving the quality of writing and reading, boosting boys' achievement through mentoring and monitoring, developing home links to support mathematics, headteacher monitoring of the quality of teaching and learning, the education of emotionally fragile children, and the use of peer counselling.

Clearly, then, there have been some exciting and powerful school improvement partnership initiatives. They are powerful because they bring together different learning organizations in pursuit of a common purpose, a theme which runs through much of Part 2 of this book.

School development planning: pulling it all together?

Throughout this chapter the importance of school culture to successful improvement has emerged, in one way or another, time and again. In particular, stress has been laid on the power of a collaborative culture: teachers working together, the involvement and empowerment of a critical mass of staff, and a collective commitment to vision, beliefs, values and purposes. In relation to the last of these, certain cultural norms have been emphasized, for example the beliefs that everyone can make a difference to student progress, that improvement is always possible, and that teachers are learners and professionals. I have also looked at how organizations can work on their structures and internal conditions in order to help shift the culture and, here, teacher development and inquiry and reflection have been put forward as major issues.

Additionally, there has been recognition that change is a long-term process, dependent on its being seen as everyone's business, and that an evolutionary and adaptive model of change is particularly appropriate to a complex educational system. Such an approach to change rests on the sort of culture described above. What is called for is a shared vision, teachers who work together, who are adaptable and who can pose and solve problems; and school leaders who are willing and able to promote and marshall the professionality of those teachers in vision building, planning and leadership roles. Finally, I have noted the potential of drawing on the knowledge, understanding and skills of the school's wider community and of other groups.

It has been argued that all of this can come together through effective school development planning, what Hopkins *et al.* (1994) refer to as an organic approach to school improvement. They suggest that a development plan most likely to make for successful school improvement is underpinned by what can be described as a Priorities-Conditions-Strategy model as illustrated in Figure 2.3.

In short, there is:

- Establishment of priorities. These arise from an audit of the school's present position, achievements and circumstances, including diagnosis of its internal conditions – undertaken in the context of the school's values, its vision of the future (though this might not be particularly clear in the first instance), and external imperatives.
- The creation of internal conditions that will underpin and sustain the change process.
- A strategy, or set of strategies, designed to achieve the priorities and to establish the internal conditions to support these: to link priorities and

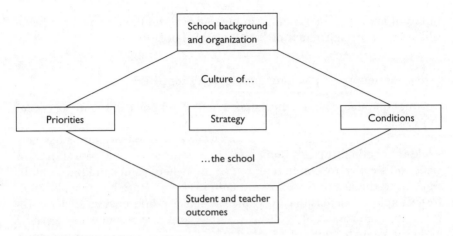

Figure 2.3 Improving the quality of education for all
Source: Hopkins *et al.* (1994: 103)

conditions. This will include attention to many of the practices discussed in this chapter. For example, in relation to establishing the condition of involvement and inclusiveness, a school might include in its strategy such activities as the promotion of, and support for, more active learning strategies; the involvement of students, parents and governors in policy development; participation in a school-LEA-HEI school improvement consortium; and the identification of a wider range of responsibility roles for students.

The last two of these are crucial. Schools can be very good at identifying priorities, but this is no guarantee of their achievement. Too often, there is a failure to translate priorities into successful action. This is often because the culture-structure dimension of schooling has not been sufficiently addressed. It is attention to the internal conditions and strategy which can remedy this. Additionally, monitoring, evaluation and research activity, including reflection on early actions taken, assists the school in clarifying and refining its values and vision – which then sets up a new cycle of priority setting.

A fundamental issue, of course, is the 'who' dimension. Who is involved in auditing, vision building, establishing priorities and strategies? Where an appropriate, collaborative culture does not yet exist, then at the outset it might be only the head and senior management team, perhaps with the governors. The aim, though, is to involve a much wider group of staff, together with students, parents and external critical friends. Here, it is the ongoing refinement of development plans that provides one of the richest opportunities of all for sharing and extending leadership roles, building a shared vision, and getting staff to work together. It is in this sense that the planning process is at least as important as the plan itself. It is the process that generates ownership of, and commitment to, the plan which is essential to successful implementation and institutionalization of change – a process predicated on transformational and invitational leadership. As Maden and Hillman (1996) observe, quoting a LEA advisor attached to one of the National Commission's case study schools, who had praised the quality of its development plan: 'but it was the richness of the discussion which led up to it which will be the real long-term benefit to the school' (p. 319).

It is possible to view the approach to school development planning described above, what MacGilchrist *et al.* (1995) refer to as a corporate development plan, as a fundamental basis for successful school improvement. However, and to return to discussion of the change process in both this and the preceding chapter, although it is useful to delineate different elements or stages of both the plan and the process, we must beware of thinking 'linear' and of becoming constrained by a 'tram line' mentality and by thinking too much of the long term. It is often because of these things that, so often, we do not achieve what is intended. In the following chapter, Cockett explores this issue in some depth.

3

Innovation and inertia

Mike Cockett

The first part of this chapter asks why, given all the past effort, schools are not already as effective as we would like them to be and suggests that the reasons might lie in the way schools behave as organizations. The second part extends this argument through a series of examples taken from actual efforts to change aspects of the system. The third part looks to the future and proposes ways in which we might establish innovation and overcome inertia.

Planning better schools?

School effectiveness research (SER) has led to the production of various 'lists' of effectiveness factors or characteristics and, while there may be differences in detail, the same factors recur. The findings have led some commentators and policy makers to conclude that, since some schools are effective and that these have the characteristics of good schools, then all schools should be encouraged to examine their practice and to enhance those factors from the effectiveness lists seen to be missing or underdeveloped. The question is, if we know what makes a school effective and if these factors do not surprise us, why is it that all schools are not already equally effective? There have been efforts to change schools and the education system for years, and yet we still do not have the system we would like. In fact, although we may feel that we are being bombarded by external and internal demands which force change on schools, for many aspects of the system and in many establishments, there is a surprising degree of stability. For those of us with long enough memories, the structure of the school day, the organization in departments, the hierarchy of heads and deputy heads and, perhaps above all, the timetable have changed little in the past fifty years. Indeed, we might go even further back than that. As Pring points out (1989), the Spens Report of 1938 expressed concern about the grip which the School Certificate Examination had on the curriculum up to 16 and the subject-based curriculum, seen as the natural pattern for the grammar school, bears a strong resemblance to the foundation subjects in the National Curriculum. There may have been changes in how the structures are expected to operate and in the details of the curriculum to be taught, but the framework has proved to be exceptionally resilient. It cannot just be argued that this is due to some collective fault in the teaching profession, some sort of change immunization which is injected during initial teacher training. We must look at the nature of schools as organizations and the way people operate within them.

Schools as organizations

The way we set about improving schools depends, among other things, on the model we hold of the school as an organization. Organizational theory applied to schools has tended to follow the development of theories applied to industrial and commercial enterprises. In this field there has been an evolution from the 'Fordist' factory model in which efficient operation is seen as a consequence of tight job specifications and hierarchical control and which attempts to rule out human error, to less mechanistic models which recognize that non-rational factors, such as the social relationships between staff and the culture of the organization, have a strong influence on performance (Westoby 1988). The popular perception of organizations, particularly those designed for efficient production, is of a rational planning leading to desired outcomes. In practice, as Weik (1988) points out, examples of such organizations are rare:

> People in organisations, including educational organisations, find themselves hard pressed either to find actual instances of those rational practices or to find rationalised practices whose outcomes have been as beneficial as predicted, or to feel that those rational occasions explain much of what goes on in the organisation.
>
> (p. 57)

Schools are not unique in this apparent resistance to change. A study of business organizations in Japan, for example, finds that there is a built-in inertia in established companies:

> When we maintain and develop existing business, we can depend on organisational inertia. The continuity of existing corporate behaviour is

consistent with the natural dynamics of organisation. In contrast, diversification, since it means change in corporate behaviour, runs against organisational inertia. Diversification involves doing things which are against the natural dynamics of the organisations.

(Yoshihara 1988: 57–8)

In common with many other organizations, schools are required to be stable. They are judged on the extent to which that stability is maintained as SER and the Ofsted manuals illustrate. Consequently, when they are asked to make changes to deeply rooted practices they find it very difficult. It can often only be accomplished through a change of staff and by working through periods of confusion and conflict. Indeed, conflict is seen as essential to an improving school (Fullan 1993). This is some way from the rational planning process implied by such things as school development plans and the required response to Ofsted school inspection reports. If we wish to improve schools we must ask why it is that schools in particular and the education system as a whole resists change, even that which is seen to be logical, well planned and well resourced.

Stacey (1996) cites the case of the British manufacturer of paint tins in the 1980s who discovered that their customers did not like the fact that their tins rusted. The manufacturer took the entirely logical step of investing in rustless tin technology but missed the fact that others were developing plastic containers. The tin manufacturers were wiped out. Logical, linear planning led to disaster. In fact, it has been long established that effective organizations do not operate in this sort of linear way and various models have been developed to explain the non-linear, dynamic processes. A full treatment of these models is not possible here (readers are referred to Stacey 1996), but it is useful to explore some of the basic ideas using examples from schools and educations systems as illustrations. Among the most recent are those based on chaos theory, perhaps better described as complexity theory. The illustrations based on this theory provide an insight into how organizations can at one and the same time apparently be constantly changing and yet remain highly stable.

It is commonplace to talk about chaos or turbulence in the education system. Sometimes this is a general complaint about the multiplicity of ill-coordinated changes with which schools feel they are inflicted. Sometimes it is a reference to what is called the postmodern condition and is used to emphasize the complexity of worldwide economic and social changes which make reading the future so difficult. Chaos here simply indicates a sense of randomness and unpredictability. However, chaos theory is as much about stability or equilibrium as it is about turbulence and instability and, in particular, it is about the boundaries between the two. There are three key ideas that are useful in considering the issue of change or the lack of it in education: positive and negative feedback, forecasting, and strange attractors.

Positive and negative feedback

These terms are not value judgements. Negative feedback is when a system operates to restore equilibrium in the way that a pendulum, damped by air resistance, gradually comes to rest. Positive feedback is when the system is driven further and further from equilibrium as when a microphone is placed too near a loudspeaker. Schools, as with all other organizations, depend on negative feedback in order to maintain a sense of order and common purpose. Deviations from the norm demand remedial action; for example, when a child misbehaves the teacher reprimands. The child may challenge the reprimand and the teacher imposes a sanction, not so much for the original misdemeanour but for the challenge. The child feels that the punishment is unfair and refuses to accept it. The teacher appeals to higher authority and the punishment is enforced. The child may still feel that the punishment is unfair but recognizes that further resistance is useless and submits. Equilibrium is restored. In very similar circumstances a positive feedback loop could also be established. Imagine that the child continues to refuse the punishment. Parents are called in but they support the child. Other children and other parents are drawn into the argument and someone alerts the local media. Now the school is faced with a situation spiralling out of control. These are simple examples but such feedback loops operate in almost all aspects of an organization. It is feedback processes which are the mechanisms by which culture and values are maintained and challenged.

Forecasting

Chaos theory originated in astronomy as a way of modelling the movement of a body subject to two strong gravitational fields. Contrary to expectations, whereas the movement of a body subject to one gravitational field was highly predictable and led to a simple repeated pattern, the influence of a second gravitational field led to unpredictable, apparently patternless movement. The advent of the computer provided the calculating power to allow the theory to be developed for various practical purposes, among which is weather forecasting. Climatologists were interested in the difference between stable and predictable conditions and unstable, and consequently unpredictable, conditions.

Edward Lorenz in the 1960s showed that the atmosphere behaves like a turbulent fluid governed by non-linear equations which can be sensitive to small changes. This is the famous flutter of a butterfly wing (Gleick 1987) which can build to a tempest. Of course, not all butterflies cause storms. Small changes do not always make big differences. The significance of Lorenz's work is that it showed how a distinction between the stable and the unstable could be recognized. By starting with a set of given atmospheric conditions and then varying those conditions slightly, it was possible to show, mathematically, the difference between those conditions which were, and those which were not, sensitive to small changes and consequently those which could, and could not, lead to confident forecasts. The point is not that in turbulent conditions the weather suddenly begins to obey a different set of laws but, rather, that it is impossible to know the initial conditions so precisely that a prediction of how the laws will operate becomes possible. Forecasters currently use about one million measures and still, in some conditions, they have difficulty forecasting the weather even twenty-four hours ahead. This is the state known as deterministic chaos (Schroeder 1991). The same laws are operating but in ways we cannot predict because we cannot have absolute knowledge of the conditions.

Although we must be wary of claiming too much, this difficulty in forecasting and this dependence on initial conditions is at least analogous to the problems in schools and education systems of forecasting outcomes of innovations. Fullan (1993) describes the historical process whereby the confidence of the 1960s that effective educational change could be achieved through well-designed and well-resourced projects was virtually destroyed as researchers began to ask about the implementation of the results of those projects. Success in pilot schools was a poor indicator of success in other schools. In spite of the emphasis on dissemination, this problem remains with us. In 1977 the Department for Education and Science identified 'ten good schools' as though somehow what those schools were doing could be transferred. What they could not describe are precisely the starting conditions for each of those schools which led to their success and consequently, while some schools may have found ideas which stimulated their development, the ten good schools did not provide a foolproof recipe for success elsewhere.

Strange attractors

When the famous Harlem Globetrotters basketball team used to play their exhibition matches they interspersed periods of serious play with periods of clowning. One of their most popular tricks was to introduce a non-standard basketball. Instead of the more or less predictable flight of the standard ball this trick ball would curve and bounce in a highly unpredictable manner. In fact the trick is easy to set up. A standard basketball is manufactured with another ball of different weight and elasticity inside it. Every time the ball is thrown or bounced the relationship between the two balls is slightly different. The subsequent flight or bounce is sensitive to the initial conditions. Forecasting the bounce or flight is virtually impossible and, of course, makes the game of basketball impossible. On the other hand, once you have seen the performance a few times, it is clear that even the trick ball is working within some bounds: it does not fly off into space, it does eventually come to rest, and there is some relationship between the bounce and the force with which it is thrown at the floor. The appearance of randomness comes from not knowing exactly what that relationship is at any given time.

Classical physics can predict the flight of the traditional basketball with reasonable accuracy, given information about the initial projecting force and the angle of projection. There is a simple linear formula which applies. In the case of the doctored ball, however, the flight of the ball would constantly have to be recalculated for every moment of its flight because how it behaves is dependent not only on the initial conditions but on the emerging relationship between the two balls, one inside the other. The system is non-linear. When mathematical models were developed for such systems, it was, at first, not easy to pursue them, for the simple reason that it required so many calculations, each one depending on the results of the previous calculation. It was only with the advent of the computer that they could be carried out sufficiently quickly for new discoveries to be made. When Lorenz fed his mathematical model of a weather system into his computer what he discovered was not a distinction between stability on the one hand and complete randomness on the other but, rather, an interim state, a sort of bounded instability. His mathematical weather system never repeated the same state twice but nor did it shoot off into some infinity. When the computer drew a graph of the calculations a pattern emerged.

In classical physics, systems are seen as being 'attracted' to states of equilibrium or stability as in pendulums or orbits of planets round the sun. In some non-linear systems, it emerged, while there was no repeated cycle, there was some sort of attractor operating which prevented absolute randomness; they were called 'strange attractors'. Apart from this bounded instability, systems governed by strange attractors have another interesting property. They are extremely stable. This may appear to be a paradox but consider for the moment the example of the beating of the heart. It is thought that the beating of the heart is governed by the laws of chaos (Gleick 1987). Each cell in the heart has it own separate beat. The overall pulsing is governed by waves of electrical energy generated in the brain which stimulates not the simple function of a man-made pump, but a complex retracting and expanding of tissues which not only moves the blood but prevents clotting and adhesion to the walls of the heart. Because of the complex of external stimuli and internal functioning, the heart never beats exactly the same way twice. On the other hand, it is extremely resilient and continues to beat even under extreme circumstances under the influence of the 'strange attractor' which governs its function. Sometimes it does fail: the heart fibrillates and loses this coordinated function. When this happens, the right electrical shock applied in time frequently restores the beat. The heart is defibrillated and the complex normal function resumes. This image of systems which at one and the same time can adapt to meet changes in the environment and yet retain a powerful stability will be developed later.

It is these images from chaos theory – the problems of forecasting due to sensitive dependence on initial conditions, recognizing the boundary between stable and instable states and the state of bounded instability, the strange attractor – which have commanded the attention of those interested in describing the operation of complex organizations. They are seen as complex, dynamic systems responding not just to two linked elements, as in the basketball comparison, but to a multiplicity of associated but independently operating elements including the individuals making up the organization, the groups they form and the forces operating from outside. Schools are good examples of such organizations.

At this stage we need to remind ourselves that chaos theory is being used as a metaphor because we are not in the position of the weather forecasters who have mathematical models and accurate measures on which to base their work. In organizational theory in general and in education in particular we lack both, and will do for the foreseeable future. The next section, through a series of examples, develops the metaphor and shows how it might help us to understand some of the forces influencing change or the lack of it in education systems in general and schools in particular.

Schools as complex organizations

The problem of forecasting is a key issue for innovators. The model of innovation promoted by the Department for Education and Employment (DfEE), for example through such mechanisms as Grants for Education Support and Training (GEST), is a case in point. Local authorities and others are invited to bid for funds by describing their starting conditions, by proposing action to alter those conditions and by setting out measures of success, performance indicators. The standard evaluation of these programmes does accept that the original plan may not work out in all its detail but ultimately success or failure is judged against those forecast indicators (Chapter 7 is a case study illustrating this issue). One effect is that the pressure to forecast outcomes in complex situations leads to a focus on manipulating the indicators rather than evaluating the effectiveness of improvement programmes. Schools employ a range of strategies to improve attainment and attendance indicators, only some of which are concerned with improving the quality of education. They have included the permanent exclusion of students, changing the definition of authorized and unauthorized absence and searching examination boards for syllabuses regarded as relatively easy.

SER has shown that schools in similar circumstances produce different results and we can, in retrospect, see differences in the operation of the schools as organizations but we cannot take any given set of starting measures and apply a formula which will model future development in any one school. We have had examples of effective schools for many years. They have been held up as models for others but attempts to repeat the success story frequently founder. The model proves too crude and an understanding of the starting conditions too limited. In SER itself the tendency is to become more complex as more is understood about the context specific nature of factors affecting schools. The original five-factor model has been superseded (Creemers 1994) and now, in studies in the US for example (Schaffer *et al.* 1994), over fifty factors are seen to influence one area alone, that of effectiveness in the classroom, and even then there is a recognition that those factors themselves are subject to influence from outside in ways which are specific to each class and to each school. Such research would appear to support the view of schools as complex, dynamic systems.

If this is so then we should be very careful about making judgements about similar but inevitably slightly different situations. In complex, dynamic systems slight variations may have major consequences over a period of time. One problem in seeking examples illustrating this phenomenon is that observing the initial variation which led to a major change is as difficult as knowing which butterfly wing started the storm. However, we are constantly faced with variations which we find difficult to explain, for which there seems to be no major cause. For example, teachers regularly recognize differences between year groups, some being 'good' and some being 'poor'. The students are drawn from the same area, many from the same families. They are taught largely by the same teachers and they follow the same curriculum and yet something makes the teaching of the second group feel less productive than the first. The same is true of classes within a school; even when the ability and interests of the classes appear similar, the experience of teaching them can be radically different.

Gleick (1987) tells the story of a group of graduate students at the Santa Cruz campus of the University of California who formed themselves into the 'Dynamic Systems Collective'. They used to amuse themselves by guessing where the nearest strange attractor might be, perhaps in the flapping of a flag or the fluttering of a leaf. To an extent our understanding of the application of chaos theory to educational systems is still at the level of that game but recognition is an important first step. For example, we might suspect that something like deterministic chaos is operating in the most stressed conditions, those created by the poverty of the area in which a school is situated. Stepping back we see a terrible familiarity about the range of problems and incidents with which such schools have to deal and yet forecasting what will happen next in any one school is almost impossible. We might expect, if chaos theory is more than just a metaphor, to find big differences between similar schools and to discover that this may not be because of major initial differences in leadership, organization or resources, but the end result of relatively minor, even unnoticed, variation in the starting conditions, or to apparently minor events in the life of the school. The differences might be as much due to accident as to design. The corollary is that the pursuit of macro changes in leadership or resources may be less effective than finding some relatively minor key which unlocks an improvement process. This notion will be developed further in the last section.

Svyantek and DeShon (1993) propose that the culture of an organization operates as a strange attractor. They suggest an analogy between organizations and biological organisms by which the organization is seen to have adaptive abilities to allow it to compete, for example for appropriate resources, and reproductive qualities which are concerned with such things as passing on ways of working and maintaining relationships. The adaptive function necessarily demands constant change, especially in a changing environment. The reproductive function maintains stability in the face of such change. The big issue, they suggest, is what happens when what we need to change is the reproduction function, that is the culture of the organization. This is such a key issue in educational innovation that I wish to pursue it through a series of extended examples.

The organization of knowledge

There is a relationship between the structuring of knowledge into subjects and time slots, and power and control in organizations (Bernstein 1971). Changing subjects, syllabuses and timetables threatens the established order; changing disciplines threatens discipline (Hoskin 1990). Bernstein's call for a change in the organization of knowledge in schools was asking for a cultural change. He was partly heeded through the development of various integrated programmes but the National Curriculum largely swept those aside, reestablishing the traditional subject as the dominant knowledge frame. The one subject which did not have an existing frame was Design and Technology and the process by which it was brought into line with the prevailing culture can be traced.

Black and Harrison (1985) summarized the problem facing those promoting technology as a core subject. They defined what for them was the essence of technology: 'Technology is the practical method which has enabled us to raise ourselves above the animals and to create not only our habitats, our food supply, our comfort and our means of health, travel and communication, but also our arts – painting, sculpture, music and literature' (p. 3). Because technology is in everything then the technology curriculum must feed on and into all other aspects of the curriculum: 'there is a broad range of educationally valid and valuable activities which both cut across boundaries of subject disciplines and yet need to draw upon those disciplines and to feed back to them' (p. 24). In the report on the Technology Education Project (Black *et al.* 1988) the same point is pursued. 'Coherence in the pupils' minds comes with the realisation, through experience, that all subjects can be exploited, often simultaneously, through appropriate tasks' (p. 21).

The National Curriculum Council Consultation report on Technology (NCC 1989) continues the positive reference to cross-curricular work, but with the first signs of a counter argument: 'Respondents strongly agreed with details in the Working Group's proposals concerning cross-curricular issues and themes. There were warnings from some respondents that cross-curricular work must not detract from teaching the design and technology profile component *as a subject*' (p. 14, my italics). This was followed by the Ofsted report on Design and Technology (Ofsted 1993) which makes no reference at all to cross-curricular matters. Its judgements are based entirely on the National Curriculum Technology as a subject in its own right and are couched in terms which would be very familiar to the teachers who taught the 'old' technology subjects. 'Most pupils used tools and equipment confidently and safely to work with wood, plastics, food and fabrics, and in about a quarter of the schools they also used metals, electronic components and mechanical systems to make a variety of products' (p. 10).

By 1995, cross-curricular references have been reduced to two mentions: teachers will help students consider 'how knowledge and skills drawn from art, mathematics and science can be applied to making' (SCAA 1995: 15). That is, the technology teacher, now entirely enclosed in the technology subject, will ask the students to look beyond the subject, but there is no longer a sense that other teachers with other specialisms might become directly involved. The timetable, the sense of subject status and the traditional notion of what a subject is have triumphed. It is true that some elements of the new subject we would not have found in the curriculum thirty years ago. The system *has* adapted to external change but negative feedback has held the technology curriculum under the influence of the attractor of the traditional subject curriculum.

Educating the disaffected and the less able

In the Review of Qualifications for 16–19 Year Olds (Dearing 1996) we find the following paragraph:

the essence of a successful response [to the problem of underachievement] involves setting alight some interest. Initially it hardly matters what the subject area is. Once interest has been captured, there is a basis for re-establishing relations with their students ... This is often accomplished by motivating learners through a new, more vocationally relevant activity. From this it may be possible to address the key skills of communication and the application of number. Since lack of progress in these skills has often symbolised failure at school, they are often not addressed head on, but introduced on the back of other studies which are motivating to the learner.

(para. 12.28)

This is hardly a new idea. The report 'Half our Future' (DES 1963), published as a preliminary to the raising of the school leaving age, makes the same connection:

They [less able pupils] can see the point of a vocational subject and often enjoy it whether they themselves are going to take up this kind of work or not. Once they begin to clear their own minds about what they are going to do, vocational takes on for them a more precise and yet wider meaning. They know that shop assistants, for instance, have to talk to customers; and with this knowledge the whole of English and not just some limited 'trade English', gains significance.

(p. 115)

Even before Half Our Future, the distinctions between grammar, technical and secondary modern schools were based on the notion that a differentiated curriculum should be provided and that it was possible to allocate children to the route which best suited their abilities.

Between the two reports there have been many projects and initiatives. With the raising of the school leaving age there was a flurry of activity to produce a curriculum suited to the needs of low achieving adolescents. The Lower Attaining Pupils (LAP) project in the early 1980s was aimed at developing a differentiated curriculum for the 'bottom forty per cent' to use the then Secretary of State for Education's phrase. While it is possible to see traces of all these in many schools, why is it that Dearing finds it necessary, not only to repeat the concern but to propose the same sort of solutions to the problem? What happened to all the old projects? The schemes have been legion, not all aimed exclusively at the less able. They included records of achievement, action planning, compacts, unit credits, negotiated learning, flexible learning, further education link courses and alternative curricula. In each of these areas teachers and others who worked on the schemes would claim to have had some success and yet the schemes come and go while the problems remain: truancy levels are high, exclusions from schools are rising, and there is a general concern that significant numbers of students are disaffected. The DfEE is concerned and continues to make disaffection and truancy priorities under the GEST programme.

I wish to propose that the reason why these attempts to improve the way schools cater for the less able have so far failed is not due to any lack of will, intention, hard work or inventiveness, but to the fact that the innovations cut across cultural attractors in such areas as the curriculum, equity, behaviour and status. By examining the way in which these cultural attractors operated we will learn something of the processes which weaken and dissipate innovatory effort.

Curriculum

The Alternative Curriculum Strategies (ACS) project in Manchester was set up under the LAP initiative. The brief in Manchester was to find anything that might interest those students in the bottom forty percent either inside or outside school. There were links with colleges, residential courses, practical programmes in school, ACS bases in which students managed flexible timetables, and so on. The rhetoric encouraged teachers to build a school within a school with its own rules and relationships and the students clearly understood this (Hustler *et al.* 1991). By 1995 the last ACS course in Manchester disappeared. In most schools they disappeared even earlier, even though the project was regarded at the time, and still is regarded by many, as very successful. It did improve attendance rates for many students, it did provide progression routes and it did keep contact with many students who would otherwise have been lost to education altogether. However, as it turned out, it contained the seeds of its own destruction. The ACS programmes in most schools, as the name itself implies, were set up in opposition to the mainstream curriculum. Consequently, they challenged the prevailing curriculum culture. At a conscious level the schools were very supportive of the programmes but at a less conscious level something like an immune reaction set in. The body of the school was uncomfortable with many aspects of the unfamiliar curriculum.

We can take, for example, the notion of the negotiated curriculum. At the time, this presented considerable problems for the teachers involved in the programme, never mind those who were not. The prevailing culture dictated that teachers decided the curriculum (sic) and that students learnt what they were told. The idea that students should be included in the decision-making process was alien. Three sorts of problems occurred. First, the teachers who attempted to negotiate were often confused. What was the status of the decisions made by the students when they seemed to be inappropriate to the teacher? Sometimes it seemed to be a sort of abdication of responsibility, with students, for example, demanding that they should be allowed to brew up or play pool, if they decided, during lesson time (both activities available in some ACS bases). Secondly, teachers would negotiate, effectively, on an activity first time round, for example deciding on the programme for a residential course. The problem came the second time round when the teacher would try to help the students avoid the problems of the first course. By the third cycle, teachers would be giving strong advice based on experience, which of course, their students did not have. Negotiation very soon became a sham or reduced to peripherals such as the menu or rules on dress. A third problem occurred between the students who had got hold of the idea of negotiation and teachers who had not. There were some vivid confrontations. Even minor matters could blow up into major storms. As these incidents accumulated, they were talked about in the staff rooms. Stories were told about 'that ACS group'. Teachers not involved were able to distance themselves. Expectations were being developed about the sort of student you would find on the ACS programme. Once again we see the process of negative feedback reinforcing the cultural norms and expectations.

Equity

'That ACS group' was also a group on which special resources were being expended. They seemed to have special privileges. They were out of school some of the time. They had space in the school for their exclusive use. All of these were very effective in convincing some, though by no means all, ACS students that they were significant in the school, and in providing them with activities they found interesting and productive. The reaction was again almost immediate. In spite of the fact that, in most cases, the ACS groups contained most of the students other teachers did not want to teach and were happy to have out of their classes, there was a resentment of the resources they were allocated. It seemed like a reward for bad behaviour. Other students also objected. Why should they not have equal privileges? A good question.

Behaviour

ACS students, it was said, were getting away with murder. They might be in school but they were not in school uniform. They were 'thick' anyway: ACS courses were examination courses in tea brewing. Staff insisted that they should be subject to the same discipline and the same sanctions as the rest of the school whatever the teachers in the ACS programme said. ACS was in the process of becoming a pejorative term to many staff and students. The message was passed on to the parents of other students who were offered places on the ACS programme. They turned them down. They had heard about ACS and they did not want their child to be part of them. In most schools the programmes were phased out, though many rationalized this as a response to the National Curriculum which could not accommodate alternative programmes.

Status

A key dilemma for schools is how to deliver alternative or remedial programmes. The problem is that the very identification of a student as in need of remedial or alternative treatment ultimately inhibits the remedial work. The *Times Educational Supplement* of 5 January 1996 carried a report on the stigma of the 'special needs' label: 'Statements of special educational need are so stigmatised in the public mind that an alternative name may soon be needed according to Professor Ron Davie' (p. 3). Whatever form of delivery and whatever the name given, the remedial or alternative programme ultimately loses status – not because of the poor quality of the programme, nor because it does not meet the needs of the identified students, but because it is the mainstream curriculum which has the high status. Even the students on the ACS courses given the opportunity to negotiate aspects of their curriculum asked for traditional maths and English lessons. They wanted to succeed in the high status territory and not simply in the newly named alternative one.

In order to make a point, the picture here has been presented in a rather harsh light. Most of the schools involved in the sorts of programme described would claim that the projects had lasting effects, perhaps not of the sort first envisaged but somehow incorporated into the normal life of the school. The argument is not that nothing has changed but rather that what has changed has done so within the bounds controlled by cultural attractors. Such changes, of course, can be beneficial, but it does not tackle those problems such as low achievement which are, at least in part, culturally determined.

Summary of Part 2

The central argument is that many aspects of the system are exceptionally stable and not subject to the logic of attempted changes even when there has been great investment in trying to bring them about. This stability is maintained both through the minutiae of school life and through the major external influences which dictate the organization of knowledge and the structures which have developed to teach and examine it. The next section asks whether there is anything to be learnt from all this about how we might plan a more effective future.

Planning to learn, learning to plan

Schools and education systems are designed for stability and are judged to an extent on how they deliver it, a point made by Elliott (1996) about the school effectiveness list of factors. They ask that schools should be calm, well ordered and disciplined working environments in which students stay on task for large periods of time and there is a sense in which schools are designed for this purpose. The structure of time, the curriculum, rules of behaviour and so on are all directed at creating order, regularity and predictability. Departures from such good order raise anxiety and provoke remedial action, negative feedback. The culture of such schools is one designed to resist any change to a different cultural attractor. It is not that they do not adapt to circumstances, but the process of adaptation is towards that which is culturally comfortable. At the opposite end of the spectrum, schools dominated by positive feedback processes would spiral off into absolute instability, a state in which nothing is ordered or predictable. In other words it would lose any sense that it was a school. The important state, it is argued, is the boundary between the two, a state on the edge of chaos in which the future is uncertain but not patternless. Stacey (1996) sums it up this way:

> It is possible . . . to predict the outcomes of group, organizational and societal systems and, therefore, to remain 'in control' of them. But this is possible only if such systems are held well within the stable zone of operation, far away from the edge of chaos. The result will be stability . . . but it will be the death of creativity and innovation . . . If it is to survive, every human system must return to the edge of chaos, where outcomes are unknowable and no one can be 'in control' . . . the true role of the leader of a creative system is, not to foresee its future and take control of its journey, but to contain the anxiety of its members as they operate at the edge of chaos, where they are creating and discovering a new future that none could possibly foresee.
>
> (p. 346)

This we can set against much of the current procedures for GEST programmes and for the follow up to Ofsted inspection and the early conclusions drawn from SER. Here, problems are seen as having solutions. It simply requires that the staff of a school, led by the head and governors, sit down and apply their minds to the problems and the solutions will emerge and progress towards those solutions planned. The two just do not 'square' with one another. The fact is that when schools which are improving are examined (Louis and Miles 1992), we find that 'following a "good planning process" is not too important. None of the schools that we looked at are text book cases of good planning – if, by good, we mean the rational, explicit model' (p. 209). What Louis and Miles found was that it was the schools with the tightest plans which improved least. The most effective planning turns conventional wisdom on its head. As Halsall points out in the preceding chapter, it often begins with a period of confusion and ambiguity in which there may have been general aims but not specific targets. Action precedes detailed planning, often on more than one front and the plan, rather than the forerunner of action, emerges as a consequence of exploratory work:

> The more narrow and specific the goals, the more likely the school is to run into problems in creating an environment for school reform. In schools with broader or vaguer goals, the multiplicity of moving parts and the overarching nature of the reform movement permits lots of positive action to generate support for reform.
>
> (Louis and Miles 1992: 206)

Effective planning, they claim, is less 'head' work conducted prior to action and more a process of evolution as accumulated practical experience among all members of staff coalesces into shared visions and common goals. In this they reflect studies from outside the education system. Mintzberg and Mintzberg (1988), for example, in discussing strategic planning propose that strategy making is a craft and 'to craft a strategy is to manage the relationship between thought and action, to nuance deliberate control with emergent learning' (p. 184). In short, then, most effective change takes place in the hinterland between stability and instability where it is impossible to be sure what is going to happen next, where change arises from multiple actions and where plans emerge rather than are imposed from the outset.

Inevitably in a short chapter some issues have been glossed over and although they cannot be dealt with in detail they should at least be mentioned. The first is that schools do not exist at either end of Stacey's spectrum. The significance of seeing school cultures as strange attractors is to imply that all schools, even the most stable, actually do change and adapt; it is the stability of a well-designed building in an earthquake zone. The second is to sound a word of caution about the studies of improving schools. These tend to be of urban schools for the good reason that these schools are those which are seen to have the greatest need to improve. The double bind here is that improvement tends to be defined according to cultural perceptions of the 'good school': those not needing improvement. However, this reinforces the feedback which makes change difficult in those schools. It could be that the key to improving the system as a whole lies in a creative destabilization of the most stable schools. The third issue is that most schools have areas of stability and areas of bounded stability and some have areas of complete chaos. It is important to recognize these if improvement measures are to have the maximum chance of succeeding.

We have now reached the point at which suggestions need to be made about how all this should affect the planning of improvement action in schools. There is a dilemma here since the conclusion of many of the writers is that long-term planning, of the sort represented by too many school development plans, does not work. One way forward is to recognize the distinction between planning to operate schools efficiently and planning long-term changes to the way the school operates. The first is that which helps current systems to operate more effectively. A lot of school improvement action is of this sort: ensuring that course work is properly managed, making sure that registration systems work efficiently, managing revision for examinations and so on. Such action is unlikely, in a serious way, to challenge the school culture. It is an adaptive process. The second sort of action either directly or indirectly challenges the prevailing culture: for example, introducing subject specialisms into the primary school, action to reduce disaffection, action to raise the attainment of boys. In this second case it is impossible to forecast accurately what the outcomes of the action will be in the long term and therefore we must adopt a step-by-step approach, modifying the action as we see its effects. Even in these areas there is a role for planning, but not as a process for providing blueprints for change. Any action needs at least a short-term plan. Planning brings people together. It helps them speculate about the future, to invent possible actions and to think of ways of carrying them out, but the purpose of the planning group is not to fix that future but rather to help develop a change culture. It is a sort of fitness exercise which helps keep people in tune with each other as they attempt improvements. The distinction is between planning which implies that we know what we want to do and how to do it and planning in order to learn. I conclude with three conditions which are essential to this process:

- People need to be free to invent improvement actions for themselves at whatever level in the organization. Balancing this need with the need to control and monitor activity is a key improvement process. On the whole, it is better to let things emerge, to deal with things as they turn up, rather than set up formal procedures.
- There needs to be a tolerance of a certain amount of tension, mess and risk because that is what living on the creative edge of chaos is like. This is difficult in schools because it inevitably affects the lives of the students, but major improvements will not happen without it. Helping people take risks, helping them to tolerate mess and to live with tensions – and to keep all of those within acceptable bounds – is a major leadership task.
- Sceptics are very significant in change programmes. Left to themselves they can generate much of the negative feedback which will eventually neutralize the programme. However, incorporated into the programme, perhaps in the process of monitoring or evaluation they can act as an important check on the enthusiasts who can find it difficult to be realistic about the outcomes of their actions.

4

Teacher research for school improvement

Karen Carter and Rob Halsall

In different but complementary ways, the preceding chapters have pointed to the need for teachers themselves to be major contributors to the school effectiveness and improvement movements. In Chapter 1, Carter has argued that facilitating this is the most important challenge in finding a way forward for school effectiveness and school improvement research (SER and SIR). Both Halsall and Cockett have built on this. In Chapter 2, Halsall has explored the centrality of collaborative cultures and certain sorts of cultural norms to school improvement and, associated with this, the importance of the interrelated themes of teachers as learners, teacher development and inquiry and reflection. In Chapter 3, Cockett has suggested that schools and their teachers need to be free to invent improvement actions for themselves.

It is our intention here to explore the possibilities provided by teacher involvement in school-based research as a strategy for school improvement. In some ways the potential for this exists more strongly than ever before. As Hopkins (1993) suggests, teacher research lies at the intersection of a number of central policy initiatives; for example, changes in the funding and delivery of teacher development, schemes for school self-evaluation, the introduction of teacher appraisal and school development planning. 'Looking across all of these "developmental changes", a major common denominator is classroom research' (p. 188). Furthermore, engagement in teacher research can be seen as contributing to a form of teacher professionalism which is needed if school improvement efforts are to succeed. Green explores this in some depth in Chapter 14; here, we briefly anticipate her argument. We agree with Hopkins (1993) that, 'systematic self-study is a hallmark of those occupations that enjoy the label "professional"' (p. 33). It has a major role to play in reasserting the value of the professional autonomy of teachers – not technicians who merely apply initiatives handed to them by others, but definers of their own reality through being able to investigate and reflect on self-chosen practices, and then modify these on the basis of professional judgement which engagement in the research process has itself informed. The matter of making 'judgements as to what is worthwhile and decisions as to what to do' (Bassey 1995: 39) is at the heart of professionalism.

We discuss briefly what we mean by teacher research and then consider the issue of the accessibility of SER and SIR findings, and some of the difficulties surrounding teachers' perceptions of the 'theory-practice divide'. In doing so, we recognize that it may be necessary to accept that a perceived view of the origins of SER and SIR as lying with 'ivory towered academics' may be just as unpalatable to teachers, as a view of its origins within an externally imposed managerialist perspective of schools, explored in Chapter 1. In the light of this, we offer teacher research as a potent tool which teachers may apply to the interpretation and local exploration of SER and SIR findings. We consider such an approach as a means of overcoming the theory-practice divide and suggest that it may prove a powerful route to establishing teachers themselves as key players on the school effectiveness and improvement stage. In exploring these issues we draw upon our own experiences as higher education partners in the North West Consortium for the Study of Effectiveness in Urban Schools (NWCSEUS, see note to Chapter 1) where we have been involved in school-based research in partnership with local education authorities (LEAs) and teachers themselves. Finally, we offer a set of questions, issues and guidelines concerning engagement with teacher research in the pursuit of school improvement.

What do we mean by teacher research?

Elliott (1991) demarcates two different accounts of how teachers reflectively develop their practices. In the first, which he associates with the idea of 'teacher as a researcher', reflection precedes and initiates action. In the second, which he associates with the idea of 'educational action research', action initiates reflection:

1 The teacher undertakes research into a practical problem and on this basis changes some aspect of ... teaching. The development of understanding precedes the decision to change teaching strategies.
2 The teacher changes some aspect of ... teaching in response to a practical problem and then self-monitors its effectiveness ... through the evaluation the teacher's initial understanding of the problem is ... changed. The decision to adopt a change strategy therefore precedes the development of understanding.

(p. 23)

Elliott clearly favours the second account. For him, the first 'constitutes a projection of academic bias into the study of teachers' thinking' (p. 23), and a separation of inquiry and practice. He also sees it as tantamount to Rome burning while Nero fiddles, the situation disintegrating while the research is being undertaken. In the second account, though, according to Elliott, there is no separation of inquiry and practice – the latter is the form of the former – and it 'may be more rational to adopt an action strategy on trust initially and then review its merits than to suspend doing something about it until all the evidence has been analysed' (p. 23).

Now, while we appreciate the essential distinction between these two accounts, we are not sure how helpful they are. The first contains only two stages: research, then action. What is missing, which would bring it closer to the second account (indeed, lead into it) is a third stage, of further research, this time into the impact of the action. It seems to us that Bassey's account of action research, presented in the following chapter, provides this. To paraphrase him, what we need to do is:

- clarify the issue of concern;
- research what is actually happening in the institution regarding this concern, including different people's understanding of it;
- introduce change on the basis of the contradiction between what is happening and what we would like to see happening;
- research the impact of the change.

Moreover, we are not as sure as Elliott appears to be in the wisdom of always acting first. It seems to us that there are occasions when the problem is that we are not quite sure of what the problem is; research is necessary at the outset to help clarify it.

More generally, we share the worries expressed by Hopkins (1993) about overly specifying process steps in research. This 'may trap teachers within a framework which [may] inhibit independent action [and] the models may appear daunting and confusing' (pp. 54–5). We prefer to adopt an eclectic view about what constitutes teacher research. Certainly, we feel that the stages involved and the appropriate sequencing of these will vary depending on the focus and purpose of inquiry. For us, then, the key issue is not to present a definitive model of the process of teacher research, but rather to identify its essential characteristics, which are that:

- as with all research, it is grounded in data which has been systematically collected and analysed for a clearly defined purpose;
- it is undertaken by teachers, though sometimes with the support of external critical friends;
- it focuses on professional activity, usually in the workplace itself;
- its purpose is to clarify aspects of that activity, with a view to bringing about beneficial change – ultimately, to improve student progress, achievement and development, this being precisely the purpose of school improvement itself;

• it may focus on, again as is the case with school improvement efforts generally, both teaching and learning at the classroom level, and supporting organizational conditions and change management capacity.

Establishing teachers as key players on the school effectiveness and improvement stage

A key factor in considering the accessibility of both SER and SIR to teachers, is their need to make sense of the findings emerging from the field in a way which informs their practice. However, the process of translating this research into practice cannot even begin until there is widespread awareness of the research among a critical mass of teachers. The teaching profession has found itself unavoidably confronted by the need to address its methods, approaches and practices as they relate to raising standards, assuring quality and demonstrating effectiveness. In this context both SER and SIR have important contributions to make in taking schools forward towards the achievement of excellence. However, for teachers, the demand to address school effectiveness and improvement in these terms has arisen largely from the impact of change following the 1988 Education Reform Act (ERA), and not from an implicit or explicit desire to grapple with the research outcomes. With the exception of circumstances where research findings may have informed documents which necessarily have to be digested as a part of the everyday demands of a teacher's role, access to SER for practising teachers would seem rather limited and its relevance questionable.

Also, if the research is perceived by teachers to have emerged in response to central government imperatives concerned with pre-defined standards, a reconcentration of their energies as teachers into managerial activity and notions of performance management, they might feel a very limited sense of ownership over its outcomes. What might be equally unpalatable to teachers, however, is the notion of school effectiveness and improvement as bodies of theory emanating from educational researchers. This could well receive an equally dismissive response on the basis that its origins do not lie in the realities of practice.

This is particularly the case with SER, where 'the take-up of school effectiveness knowledge by practitioners within the educational system within schools has been very limited indeed' (Reynolds 1992: 17). Reynolds argues that this may be partly because SER in the UK 'is heavily academically dominated' in contrast to the school effectiveness movement in the US where practitioners have taken a more central role in the development of the research. Stoll and Fink (1996) go further, suggesting that the limited use of SER findings by educators may be as a result of 'the traditional inaccessibility of researchers who turn teachers off with their use of complex language to explain relatively simple phenomena' (p. 40). The solution which they offer to the thorny problem of the accessibility of research findings and the need for teachers to derive their own meanings from this research, is 'for researchers to work closely with schools, introduce the research findings to them in meaningful ways, and work with them using action research to try out, reflect on and evaluate the findings in projects tailored to schools' unique contexts' (p. 41). In this way it might be possible to utilize the methodology of school improvement to explore the findings of school effectiveness. This in itself might provide one accessible doorway to the more active involvement of teachers themselves in examining, and perhaps even challenging, the multiple meanings of school effectiveness and improvement as they impact upon the real lives of schools and the teaching profession itself.

Developing understanding and ownership through involvement

The process of translating this research into practice, however, also depends upon a recognition of teachers themselves as the potential key contributors to any moves towards school improvement. A long-term view of the involvement of teachers requires that they are supported in moving beyond mere access to, and acceptance of, SER in a way which enables them to contribute to an *extended* debate, where practitioners are given a participative voice alongside academics and policy makers. Teachers themselves need to be contributors to SER and SIR. This demands a shift from the current role of the profession, where teachers are often given no other option than to act simply as interpreters or recipients of established theory. As Dadds (1996) explains, teachers' voices can be easily silenced against the deafening chorus of established expertise:

> Many feel increasingly surrounded by outside organisations claiming 'to know', about their insider work, and to 'know better'. They research, thus within multiple structures of 'outside expertise'. These conditions may make it more difficult, but more imperative, to foster good quality practitioner research that generates action from the inside.
>
> (p. 6)

In taking this longer term view we are reminded that 'the fact remains that it is the individual teacher who still holds the key to the successful long-term impact of change within his/her own classroom (Day *et al.* 1990: 134–5). In this respect teachers cannot be considered as anything other than 'key players' on the school effectiveness 'stage' and as such there is a need to recognize, and give status to, their knowledge of what makes a school effective at a practitioner level. In short, while accessibility of the profession to the outcomes of SER is important, the research itself will not have the impact upon schools desired by Reynolds and others, unless it is deemed acceptable to teachers on the basis of its relevance at practitioner level in making a real contribution to improvement. As Carter has acknowledged in Chapter 1, in addition to addressing the issues of accessibility and acceptability, it is also necessary for those involved in school improvement projects such as ours, to consider the need for 'adaptability' of the sort which acknowledges the changing and uncertain nature of the current organizational climate in schools and recognizes the individual contexts in which schools operate.

It is on this basis that NWCSEUS has acknowledged the importance of teachers entering the debate about school effectiveness now, at a time when research is still evolving. This is based upon a belief that the performance of teachers as key players needs to evolve from a thorough understanding of their roles and facilitate not just an interpretation of the 'script', but some contribution to its production in the first place. One must be careful, however, in promoting such involvement as part of a framework of professional development to ensure that such ventures avoid what Frisby (1987) describes as:

> A model of INSET [inservice education of teachers] from the repertory theatre where actors rehearsed one role while performing a different role and then on the following Monday night opened with their new role, having trained for it, while simultaneously dispensing with their old one. Such a model will not do in schools. School based INSET is a drip-feed, we put in new things a bit at a time. In schools, thinking about things, talking about things and above all trying things out is in-service training.
>
> (p. 104)

Just as INSET requires a 'drip feed' and a carefully considered evolving approach, so does any attempt to involve teachers in addressing aspects of school improvement and effectiveness. If teachers are to have ownership of the quest for effectiveness then they need to be actively involved in the discovery process. As 'key players' they need to be able to have access to SER and SIR in a way which enables them to explore the 'script' and contribute to the 'rehearsals'. Otherwise, there is a danger that teachers will find themselves firmly cast in the understudy's role, being thrust on to the stage for the opening performance with no support from the rest of their fellow players from academe, who have retreated to their dressing rooms, research complete, funding exhausted and awaiting the next offer of a starring role!

This is to acknowledge the important role which teachers can play in establishing themselves within the school effectiveness and improvement debate, as 'intellectuals and representatives of life long learning,' in the way described by Sachs (1996), where teachers are provided with opportunities to reposition themselves quite differently within both social and political arenas:

Redefining themselves, rather than being externally defined can provide teachers with: opportunities in a variety of arenas to voice and make public their expertise and professional knowledge which may come to develop during the course of their careers. Furthermore, rather than relying on the conventional wisdom of experience as the basis for justifying their practice there is a place for teachers to construct themselves in public and professional domains as intellectuals and as representatives of life long learning.

(p. 4)

The case for a research partnership

The arguments presented so far underline the need for a real partnership within the research process between those in higher education, those charged with policy making at a local and national level and, most importantly, teachers themselves. Mortimore (1995) underlines this, pointing to the limitations of current approaches to national policy formulation and development, which have failed to take account of these various voices within the partnership. He claims that the strained relations between government and both practitioners and academics over the last decade, have led to 'the adoption of a series of untested policies' resulting in a situation where, 'many have had to be unscrambled, and costs and casualties have been high'. If, as Mortimore suggests, this makes the case 'for those involved in the work of effective schools to play a more prominent role in the formulation of policy', this involvement must include both academics and teachers, who can contribute a powerful combination of research and practitioner expertise. Dadds (1996) goes further in expressing the rationale for fostering such a partnership approach to research:

There are good reasons for fostering our partnerships with other practitioners. First, as central control over professional life increases, the need to work together, across institutional boundaries becomes stronger, in order to guard, as well we can, against uncontested, monolithic government views of professional work. Second, our efforts to do those good jobs of work through research can be enhanced if we join forces wherever there is a common will for change. Together, we ought to be able to achieve more than we can as separate professional groups. Together we bring a variety of experiences and expertise which can be drawn upon collectively for the greater good of the beneficiaries'.

(p. 7)

The importance of involving teachers within this partnership is further emphasized when one considers that when the national priorities change, the funding runs out, and the policy makers and researchers move on to other things, it is the teachers who are left with the job of implementation.

This notion of attempting to embed the research process itself with those who are involved at an operational level in schools has much to commend it, if only on the grounds that it is they who will still be there 'performing' when the rest of us have left the theatre. This point is explored by Brighouse (1994) in his discussion of the funding arrangements associated with developments in urban education and urban renewal programmes: 'those who view cities from afar fling money at the problem in time-limited dollops – the equivalent of food parcels to the third world' (p. 1). He goes on to stress the limitations of such an approach in bringing about any real change and suggests that if this trend is to be reversed there needs to be closer attention given to local priorities and decisions and 'the involvement as participants as far as possible of those affected'.

Such an approach is reflective of the work of the Australian National Schools Network whose involvement in collaborative, 'facilitated practitioner research' has acknowledged the importance of building 'a culture of research in member schools as an integral part of their rethinking processes' (Harradine 1996: 1). In this respect the NWCSEUS has been keen to address ways in which our collaborative work can contribute to establishing a culture of research within participating schools. Our intention, here, is that the processes and methods utilized by teachers within an action research framework will continue to be used beyond the life of individual projects, being internalized within the normal procedures of school and classroom review and evaluation. If such critical partnerships are to be built, it is vital that *all* concerned, including teachers, heads, students, parents, governing bodies, businesses, LEAs, national policy makers and higher education, learn from each other. Such an approach to partnership may also prove productive in creating a model for school effectiveness which is truly based upon the creation of a community of learners of the sort described by Glover (1995) in his review of the perspectives of Barth (1990) and Rosenholtz (1989):

> Barth . . . like Susan Rosenholtz presents a model of effectiveness which looks at school, not as a place, 'for important people who do not need to learn and unimportant people who do', but as a place 'where students discover, and adults rediscover, the joys, the difficulties and the satisfactions of learning'. This is a model of school effectiveness dependent on the creation of a 'community of learners' or in Rosenholtz's terms, the building of learning enriched as opposed to learning impoverished environments.
>
> (p. 18)

The promotion of such a model of school effectiveness, however, is clearly dependent upon an acknowledgement of the part played by teachers and their own learning within the educative process. This approach needs to be encouraged at school level as part of an internal, context-specific process, not only to facilitate the exploration of current theory as a means of informing future practice, but in giving teachers some ownership of any new theories which may emerge from this exploration of their practice. As Groundwater-Smith (1996) concludes, 'In an educational world where the activists in education are more likely to be governments than educators it is essential that the professional voice is strengthened' (p. 16). In referring to Popkewitz (1991) she endorses a concern shared by the NWCSEUS which is 'to broaden the opportunities for debate about reforms, so that many voices can be heard' (p. 16). Just as collaborative facilitated practitioner research projects in Australia have achieved this aim, it is our hope that the involvement of partners from schools, LEAs and universities within our own action research work will also provide a basis upon which teachers' voices, along with those of others, can be heard and can, as a result, make a real contribution to the school effectiveness and improvement debate.

Resolving the theory-practice issue

Teacher research has much to offer in enabling teachers to resolve what they might perceive to be a divide between the theory of SER and SIR and their own practice. By adopting this approach the intention is to make current research accessible, while placing teachers at the centre of the research process itself. Scheerens (1992) draws our attention to the need for teachers to interpret school effectiveness studies and improvement strategies emanating from research, within the context of their own schools. The rationale which underpins his argument is that much of the research may have identified effectiveness factors and improvement strategies which are so contextually bound that they may not be directly transferable. Scheerens concludes that improvement requires schools to adapt strategies appropriate to their local conditions, in the light of the interactions investigated in effectiveness studies.

This emphasizes the need, not only to address ways in which SER and SIR can be made more accessible to teachers, but ways in which, through their involvement in school-based research, they can be encouraged to play a more central role in thinking through school effectiveness and improvement issues for themselves. In acknowledging the potential of contributions which practitioners can make, we are mindful of the need to promote ownership of the research process by teachers themselves, in a way which encourages an adaptive response to the investigation of established theory emanating from SER and SIR. Such an approach promotes the notion of teachers taking charge of the formulation of their own theories, in the way envisaged by Fullan (1995) where teachers 'immerse themselves in real situations of reform and begin to craft their own theories of change, constantly testing them against new situations and the experiences of others'.

Teacher research, then, and especially action research, can be seen as providing a potent means of facilitating such teacher involvement, giving them access to established SER and SIR theories, while promoting their participation in contributing new research in these fields. Furthermore, it is more likely that such research will have a more significant impact upon teachers in real terms if they are given the opportunity to explore the issues central to these fields in, and through, practice at school level. For teachers, validation of school effectiveness and improvement theory through practice is likely to have a more meaningful impact than attempts to generate an understanding and acceptance of theories which have been validated by those external to the school and then presented as established or recommended practice. Elliott (1991) suggests that teachers often feel threatened by theory when it is presented in this independently validated form:

> Teachers feel 'theory' is threatening because it is produced by a group of outsiders who claim to be experts at generating valid knowledge about educational practices. Phenomenologically speaking, from the perspective of teachers, 'theory' is what outside researchers say about their practices after they have applied their special techniques of information processing. As such it is remote from their practical experience of the way things are. To bow to a theory is to deny the validity of one's own experience-based professional craft knowledge.
>
> (p. 45)

In this context one can see why teachers may feel that theory, particularly that concerned with school effectiveness, has little relevance to them, being remote from their professional experiences, knowledge and skills. The situation is further exacerbated when research findings are reported upon or published in a manner perceived to be inaccessible to teachers. As Gurney (1989) points out in referring to Rudduck (1985), teachers often describe their 'inability to speak the conventional language of research reportage' as a significant barrier to gaining access to research findings, let alone to contributing to them. This, Rudduck claims, leads to 'a lack of self-image with regard to whether or not we have anything of value to contribute to the body of educational knowledge and understanding' (p. 18).

Teacher empowerment within the research partnership

For the NWCSEUS an important aspect of the process of adopting an action research approach has been the need to address the theory–practice divide as being embodied by the perceived differences between the work of its partners from higher education and schools. These have been very real concerns and have influenced the Consortium's approach in developing action research in the participating schools, through a partnership of players. These partners, some of whom are associated in teachers' minds with the accountability element of school effectiveness such as local school inspectors, and some of whom like ourselves come from academe, have had to grapple with these issues of perceptions regarding SER and the theory–practice divide. As Sachs (1996) describes, however, a partnership approach to research projects such as ours provides an effective means of overcoming this divide:

> Successful school-university collaborations provide a means of overcoming the credibility gap between . . . the castle of the school and the castle of the academy. Partnerships enable a new kind of professional learning to occur between teachers and academics and also help in the creation of new, more powerful kinds of knowledge to inform teaching and schooling.
>
> (p. 10)

Our approach has been to develop the projects in a way which has focused the attention of teachers on school improvement in areas which they have prioritized as important, rather than forcing an effectiveness agenda through externally imposed criteria. Here we have emphasized the development rather than the accountability dimension. As academics, the challenge has been to dispel an 'ivory tower' perception of our work, through our involvement with teachers in their own research. In this way we have viewed the action research method as an effective tool for bridging the theory–practice divide, with the intention that it will help teachers make sense of school improvement and effectiveness research in the context of their own situations, in a way which is clearly rooted in practice:

> The Consortium has from the outset seen research – and especially action research – as one door into school improvement, because we believe it provides a framework for a rigorous, systematic and thoughtful pursuit of the improvement process . . . It is about giving ownership to the practitioners. It is about developing the skills of effective change management. It is about providing a shared methodology for research. It is about change based on evidence rather than on a hunch or an externally dominated agenda.
>
> (NWCSEUS 1995: 7)

Haggarty and Postlethwaite (1995: 171) in describing their collaborative research work with schools, refer to Carr and Kemmis (1991) who write that, when facilitators work with teachers 'they often create circumstances in which project control is not in teachers' hands'. Different facilitator roles establish different kinds of action research: technical, practical or emancipatory. Technical action research it is argued, investigates issues raised by the outsiders, whereas in emancipatory action research 'the practitioner group takes joint responsibility for the development of practice' (p. 202). In the process of negotiating the focus for the school-based projects with which we are involved, we have aspired to the latter model, on the basis that such an approach encourages teacher empowerment and involvement in SER and SIR. Participating staff have been encouraged to define the original problem, the focus for their research, starting from the school context and their priorities for school improvement but with an eye to the effectiveness factors identified in established research. So, while SER and SIR findings have provided the backdrop to this teacher research, and have as a result often influenced the school's choice of project, the adoption of an action research approach has enabled the staff to identify their own school-based problem as a means of investigating the validity of such findings within their real situation.

It is necessary to recognize that such an approach requires that teachers as contributors are empowered in two important respects. First, through the research process itself, which should provide contributors with a means of bridging the theory–practice divide and, secondly, through a supportive endorsement of the fact that teachers are well placed to challenge established theory and research findings from within the real contexts of their schools and classrooms. Empowerment of this kind reinforces the role of teachers in the adaptation and even reconstruction of theories or strategies espoused by SER and SIR.

As Elliott (1996) suggests, the facilitation of reflexivity through action research is empowering to teachers, in enabling them to explore effectiveness and improvement theory in relation to, and in the light of, their own practice and their understandings of this practice. In referring to the work of Brown *et al.* (1995) he suggests that 'research findings are useful not when they confirm existing understandings, but support the development by the teacher of new ones'. In this we can see the importance of the reflective process which action research promotes, in providing a basis upon which a teacher may 'examine the understandings which shape his or her practice [and be] able to reconstruct them as a basis for improving practice' (p. 219).

Action research – indeed teacher research more generally – offers us a way of resolving the theory–practice issue for teachers. As such it would seem to have a lot to offer in making SER more accessible, by enabling teachers to come to a more meaningful understanding of work in the field and by involving them as active partners. It is for this reason that the development of consortia, embracing schools, LEAs and universities, may prove to be central to the continued work of the school effectiveness and school improvement movements. Indeed, as Elliott suggests, such an approach may well provide just the kind of creative outlet for responding to the current imposition of a paradigm of school management and development based upon a rational systems and control surveillance model:

> I would argue that the widespread emergence of collaborative action research as a teacher-based form of curriculum evaluation and development is a creative response to the growth of technical-rational systems of hierarchical surveillance and control over teachers' professional

practices. Out of the still smouldering embers of the traditional craft culture the phoenix of a collaborative reflective practice arises to offer creative resistance to the hegemony of the technocrat.

(1991: 56)

If this potential can be fully realized then Elliott's vision of the resolution of the theory–practice issue as one of the unintended outcomes of government interventionism in education may well become more than a popular aspiration. It may provide the key to open the door for teachers to school effectiveness in a research context, where they will be able to explore their own understandings and derive their own meanings about what makes schools effective and what might lead to their improvement.

In short, then, our argument is that teacher research, especially when it is undertaken within the context of a partnership of 'players' from all sectors of education performing together on the same 'stage', seems a very attractive proposition for the future of school effectiveness and improvement work. Opening the doorway to improvement from the inside of the school, through the active involvement of teachers in school-based improvement research in collaboration with others, may well prove to be an important 'point of direction' in encouraging a well rehearsed and informed performance by the company's key players. 'After all, it is the teachers who ultimately hold the key to the success of the educational enterprise and it is surely time that we began to see the world of schooling from their viewpoint' (Hargreaves and Goodson 1996: 24).

Teacher research for school improvement: some questions and issues

Our argument is that teacher research can be a powerful strategy for school improvement. However, there is no guarantee that its potential will be realized. We offer a set of questions and issues that we feel are worth considering in order to help prevent a situation where, to paraphrase Elliott (1991: x), a thousand flowers might bloom but without vigilance can die. Most arise out of what has been presented in this book so far, especially in Chapter 2.

It was tempting to put them forward as a list of conditions regarding teacher research for school improvement, but we resisted. We have no wish to repeat the error that some writers have made, especially with lists of effectiveness factors or characteristics: of seeming to offer a blueprint for success. The resolution of one issue will be a particularly pressing need in one school while that of another will be more important elsewhere. Also, of course, the absence of the 'right or best conditions' does not necessarily mean that teacher research will not happen, nor that it will not help promote school improvement. It is sometimes the case that a flower *will* bloom and survive against the odds, and even propagate. It is with these health warnings that the offer is made.

Is the culture right?

Teacher research has the potential to help shift the organizational culture in a direction supportive of school improvement. This is a major reason for urging its adoption as an improvement strategy. However, there is a chicken and egg situation because, at the same time, it is likely that if the culture is not supportive of teacher research then the chances that the flower *will* die are increased. It is useful, therefore, to establish, or work on, certain elements of the sort of collaborative culture and certain of the cultural norms that are explored in Chapter 2. Thus:

- Is there practice of teachers working with and for each other, and is there a cooperative set of relationships?
- Is there a belief that teacher research is a meaningful activity, that it can make a difference to student progress?
- Do teachers believe that they are, or should be, (continuing) learners, and that learning comes about from self and peer assessments of how well their judgements are working?
- Is there openness and trust, a willingness and ability to speak one's mind and to listen to others? Here, Elliott (1991) points to the constraining nature of two features of what he calls the traditional craft culture: 'what I do in my classroom is my business and what you do in yours is your business' (p. 58), and a hierarchical structure of professional authority. Gathering data and eliciting critiques from students, parents and colleagues, he says, challenges these understandings.
- Is there a willingness to take risks, to try something different? This is especially important in action research where the whole point is to try something different, whether as a result of research and/or as something which is to be researched.

Are the structures right?

As Halsall has written in Chapter 2, it is the existence of the sorts of internal conditions in a school that Hopkins (1996) has described, which can support improvement efforts. Two of these seem to us to be particularly relevant to the undertaking of teacher research.

Teacher development

- Is there a commitment to teacher development, for example in the school development plan; has the school established an appropriate infrastructure for this; and is teacher research seen as a significant element within a strategy for teacher development?

- Is teacher development facilitated by the adoption of the sorts of guide-lines advanced by Moore (1988), as described in Chapter 2? To summarize these, is there a collaborative approach to diagnosing needs and activities; are teachers' own experiences used as a starting point; are staff encouraged and enabled to define their own learning objectives, to develop reflective thinking skills, and to integrate learning with action?
- Is attention paid to the integration of the school's development needs and those of the teachers themselves: to interrelating school and teacher development in mutually supportive ways?

Senior management support

Do senior managers encourage teachers to be proactive, to take the ini-tiative, to be involved in various forms of leadership roles, and to use their professional judgement? Are teachers seen as professionals who possess problem-posing and problem-solving skills? Do senior managers themselves engage in research and reflective practice?

Elliott's (1991) account of the teacher research-based Ford Teaching Project (FTP) and Teacher-student Interaction and Quality of Learning (TIQL) project is informative. As he suggests, teacher research implies both self critique and institutional critique. However, in the FTP few schools had organizational forms which fostered institutional self-critique, nor were senior managers active in the project. One result was that the teacher researchers found it difficult to establish a critical discourse within the schools. Another was that in most schools, once the funded life of the project ended and the support structures provided by the project were removed, research activity ceased. It had not become institutionalized. Building on this experience, the TIQL project selected schools in which senior managers were very involved in teacher development policy and practice, and had themselves under-taken teacher research as part of an award bearing course. They were also used as internal facilitators, their role being to develop strategies which would enable the schools to support teachers' research activity. Again, though, project cessation was accompanied by disintegration of the internal facilitator role. 'It was if the internal facilitators required their strategies ... to be validated by a strong external support team' (Elliott 1991: 41). This might have been so, but equally it might have been because the project, and the internal facilitator role within it, were 'bolt-on' activities, not part of the 'normal' institutional culture or organizational arrangements, nor a usual aspect of the senior manager's role.

Is the research linked to whole school priorities?

The focus of any research should be one to which the individual or group of researchers are genuinely committed, especially given the ever-increasing demands on teachers' time and the increasing complexity of their role. For this reason alone it would be unwise and inappropriate to eschew the notion of teachers undertaking highly 'individualistic' research which might well be unrelated to colleagues' concerns or those of the school more generally. Indeed, this has been a fairly common feature of teacher research. Additionally, it *can* be the case that this sort of endeavour acts as a catalyst in the identification of new whole school priorities. However, it is more likely that research which is linked to existing whole school priorities will have most chance of being supported within a school, and of having a wider impact on practice and on school improvement. We agree with Hopkins (1993) that, 'The main difference between the 1970s and the 1990s is that classroom research has increasingly to be seen within a whole school context' (p. 2), and that one should 'try and link . . . to a well-known or identifiable need at the school level' (Hopkins 1989: 193).

Research at the classroom or school level?

We have acknowledged, in most cases, the primacy of a research focus on whole school priority areas. However, this still begs the question of whether there should be classroom-focused research (e.g. to do with a whole school priority of introducing more differentiated work), or a more 'management' focused research at school level (e.g. to do with a whole school priority of developing an infrastructure for teacher development). This issue connects with the discussion in Chapter 2, of the existence of different sorts of development priorities: the need to work on the curriculum and teaching-learning *and* on the school's internal conditions so as to support this. Just as both are important in school improvement efforts, so too are both types of research focus.

It has been the case that most writers on teacher research have emphasized classroom research. Thus, while Hopkins argues that teacher researchers increasingly need to take a whole school perspective, he seems to suggest that this means linking *classroom* research to whole school priorities. Similarly, Elliott (1996) argues that 'the priority for school improvement . . . is how to support and encourage a process of deliberative reflection . . . on the part of teachers at *classroom* level' (p. 219, our italics). We do not wish to dissent from a view that classroom research warrants such emphasis; far from it. However, we do feel that teacher research at the *school* level warrants greater consideration than seems to have been the case.

Where this is so, however, it is important to remember the importance of teacher researchers being committed to the research focus. The issue here is whether they see such research either as relevant to teaching and learning in the classroom or more broadly, as being in the interests of their students and others such as parents. Carter's account in this chapter of the early problems she encountered in her work with one of the NWCSEUS schools highlights this. One of the major factors affecting whether Consortium projects have actually 'gotten off the ground' has been whether the wider staff body has been supportive of the focus. Where they have not been then there has not been 'acceptability' of ownership and the projects have not progressed. Here, then, the issue is not just one of agendas imposed by central government but also by heads, sometimes acting as Elliott (1996) has suggested as line managers of the state. Here, a key point is that it is not enough for a research project to be rooted in the school development plan, but that the plan itself has been developed in consultation with, and has the support of, the wider staff body. If it is, then research other than that at the level of the classroom can equally gain their commitment. In short, 'acceptability' can be associated with 'non-classroom' research.

What are the purposes of the research?

As previously explored, school improvement is about enhancing student progress, though to succeed in this schools often need to work on their capacity for managing change. This points to two broad purposes of teacher research in relation to improvement: to assess student outcomes and to assess the change or implementation process. The former can be seen as research about school improvement, the latter as research for improvement.

There are several basic issues to do with assessing outcomes. To begin with, one needs measures. These can be relatively straightforward but more often are not. Thus, while it is fairly unproblematic to 'measure' attendance, it is more difficult to measure such things as underachievement, truancy or cooperation, simply because defining them is a complicated affair. Secondly, we often wish to measure progress. This involves comparing baseline and 'post change' data, which can present problems. For example, it is not always possible to obtain the same sort of data and, in some schools much more than in others, it is not always possible to retain the same populations for comparison purposes. More crucial, how can one be sure that it is the change that has been implemented and studied, and not some other factors, which has been the major influence on progress?

Much attention is rightly given to the assessment of outcomes. However, there is a tendency to ignore the change or implementation process. Hopkins (1989) quotes from Berman and McLaughlin (1976: 500):

Although student outcomes might be the ultimate indicator of the effectiveness of an innovation ... projects must go through the complex and uncertain process of implementation before they can affect students, it makes sense to put first things first and to measure the effectiveness of implementation.

In particular, there is a need to 'define' the change itself. What has actually been implemented might not exactly be what was intended. Also, what can we learn from discovering what factors have been either supportive or inhibitive of the change?

How to report the research for impact?

Here, we assume that the research that has been undertaken has been related to the goal of school improvement, and is not of relevance only to the teacher researcher him/herself. A corollary of this is that some form of research report will be necessary. The issue is how best to approach this in order to ensure that the research does lead to action. It might be the case that a verbal report alone will suffice, but in most cases it is likely that a written report will have greater impact. In order to maximize impact:

- The report should not be too lengthy. Nor should it be written in a highly technical style; although it might form the basis of a journal article, it *is* a report.
- The report should include, though not necessarily in this order,
  - a statement of what the research was trying to find out and the reasons for this;
  - a summary of the main findings and recommendations for action;
  - a brief explanation of how the research was designed and conducted, what data was collected, how and from whom it was collected and for what purposes;
  - clarification of any terms or concepts that might be variously interpreted by different people;
  - acknowledgement of the limitations of the research;
  - full details of the findings, recommendations and data collection instruments, possibly as appendices.
- The focus and purposes of the research on which the report is based should have been made known to, and received the agreement and support of, all those people to whom the report's implications and recommendations will relate. Related to this, there needs to be sufficient motivation and intent to consider seriously, and possibly act on, these.
- If circumstances, for example resource constraints, are likely to make it impossible to act on recommendations then avoid making them! To do so risks causing resentment and a feeling that the research has been pointless.
- The report should not be issued and/or spoken to before a decision is made on the next steps to be taken. For example, will discussion groups be established to help generate a considered response to the report or to identify the sorts of task groups that will need to be formed to work on action steps relating to recommendations?

How is time to be found?

This is a crucial question to consider for it is often a lack of time which is the key factor in the 'wilting of the flower', even if teacher research is not a 'bolt on' activity. Although it is pertinent to ask it of all research activity, some of the possible responses closely relate to a number of the major school improvement 'messages'. The fact is that there are no easy ways of resolving the issue but it can be helpful to consider the following.

Funding

If there is a genuine commitment to the research at the school level, whether because its focus and purposes relate to school priorities or because teacher research is seen as an important element within a policy for teacher development, then it would seem reasonable that time for teacher research should be funded, to some degree at least, from within the school's own resources. This might be the most acid test of senior management support! Additionally, while most schools look to external sources for financial support regarding a host of purposes, very few do so to support research activity; yet such sources do exist. For example, a number of charitable trusts are responsive to teacher research proposals, and possibilities can exist by way of proposals from schools or consortia of schools in the context of Single Regeneration Budget projects within their Training and Enterprise Council area. The most visible example in the UK recently, however, is the Teacher Training Agency's (TTA) teacher research grants scheme and its funding of school-based educational research consortia. Such funding is likely to increase in future, especially if the arguments put forward by David Hargreaves hold sway: 'a substantial proportion of the research budget can be prised out of the academic community [and] transferred in phases to agencies committed to . . . full partnership with teachers in the interests of improving practice' (1996: 7).

In-kind support from partners

This brings us in particular to the matter of collaboration with external partners, a theme that runs throughout this book. Time might be 'saved' simply through having an *extra* pair(s) of hands, for example by utilizing the 'outsider' as a data gatherer, as a contributor to the construction of data collection instruments, as an initial commentator on the research report or whatever. Alternatively, he/she or they might be used *instead* of the teachers for any one of these activities, or for training a group of teachers in research skills. The possibilities are numerous.

How, though, does a school obtain such support? It might be by convincing local authority staff or school governors who possess relevant skills that it can form part of their advisory or support remit – and many will not need convincing. Or, it might be by securing the services of higher education colleagues on the basis of, for example, a *quid pro quo* arrangement in the light of the school's support for their institution in the initial or continuing professional development of their own students. Engagement with the school's research activity might also be an attractive proposition for higher education staff if it relates to their own research interests (and provides an opportunity for publications!). Involvement in the more formally constituted research-based consortia, such as the NWCSEUS, presents a particularly valuable opportunity to obtain in-kind support.

There are, of course, other benefits that such partnerships bring. For example, external critical friends can help combat some of the possible disadvantages of teacher research. They can provide an element of 'distance' and, if not objectivity, a different subjectivity. They can help identify any self-deceptions that teacher researchers might have concerning their motives and intentions. They can help reduce any insularity by bringing to bear other perspectives on, and understandings of, the situation. Finally, they can sometimes more easily gain access to, and elicit more honest responses from, certain sorts of data providers, for example the head him/herself.

Using internal teams

Very often, teacher research is undertaken by an individual or, occasionally, by a pair of teachers. However, the use of a larger staff team can mean that, while the total amount of time needed for research remains unaltered (or even increased slightly), as with the use of outsider collaborators, the sharing of research planning, instrument construction, data gathering and analysis, and report writing means that the time commitment for any individual member of the team can be reduced. Their involvement becomes a more feasible proposition. Such internal collaboration is in any case likely to be particularly appropriate to teacher research for school improvement: it is a manifestation of, or a contribution to, a collaborative culture and a shared purpose and commitment. It is also likely to help maintain the research effort through the mutual support it provides, and to lead to the more active participation of a broader group of staff in debates following the conclusion of the research.

These, then, are for us some of the key questions and issues for teacher research and school improvement. Halsall revisits several of them in Chapter 13 in reviewing the case studies of teacher research which follow as Part 2 of the book.

Part 2

Case studies of teacher research for school improvement

Introduction

Part 2 does not begin with a case study, but with a chapter by Michael Bassey which provides an introduction to action research. It includes a description of just one action research model. This is followed by an account of brief, *invented* examples of research for improving practice which use this model, as a way into illustrating a variety of research methods that can be employed by teacher researchers.

The case studies which follow are not, in fact, rooted in the framework put forward by Bassey which is for the purpose of illustration only. Nor are they rooted in any other single research model. The approaches that have been adopted are quite simply those that have been appropriate to the research focus, the school context and circumstances and, indeed, to the researchers' own 'idiosyncrasies'. As with case studies generally, there is no intention to generate generalizations concerning their various foci. Nor, indeed, is there an attempt to seek to generalize about, or suggest a particular model for, teacher research for school improvement from the set of case studies. Their value as separate contributions rests on the notion of relatability. We hope that others, working in similar situations, will find it possible to relate their decision making to that described in the chapters. Their value as a set of case studies lies in their contribution to:

- the debate about school improvement – with one exception, they have arisen directly out of a particular improvement thrust within the schools concerned;
- consideration of the role of collaboration with the school improvement debate – they all involve internal and/or external collaboration in one form or another;

- an exploration of the particular relationship between teacher research and school improvement – and, here, Chapter 13 reviews the case studies in the light of some of the questions and issues discussed at the end of the previous chapter.

5

Action research for improving educational practice

Michael Bassey

Educational action research is an inquiry which is carried out in order to understand, to evaluate and then to change, in order to improve some educational practice. It is a form of research that people can do by themselves, about themselves, and for themselves. In schools all over the country it is being carried out by teachers as a tool for school improvement and for enhancing classroom practice. This chapter is concerned with the first of these, that is school improvement. Such an endeavour usually entails someone with a managerial responsibility in the school taking the initiative and leading the research inquiry.

It is a powerful method for determining change, and for monitoring change to ensure that it is worthwhile. Its great merit is that it enables people to own the change. However, it requires a share of that precious commodity, personal time, and it can be painful – if the evidence collected points to uncomfortable conclusions. It is not, of course, the only method of promoting change. Change by fiat may be quicker, by subterfuge easier, and by discussion simpler, but because action research depends upon the authority of evidence, rather than the authority of people, it is often more successful in the long run.

The following section sets out a framework for doing action research. There are lots of descriptions of action research; this is one that many people have found particularly helpful. It is based on three key questions and eight stages of research. Next come seven invented examples of action research which could be initiated by teachers in managerial roles in schools. In particular these might be headteachers of primary, secondary or special schools, heads of department, or heads of year in secondary schools. I use invented examples because these enable a range of possible inquiries to be covered which illustrate a variety of research methods in a simple way. These are written as brief 'diary entries' by the person who conducts the research. The examples are followed by an account of some of the methods of action research which have been found useful in schools. Finally, there is a list of situations in which action research is unlikely to work.

A framework for doing action research

This framework of eight stages is based on three key questions:

- What is happening in this educational situation of ours now? (Stages 1 to 4)
- What changes are we going to introduce? (Stage 5)
- What happens when we make the changes? (Stages 6 to 8)

It is important to recognize that, unlike research in the natural sciences, action research has a subjective quality in which personal involvement is essential. Hence pronouns such as 'I' and 'we' inevitably feature in the formulation of research questions. Also, unlike the natural sciences, it has a value orientation which enables judgements to be made as to whether an innovation is worthwhile.

Stage 1: Define the inquiry

What is the issue of concern? What research question are we asking? Who will be involved? Where and when will it happen?

Stage 2: Describe the educational situation

What are we required to do here? What are we trying to do here? What thinking underpins what we are doing?

Stage 3: Collect evaluative data and analyse it

What is happening in this educational situation now as understood by the various participants? Using research methods, what can we find out about it?

Stage 4: Review the data and look for contradictions

What contradictions are there between what we would like to happen and what seems to happen? (It will be very unusual if none is found, and will probably be because the situation has not been critically examined in sufficient detail.)

Stage 5: Tackle a contradiction by introducing change

By reflecting critically and creatively on the contradictions what change can we introduce which we think is likely to be beneficial? (Wisdom is needed here to ignore the things which cannot be changed and to work on ones that can.)

Stage 6: Monitor the change
What happens day-by-day when the change is introduced?

Stage 7: Analyse evaluative data about the change
What is happening in this educational situation now – as understood by the various participants – as a result of the changes introduced? Using research methods what can we find out about it? (This is similar to stage 3, but now focuses on the effect of the change.)

Stage 8: Review the change and decide what to do next
Was the change worthwhile? Are we going to continue it in the future? What are we going to do next? Is the change sufficient or are we going to carry out another cycle of research with a more closely focused research question? Who are we going to tell about the results of this research?

(See Figure 5.1.)

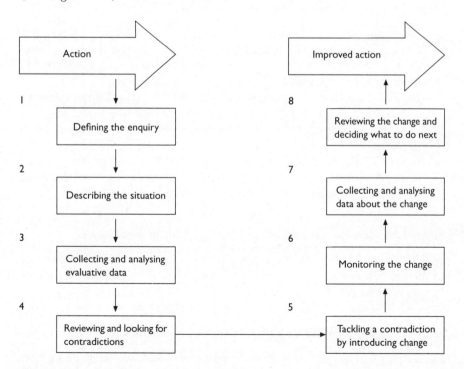

Figure 5.1 Eight steps in action research

Invented example 1: Curriculum monitoring

Research led by a new primary school headteacher or a new head of faculty in a secondary school. The following represents diary entries, made at each of the eight stages described above.

Stage 1: Define the inquiry

Initial question: How do I, as head, know what is going on in classrooms?

Stage 2: Describe the situation

I have recently been appointed. Previous head much respected, but aloof and ran things from his office. He left all decisions about teaching to individual staff in relation to their own classrooms and visited classrooms only when taking visitors round. I intend to provide educational leadership, to ensure that we respond effectively to the national curriculum and provide for each child appropriately in terms of his and her potential.

Stage 3: Collect evaluative data and analyse it

(a) We had a general discussion at a staff meeting to initiate the project. I described my proposed procedure for exploring the question, 'How do I, as head, know what is going on in classrooms?' I referred to Ofsted expectations and governors' responsibilities.
(b) During a fortnight, I chatted (i.e. ten-minute informal interview, or purposeful conversation) to each teacher in turn about the question and made notes which were agreed with the teacher. Difficult, but I persisted.
(c) I wrote a short paper for staff on the findings. Anonymized data avoided making references too easily identifiable. There was a wide range of views from 'welcome' to 'please keep out'.

Stage 4: Review the evaluative data and look for contradictions

At a staff meeting we discussed the paper and I tried to focus on the contradiction between my view of my role and the range of responses made by members of staff.

Stage 5: Tackle a contradiction by introducing a change

I said that I had decided to visit each classroom for about ten minutes from time to time, keeping a low profile, looking at children's work and talking with them, and making sure that I share my perceptions with the teacher before the end of the day. I asked each member of staff . . .

Stage 6: Monitor the change

. . . to monitor the progress of this change by keeping a diary (five-minute entry once a week) until the end of term about the experience of my visits.

Stage 7: Analyse the data

GG had offered to read through the diary entries and so she reported at the beginning of next term on how the staff perceived my visits. I gave my own report on how I felt that this was facilitating my role of educational leadership.

Stage 8: Review the change and decide what to do next

Staff meeting discussed the reports and decided . . .

Invented example 2: Communications

Research led by deputy head. This could be in a large primary or a small secondary school.

Stage 1: Define the inquiry

The starter was an overheard remark: 'Communications in our school are abysmal.' My first question was, 'How effective are communications in our school?' but soon this was redefined as: 'What kinds of communications are used in our school, what are the purposes of each, and to what extent are these purposes served?'

Stage 2: Describe the situation

This was my analysis of communications:

(a) Communications from head to children:
    (a1) Notice via class teachers to read to class.
    (a2) Notice at school assembly.
(b) Communications from head to teachers:
    (b1) Word of mouth in staffroom, corridor, classroom, etc.
    (b2) Staff room noticeboard.

    (b3) Staff meetings.
    (b4) Note taken round classrooms.
(c) Communications from head to other staff:
    (c1) Note passed round (e.g. dinner staff).
    (c2) Staff room noticeboard.
(d) Communications from head to governors:
    (d1) Letter posted to each governor.
    (d2) Statement at governors' meeting.
(e) Communications from head to parents:
    (e1) Letter to parents delivered by children at home time.

There was too much to research into so I focused the inquiry on (b), that is communications from head to teachers. The head agreed to discuss this at the next staff meeting.

Stage 3: Collect evaluative data and analyse it

We had a general discussion at a staff meeting and agreed that 'communications' was an important issue. As deputy head I suggested the following method of inquiry.

> Structured conversation between interviewer (myself) and four volunteer teachers for say ten minutes. Effectiveness of each of the four modes to be enquired into. E.g. 'Can you tell me how effective the staff room noticeboard is?' 'How often do you look at it?' 'What are the difficulties?' 'How could it be improved?' 'Do you feel the head passes on all that we need to know?' Interviewer writes responses onto a proforma – i.e. duplicated sheet with these questions on. From the interview responses I would design a questionnaire and send it to each teacher. I would analyse the responses, discuss with the head and together we would write a report for staff meeting.

This was agreed. The head was apprehensive but said he felt it would be important 'to find out what the problem is'. Three weeks later it was all done.

Stage 4: Review the evaluative data and look for contradictions

I reported at the staff meeting. There seemed sometimes to be contradictions between what the head thought she had done and what the staff considered to be the case, between what the head passed on and what the staff felt they needed, and between the head feeling that a note pinned to the board told everybody something important and the likelihood of everyone reading it immediately.

Stage 5: Tackle a contradiction by introducing a change

At the meeting somebody suggested this change. Every note put on the board by the head will carry a sticker with staff initials on. It will also carry the date and time of putting on the board. A pencil will hang on string by the noticeboard and staff should tick the notice once read – and draw the attention of 'unticked' colleagues to it.

Stage 6: Monitor the change

HK volunteered to monitor the staff room noticeboard and at regular time intervals keep a check-list of who has and who hasn't ticked the 'I've read it' sticker. This would provide evaluative data.

Stage 7: Analyse the data

HK and I went through the data and showed that one department tends often to be two or three days behind everybody else in reading the notices. It might have been obvious before, but no one had thought of it – it's because they tend to make their own coffee at break, being somewhat isolated from the rest of the school. Also RS and TT only read the noticeboard when someone else tells them to!

Stage 8: Review the change and decide what to do next

The staff meeting decided that the 'I've read it' stickers were useful and asked the head to continue with them. Also the isolated department will get a special photocopy of all notices.

Invented example 3: Differentiation in the delivery of the curriculum

Research led by head. This could be in a primary school.

Stage 1: Define the inquiry

How do we plan for differentiation for individual children on a day-by-day basis?

Stage 2: Describe the situation

The curriculum of the school is religious education plus the national curriculum interpreted as: mathematics, English, topic (embracing science, technology, history, geography, and art with some maths and a lot of English), physical education, music, and art. The teaching methods are a mixture of whole class lessons, group work and individual work. The learning activities are: (a) tasks set for everybody in the class which different children will achieve differently; and (b) different tasks set for different groups of children, decided according to their perceived ability to learn from the tasks. I decided to redefine the enquiry by focusing on (a) and (b) in topic work.

Stage 3: Collect evaluative data and analyse it

We had a general discussion at a staff meeting to initiate the project. I put forward the following procedure.

> During a fortnight, I would chat (i.e. informal interview, or purposeful conversation) to each teacher in turn about the current topic and the extent to which (a) and (b) operate in his/her classroom. Specifically I would ask 'What are the problems of (a) and of (b)?'

This was agreed and in addition I was urged to collect examples of the two kinds of task and make them generally available. I wrote a short paper for the staff on findings. Data was anonymized in order to avoid making references too easily identifiable. But inevitably some people were recognizable – I got their agreement before distributing the paper.

Stage 4: Review the evaluative data and look for contradictions

The school mission statement says, 'We try to treat each individual child according to his or her needs', but the evidence of topic work is that in most classes children are given work as if they are all at the same stage of development. I'd written a fairly bland report, but this view was articulated by several teachers at the meeting.

Stage 5: Tackle a contradiction by introducing a change

The change was agreed at the meeting. Everybody would try to set tasks at different levels of complexity during the next half term's topic work . . .

Stage 6: Monitor the change

. . . and to monitor the progress of this change by keeping a diary (ten-minute entries twice a week).

Stage 7: Analyse the data

PQ has offered to read through the diary entries and report at the beginning of the next term on how well the introduction of different levels of task has gone.

Stage 8: Review the change and decide what to do next

Staff meeting discussed PQ's report and decided ...

Invented example 4: Marking of children's work

Research led by head. This could be in a primary school.

Stage 1: Define the inquiry

How do we ensure that the marking of children's work by teachers achieves educational purposes?

Stage 2: Describe the situation

There is as yet no school policy on marking and my overall impression is that the marking of children's work serves only the purpose of ensuring that tasks set are completed. Reflecting on this I redefined the inquiry: What evidence is there of children trying to improve their work as a result of what their teacher has said or written about their work?

Stage 3: Collect evaluative data and analyse it

We had a general discussion at a staff meeting to initiate the project. Everyone agreed that it was an important issue and we chose a fairly direct way of investigating it, as follows:

> At the beginning of a particular lesson teacher A will return work to children, teacher B will observe what happens, and the head will release teacher B by taking his/her class. During the lesson teacher B will endeavour to chat to a number of children, asking 'What did teacher A say to you about your work? What are you going to try to do about it?' (It is expected that according to the age of the children, teacher A's comments will be spoken or in writing.) Afterwards teachers A and B will write a short report together on the findings. During the course of several weeks every member of staff will play the role of A and B, so that everyone has participated and a set of reports are prepared. The head collects in the reports and writes a covering note before distributing the complete set to each member of staff.

It took most of the term to do this, because the occasions when 'teacher A' was returning work, 'teacher B' could leave his/her class, and when I could be free, were few and far between! But it worked and I got my report written – giving every teacher a pseudonym (even though some were thinly disguised).

Stage 4: Review the evaluative data and look for contradictions

A special staff meeting discussed the report, focused on the initial question and . . .

Stage 5: Tackle a contradiction by introducing a change

. . . then chose a working party to draft a marking policy for the school.

Stage 6: Monitor the change

Staff monitored the progress of this change by keeping a diary (ten-minute entries once a week) for half a term.

Stage 7: Analyse the data

MM offered to read through the diary entries and report at the beginning of the next term on the implementation of the marking policy. She used pseudonyms again.

Stage 8: Review the change and decide what to do next

Staff meeting discussed MM's report and decided . . .

Invented example 5: Preparing for a school development plan

Research could be in any school which has not yet prepared a school development plan, or which decides to rethink its planning.

Stage 1: Define the inquiry

Initial question: How do we evaluate the school prior to devising the school development plan for the next three years?

AUDIT OF OUR SCHOOL

These 10 items were identified by the National Commission on Education as characteristics of successful schools. **This questionnaire asks in which of these areas should we particularly aim to improve in the future.** The purpose of the enquiry is to give staff and governors some directions we should aim for in preparing the school development plan for the next three years.

Please identify between 2 and 5 items on this list which you think should be **areas for development** during the next three years. Put a circle round the item numbers to indicate your choices. Don't put your name on the sheet, but do indicate whether you are teacher or governor (teacher-governors should respond as teachers).

1   Strong, positive leadership by the head and senior staff.

2(a) A good atmosphere or spirit, generated both by shared aims and values . . .

2(b) . . . and by a physical environment that is as attractive and stimulating as possible.

3   High and consistent expectations of all children.

4   A clear and continuing focus on teaching and learning.

5   Well-developed procedures for assessing how children are progressing.

6   Responsibility for learning shared by the children themselves.

7   Participation by children in the life of the school.

8   Rewards and incentives to encourage children to succeed.

9   Parental involvement in children's education and in supporting the aims of the school.

10   Extra-curricular activities which broaden children's interests and experiences, expand their opportunities to succeed, and help to build good relationships within the school.

I am: a governor [   ]   a teacher [   ]

Figure 5.2   School audit example

Stage 2: Describe the situation

As head I think we have a good collegial atmosphere among the staff, who work hard and ensure that the children do the same. But am I deluded because as head I need to think that?

Stage 3: Collect evaluative data and analyse it

The report of the National Commission on Education, *Learning to Succeed* (1993), gave an interesting list of ten characteristics of successful schools. I propose to use these ten items in a questionnaire to be distributed to all staff and to all governors, seeking their views (see Figure 5.2). The responses are to be anonymous and the results (prepared by the deputy head) will be separate collations for staff and for governors, which will be reported to a staff meeting and to a governors' meeting. The reader is left to imagine the rest!

Invented example 6: Improving staff meetings

Research led by new deputy head in a large secondary school.

Stage 1: Define the inquiry

There is a general feeling in the school that staff meetings were too long-winded; could they be shortened, but still serve their purpose?

Stage 2: Describe the situation

For years the practice has been that all the teaching staff of the school meet once a term on the first Wednesday afternoon at 4pm, with the head in the chair. An agenda (one page) is distributed beforehand and the secretary issues minutes (usually two or three pages) about a fortnight after the meeting.

Stage 3: Collect evaluative data and analyse it

I suggested at the staff meeting in the Autumn term that, if the staff agreed, one meeting should be thoroughly studied. This proposal was met with a measure of anxiety by the head and cynicism by older members of staff, but – if I was prepared to do it – I was given the go ahead. At the next meeting an audio-tape recording was made, a junior colleague kept a note of who spoke and for how long in relation to each item on the agenda (I deliberately asked someone who normally doesn't speak at the meetings), and a simple questionnaire (asking 'What were the valuable items on the agenda for you?') was given to everybody at the end of the meeting.

A who-spoke-for-how-long analysis gave these results: head 40 per cent, deputy heads 30 per cent, heads of year 15 per cent, heads of departments 10 per cent, other teachers 5 per cent. The meeting lasted for two hours. Different people noted different items as valuable, but everybody said it lasted too long. Analysis of the tape (2.5 hours spent on this – trying to listen without stopping it) suggested that information giving took 40 per cent of the time and decision making 60 per cent.

Stage 4: Review the evaluative data and look for contradictions

My summary of the data had three points: everybody wanted to participate in decision making; everybody needed information (but not everybody needs every bit of information); and everybody wished the meetings were shorter.

Stage 5: Tackle a contradiction by introducing a change

At the next meeting, when I presented my interim report, three points were agreed.

1 Wherever possible information will be put on paper and distributed at least three days before the meeting. Everybody undertakes to read through these papers beforehand – so that the same ground doesn't need going over again.
2 Suggestions for decisions will be put on the agenda paper (like the motions of more formal meetings).
3 The meetings will end after one hour irrespective of whether all the business has been completed.

Stage 6: Monitor the change

After two meetings run by the new rules the head suggested that a question-naire be issued to all staff by a research group of three (excluding me) . . .

Invented example 7: Struggling to reduce pressure of work in a department

Research led by a head of a department in a secondary school.

Stage 1: Define the inquiry

The issue was a familiar one: how could the administrative pressures on staff be reduced so that they could concentrate on their teaching and the pastoral needs of the students?

Stage 2: Describe the situation

I am head of a science department with nine members of staff, several of whom carry senior responsibilities outside the department. Sadly, the research began as a result of Bill's heart attack. At the staff meeting when we learned that he had been whisked into hospital suddenly there was an outpouring of complaint about the pressure of work in the department. I offered to carry out a small piece of action research into the problem if everybody would agree to provide some data. I said, 'We have a crisis and

---

DIARY Name_____ Routine time of day for entry_____

Please spend no more than five minutes each day entering a note of your major work frustrations of the previous 24 hours.

MONDAY

Figure 5.3 Diary

should use our intelligence to climb out of it. First we need to study the crisis itself.'

Stage 3: Collect relevant data and analyse it

I devised a 'points of frustration' diary and asked everybody to make an entry once a day, preferably at the same time each day in order to establish a routine – and to spend not more than five minutes making the entry. I asked if everybody would do this for the next three weeks and then give me the diaries for analysis. I said I couldn't guarantee anonymity in my report but would reproduce the raw entries without naming the authors. (See Figure 5.3.) I made sure that I kept reminding people about the diaries. I won't repeat the nickname they gave me!

Stage 4: Review the data and look for contradictions

After three weeks I collected the diaries and had them typed out. Where the diaries referred to other members of staff as the source of frustration I had XXX put in place of the name. This raw data was a twelve-page document! This was marked 'confidential to department staff', distributed, and then discussed at a special staff meeting. All hell was let loose! After an hour we stopped and agreed to meet a week later. By then sense had begun to prevail. Three people had got together, analysed the frustrations, and showed that about half of them focused on the difficulties of staff getting access to three senior members of staff who were frequently unavailable. It was a larger issue than the department and so I persuaded the head (with difficulty) to put our report on the agenda of the senior management team.

Stage 5: Tackle a contradiction by introducing change

The senior management team meeting started like our first staff meeting – with everybody shouting at once. But when it calmed down we began to face up to the contradiction. Senior staff are frequently needed for quick decisions. Senior staff are often not available. Eventually it was decided to redefine one of the secretary's jobs to include 'message-relay-and-monitor'. Members of staff failing to contact a senior person would give details to the m-r-m secretary who would search, find, relay the message and report back. (We had to spend some of our meagre funds hiring extra help in the office.)

Stage 6: Monitoring the change

I have been asked to monitor this and to report to the senior management team at the beginning of next term.

Carrying out action research on a limited time budget

The starting point for any action research needs to be a concern about a worthwhile issue and a personal commitment to spend some time on it. Many people find that writing research times into their diary of future events helps ensure that it happens.

The essential tool is an 'inquiry journal', that is a notebook. This is where you keep notes stage-by-stage as the research unfolds. It includes accounts of what you did, what data you collected, what thoughts you had, what conclusions you came to. It is a working document which provides the source for subsequent reflective thinking and report writing. A notebook is much much better than scraps of paper or backs of envelopes which too easily get lost!

There is nothing necessarily sophisticated about research inquiries. Most action research depends upon piecing together bits of conversations, careful observation of people in action, analysis of school documents or of writings of children and teachers, and trying to make sense of what is happening. Asking pertinent questions is an important part of it, but also listening to the questions that others are asking is valuable.

Keeping records of these inquiries is essential and here it obviously matters that you work to a code of ethics which is often described as 'respect for persons and respect for truth'. This means that while pursuing the truth, you do it in such ways that the confidences of people are respected and they feel neither deceived nor betrayed.

It is important to try to let everyone concerned be on the inside of the research. Action research is a democratic process, meaning that it is one way of enabling people to organize their affairs themselves. Change comes more easily if people feel that they own the change. If they have felt that the research preparing for the change is theirs, they will more readily accept change, and may welcome it. Unlike some other forms of research, action research is not seeking objective descriptions of the *status quo*, it is using research methods to initiate worthwhile change.

Here are nine methods of action research appropriate in schools:

1 Staff discussions (part of the democratic, open style of action research).
2 Reflective thinking. (What am I trying to do? Why? What will happen if? etc.)
3 Written-up chats, purposeful conversations, or informal interviews (always short) – with teachers, governors, parents, children.
4 Observation of children or teachers (which requires careful agreement on what is to be observed).
5 Analysis of children's work.
6 Analysis of teachers' writings (plans, evaluations, annotations on children's work) – with their agreement.
7 Keeping of diaries – restrict the time for making entries!
8 Questionnaires to parents, teachers, governors, older children. (Open-ended questions, closed questions, check-lists to prioritize, etc. Only anonymize if necessary to protect individuals or to enhance validity of replies.)
9 Progress reports to staff, governors, maybe parents and older children – brief, chatty, informative; they can serve as change agents.

Some of the situations in which action research will not work

It will be obvious from the examples that action research will not work if the social climate is not conducive to free inquiry. Here are five situations in which attempts to use action research as a means of school improvement are likely to be disastrous:

1 Where there is a lack of democratic intention by the head.
2 Where there is insularity among the teachers, and a lack of collegiality.
3 Where there is a lack of trust and of mutual respect for each other's professionality.
4 Where there is non-acceptance of professional commitment to improve practice.
5 Where the pressure of day-to-day life is such as to preclude opportunities for data.

6

Getting the measure of bullying

Mike Cockett and Kevin Brain

Most improvement programmes do not lend themselves to simple processes of investigation. Most action takes place in complex contexts and schools are not in a position, even if they wished, to make changes one at a time. Add to that the fact that a lot of evidence is based on subjective perceptions at some level or other and it is clear that evidence gathering cannot be for the purpose of proving or otherwise that an innovation is appropriate or effective. This is not to say that it cannot be valuable, but the limitations on the validity of the evidence need to be understood. In particular, evidence gathering can be specifically aimed at challenging or uncovering common or culturally determined perceptions. While tackling bullying is a legitimate concern for a book on school improvement the purpose here is not so much bullying itself but what the process of investigating bullying might tell us about the value of evidence and information gathering in general. The issues raised about methodology might equally apply to other foci, for example discipline procedures, work patterns of students, teaching and learning styles or student–teacher relationships. There is a brief discussion of these matters at the end but the bulk of the chapter is a summary of the bullying case study itself.

Defining bullying

Bullying has emerged, over the past few years, as an issue of national concern and there is pressure on schools to respond. Since 1989 numerous studies have been carried out and a range of texts published on how to deal with bullying (e.g. Besag 1989, Ahmad *et al.* 1991, Olweus 1993). Within the literature the importance of raising awareness of the nature and extent of bullying is stressed as being the first step on the road to tackling it. This study shows how raising this awareness is a complicated process. It involves understanding how the context, student–teacher interactions and the subjective interpretations of all parties, determines what is identified as bullying. Ultimately, bullying cannot be regarded as a distinct form of behaviour which anyone can recognize. The term covers a complex range of social behaviours which may or may not, in fact, be classified as bullying. What is defined as bullying depends, in part, upon individual perceptions and the context in which the behaviour takes place.

The school context

The research was undertaken at an all boys, 11–16 comprehensive school in a northern city. It was conducted at the request of the school and the intention was that it should be the basis for policy and action to reduce bullying. The concern with bullying was part of a wider concern about the extent of violent and abusive behaviour within the school and the social context in which many of the students lived. This was perceived as one in which violence was taken for granted. As the head said, 'The staff have grown very deeply anxious about the behaviour and discipline in school . . . This is a symptom of the wider community culture.' The head's purpose was most clearly expressed by his desire to make the school a 'place of safety'. The difficulty of the task was most clearly expressed by some student graffiti: 'If someone is afraid of you, remember you can do anything.' Prior to this study the staff had spent a full day in examining the issue of bullying within the school. Some aspects of the outcomes of this day will be referred to later. It was intended that action should follow the day but illness of a key member of staff meant that no action was taken. This study was a stage in trying to restart the programme.

Methodology

Much of the research into bullying has relied on surveys. In a review of methods for investigating bullying Ahmad and Smith (1990) argue that the anonymous questionnaire is the best method for investigating incidence of bullying. The surveys usually pre-define bullying in an attempt to ensure that all the students surveyed are answering questions about the same type of behaviour. However, two immediate problems arise with this approach. First, pre-defining bullying means that you do not get information about what students treat as bullying in the day-to-day context. Secondly, the surveys tell us little of the processes leading up to, and the context of, bullying incidents. As we hope to show later, understanding these contextual factors is crucial in grounding a definition of bullying in the specific school context.

This is not to assert that bullying is a purely subjective phenomenon of which no measure can be made. Rather, as Sian *et al.* argue, 'when an individual applies the label bullying to an interpersonal interaction, there is bound to be *at least an element of subjectivity* which relates to an individual's social construction of the incident' (1993: 133, our italics). Neither providing a pre-given definition, nor simply asserting that bullying is in the eye of the beholder, will allow us to tackle the issue of bullying. Each of these approaches captures something of the truth. Being bullied is a subjective experience but it is not purely individualistic. What students and teachers regard as bullying will be conditioned by the prevailing norms of their own specific cultures and by wider factors such as the school culture as a whole and wider social processes such as gender, race and class. (We know for instance that if bullying is defined as physical aggression then girls will under-report being bullied since they tend to be bullied in less directly physical ways, e.g. Olweus 1993.)

Because of this it was decided that three ways of gathering information should be used: participant observation, a questionnaire and structured interviews. In this way it was hoped to make apparent the differences between the external definition and the context specific operational definitions used by students and teachers. The expectation was that it is out of this sort of multi-dimensional investigation that appropriate models for action can be developed.

The first phase of the research began with six weeks' participant observation undertaken in the school from September to mid-October. A group of Year 7 students were followed for five weeks. The purpose was to gain an insight into a number of processes: how new students adjusted to the school and perceived it; how they behaved towards each other and established norms of behaviour; and how they were treated by others. The participant observation also included observing staff rooms, playgrounds and corridors especially at break times and talking to a wide variety of students in different settings: on the bus to and from school, in the playground and around local shops. From mid-October to December occasional visits were paid to the school and informal conversations with students and staff held to continue the momentum of the participant observation. During this period, the questionnaire was designed and piloted.

The questionnaire was based on a modified version of the Olweus (1989) bullying questionnaire used by Smith and Sharp (1994). It contains a pre-given definition of bullying as follows:

We say a young person is being bullied or picked on when another young person or group of young people say nasty or unpleasant things to him or her. It is also bullying when a young person is hit, kicked, threatened, locked inside a room, sent nasty notes, when nobody ever talks to them and things like that. These things can happen frequently and it is difficult for the young person being bullied to defend himself or herself. It is also bullying when a young person is teased repeatedly in a nasty way. But it is not bullying when two young people of about the same strength have the odd fight or quarrel.

(p. 13)

Subsequent to the survey, structured interviews were undertaken with 14 students who were suspected by staff of either being bullies or victims of bullying. These came from Years 7, 8 and 11. The interview schedule explored both the specific experiences of bullying and being bullied as well as more general issues to do with behaviour in school. Although students who were suspected of being bullies and victims were chosen by the school staff, the interviewer did not know which students fitted into which category unless the students specifically identified themselves as being bullies or victims.

Summary of the evidence

The participant observation allowed a picture of aspects of school and classroom behaviour to emerge. Activities such as pushing, hitting, and name-calling were found to be part of the daily run of classroom life. They were not regarded by the students as being abnormal. From informal interviews and observation it became clear that their aim was often to resist teacher authority, alleviate boredom, form group identities and provide for ways of achieving status and significance with each other. The participant observation also provided some evidence of the way student behaviour was dealt with in practice by teachers. This showed that teachers do not work to a simple definition of bullying and non-bullying behaviour. The reality is much more complex. They interpret and deal with behaviour through a number of frameworks such as levels of maturity, gender, perceived normal classroom behaviour and so on. Thus behaviour which could, on the survey definition, constitute bullying will, in practice, be classified in a variety of ways, for instance as an example of 'immaturity', or of 'just being the way they are around here', or 'that's the way boys are'.

The survey covered 563 students across the five years of the school, roughly 80 per cent of the school population. 19.6 per cent of students reported being bullied at least once a month. The most frequent form of bullying was name-calling followed by being hit. Bullying was seen to be most likely to occur in the playground but 48 per cent of bullies said that the place they most often bullied in was the classroom. This finding proved interesting to the staff and the researchers, since staff generally did not think that students were left unsupervised in classrooms long enough for bullying to take place.

The formal interviews revealed that students, whether bullies or victims, had elaborate and context-specific rules for classifying different kinds of actions. For instance, all of the 14 interviewed operated systems of rules for justifying particular kinds of aggressive behaviour. These revolved around such things as 'having a go at someone if they called your family', and distinguished between pushing and shoving that was designed to inflict harm and that which was just part of messing around. As part of messing around, it was clear that they expected other students to have a degree of acceptance of these actions. While it was possible to go too far in messing around, it was also considered possible for students to be too soft.

All the students normalized aspects of aggressive behaviour as being part of school life, valued expressions of toughness such as being able to stand up for yourself, and considered a variety of activities such as name calling and taking people's belongings in class simply as ways of having a laugh. Even two of the interviewees who were victims had difficulty seeing name-calling and taking people's belongings in class as bullying. As one boy put it, 'it's not proper bullying is it?'

The contextualizing of the survey results using the evidence of the participant observation and formal interviews illustrated how behaviour was classified by students and teachers according to the context of that behaviour and the meaning it held for the participants.

The problem of recognition

Teachers and students and school authorities recognize, classify and explain behaviour in different ways. This is a simple but important point. If the behaviour is to change, then there must be some attempt to bring those different perceptions into closer alignment. Not to do so risks inappropriate responses from students and teachers. For example, seeing a particular incident as an example of bullying would elicit a serious response from teachers to what is agreed to be serious antisocial behaviour. If the students, on the other hand, including the supposed victim, interpret the same incident as 'a bit of a laugh' then the teacher's response will be seen as inappropriate, even as a use of power akin to bullying. Consider the following extracts from the participant field notes, keeping in mind the external definition of bullying as given in the questionnaire.

Incident 1

Jack and Walter start arguing over whether or not Jack 'nicked' his pen. Jack taps Walter lightly with his pen and Walter says threateningly,

'Don't hit me, Jack.' John asks Lee for a rubber, tries to grab it but Lee won't let him have it. Lee says, 'Sir, he's nicked me rubber.' John shouts out, 'Sir, I'm only using it for a second.' Dan says to me, 'Steve is doing this to me' (he makes a punching gesture). I ask him why and he tells me it is because he won't give him a toffee. Dan and Walter start arguing over whether work has been done. John writes on the back of the chair. John climbs on the desk and jumps off. Dan takes Lee's ruler and starts banging it. Another student tells him off. John hits Dan and they start wrestling. Peter shouts to John, 'Leave him, you puff!' John hits Pete.

Now imagine oneself as a busy teacher aware of this behaviour while trying to engage in setting a work task. Does any of this behaviour constitute bullying? If we take the survey definition then there certainly is threatening behaviour. Two students have their belongings taken. Two students get hit and another gets called names. The crucial point is that it all depends upon how the action is interpreted. To demonstrate this we could as an exercise weave our own narrative around some of these incidents. Take the following: Lee says, 'Sir, he's nicked me rubber.' John shouts out, 'Sir, I'm only using it for a second.'

Interpretation 1

For Lee having his rubber 'nicked' is an indication that he generally cannot prevent students doing things that he does not want to happen. He is a victim of students who are more assertive and forward than him. He clearly feels that his rubber was nicked, not borrowed, and needs to seek the support of a significant other, in this case the teacher, to prevent this happening. The fact that John protests that he is only borrowing indicates that he is trying to cover up his actions.

Interpretation 2

Lee is trying to get John into trouble as part of his idea of a joke. He knows that reaching over and taking someone's rubber is part of the general, taken for granted, way in which all students including himself behave. John's protest that he is only borrowing the rubber is in fact true.
   This is what the teacher said about this kind of behaviour:

> You need to get a grip right away; they still haven't learned the difference from junior school. It's very different in co-ed. The girls have a moderating effect . . . Here even the year 10 behave like year 8 in a co-ed school – very childish, very unruly.

The overall concern for the teacher is in maintaining classroom control, not in investigating whether or not any of these incidents are indicators of bullying. The key lies in 'getting a grip right away'.

Teacher classifications

The informal discussions with teachers and observations of their behaviour revealed some of the ways in which teachers perceive and interpret this type of student behaviour. For instance, one teacher described a disruptive student who always took other people's belongings as 'just stupid; a bit of a twit'. This was a common interpretation for teachers taking this particular Year 7 class. Comments made to students engaged in pushing and shoving, kicking each others' chairs and hitting each other with rulers included, 'stop being stupid', 'stop being a twit', 'you're being an idiot', 'you've proved to be a damn nuisance'. Similar comments were made to the whole class. 'This is a particularly badly behaved class', 'You are all extremely rude and bad mannered', 'I have never seen such a badly behaved class in all my time.' The theme of maturity versus immaturity loomed large in teachers' classifications of behaviour. Typical comments were: 'You're not in baby school now', and 'You are in senior not junior school now.'

In addition to the themes noted above, informal discussions with teachers revealed that a certain degree of physical aggression was expected because the school was a boys' school. Thus boys fighting, pushing and shoving each other was 'part of the ways boys are' and to a degree 'to be expected in an all boys school'. Also, this level of physical robustness could be explained by referring to the type of local community the school was in. This was seen as one which supported the expression of violence. As the head reported, with some exasperation, it is difficult to tackle bullying when faced with a parent who is angry because he (the head) can't beat the child in school. Another teacher argued that some of the local families only existed on a physical dimension where fathers 'come home, go down the pub, fight, come home and slap the wife about' and this explained the level of aggressive behaviour in school. For other teachers there was little you could do 'because that's the way they are brought up round here'.

Such explanations come readily to the teachers. They served to build up a picture of what was normal behaviour within the school. One teacher said that students jumping on each other was:

Just how they greet each other . . . now that's not what I call bullying. Perhaps my definition is too narrow . . . I tend to go on the physical side. If it's a bigger boy against a smaller boy then that is more likely to be or become intimidating.

Another commented:

You've seen what it's like at break in the corridor. I get pushed and shoved . . . the number of times I get bumped in a day . . . if we considered pushing and shoving, I would be bullied.

The ways in which behaviour is classified and explained by teachers directly impinges on the ways in which they deal with incidents of aggression or bullying.

Teacher responses to aggressive behaviour

Since bullying is not apparent in the behaviour itself and since the teachers in the school recognized a level of physical violence as normal, then they are left somewhat adrift in trying to deal with aggressive and violent behaviour and in trying to identify bullying in this generally aggressive context. Four incidents captured in our field notes illustrate this confusion.

Incident 2

In class, Dan takes Lee's belongings. Lee tries to get them back. Dan starts hitting Lee on the leg, then he grabs Lee's arm and twists it. Despite Lee asking him to stop and saying, 'It hurts', he does not stop. Lee begins to cry. Dan stops and Lee puts his head on the desk and continues crying. The teacher notices this and comes over.

After the incident the teacher was interviewed:

Interviewer: Did you speak to Dan about the incident?
Teacher: Yes, I spoke to Dan and tried to explain that his behaviour was unkind. I didn't speak to Lee.
Interviewer: Why not?
Teacher: Because I didn't want to embarrass him. That's why I let him move later.
Interviewer: How serious do you think it was?
Teacher: It was not a major incident.
Interviewer: Dan's form teacher thinks Dan is a bully, so do you think he is a bully?
Teacher: I am concerned that he is not totally a bully. There's a bit of good in him somewhere.

Subsequent to this, no teacher made any attempt to follow up the incident with Lee or Dan.

Incident 3

Steve was sent out for grabbing another boy. The teacher shouts very loudly and aggressively at him, telling him that this constitutes assault. The teacher goes on and says, 'This school does not stand for physical violence in any form whatsoever . . . there's no excuse for hitting some-body ever.' After telling Steve this, the teacher makes him stand outside the class for five minutes.

Steve clearly feels aggrieved at this incident. He explained to me that he'd only just chopped someone on the back messing about and couldn't understand why he had been sent out.

Incident 4

Two of the lads start arguing over who gets to use the pestle and mortar. Steve keeps hold of the pestle and Phil grabs it. A couple of other lads tell Steve to let go, he ignores them. A mini fight starts. Phil pushes Steve and Steve hits Phil in the stomach with venom. The teacher notices and tells them to keep their hands to themselves then returns to writing on the board. There is no animosity between the two lads after the incident as they start to laugh and joke with each other.

Incident 5

The teacher spoke to Walter about being locked in the toilet.

Teacher: That's a silly place to get locked in. All that water.
Walter: Yes, miss.
Teacher: Who did it?
Walter: 5th year, miss.
Teacher: Who let you out?
Walter: 5th year, miss.
Teacher: What would have happened if you'd have been in there all weekend?
Walter: Miss, don't know miss.
Teacher: You'd have been hungry. Next time you hear the keys rattling in the door call out, ok?
Walter: Yes, miss.

Throughout, Walter has the demeanour of someone who is being told off.

These incidents speak for themselves. They illustrate just how varied teachers' reactions to and treatment of student behaviour can be. The, seemingly, most trivial of the incidents was dealt with most forcefully by one teacher. The incident that resulted in most physical harm was not felt to be a major incident, while the incident of being locked in the toilet by an older student was neutralized by the teacher and the victim seemed to get the blame. What constitutes bullying or unacceptably aggressive behaviour is, as one teacher argues, 'all a question of definition'. It would appear that in this school teachers are working to very different definitions and con-sequently the ways in which student behaviour is dealt with varies widely.

Student interpretations

As with teachers, we find that students actually interpret and classify behaviour in a number of ways:

> When you're just walking along, people just come up to you and shove you. It's not bullying you just treat it as a bit of a joke.

> Everybody pushes and trips people up, it's just messing. They just, like, have a laugh and a joke in class, take your stuff and leave it in their pockets. Then when it goes to the end of the lesson you get it back . . . In the dining room they, like, trip you up, you know, like, have a laugh and a joke.

> When you call people, it's just part and parcel of school life . . . You can't get rid of being called. You just laugh it off.

> When people walk past, you try and trip them up, things like that . . . You just get them all running round, the little first years, and everyone trips them. Everyone does it. You think it's funny.

This material from the formal interviews with students illustrates how they all, including those who said that they had been bullied, accept quite readily name-calling, pushing, shoving and fighting as being part of school life. Such behaviour is normalized and regarded as part of the way in which you have a laugh in school. As Sian *et al.* (1993) point out, for students, what is to count as an incident of bullying depends upon the individual social constructions of playground, classroom and school life. In this school we found:

- Violence justified in defence of family honour: 'Fighting's all right . . . You can't just go about fighting all the time, like, but if there's a cause, say someone calls your family . . .'
- Fighting and bullying as one of the ways in which a social hierarchy is established: 'Sometimes they are all egging you on to fight and if you don't fight you get called', and 'He's not hard and he can't batter no-one. He's the softest in the school. If you ask him for his money he goes, "Don't batter me will you?"'
- Bullying for pleasure: 'When I bully someone it's alright. I like bullying them, just to see them on the floor crying. You get a laugh, a buzz, off pushing people around.'

Student perceptions of teacher responses

The survey contained a question on teacher responses to bullying. Despite the fact that 58 per cent of those students who said that they had been bullied also said that they had told a teacher, only 4.7 per cent of them thought that bullying would stop because of this. Similarly, in the formal interviews students stated that teacher action had little effect on bullying. The following quotes are all from victims: 'Teachers won't do anything about it'; 'Nothing really happened. They got shouted at but that does nothing really. It doesn't tell them that bullying is a very serious thing ... It doesn't get imprinted to their minds'; and 'I've complained to the teachers. They just bring them into the office and tell them to stop it but they carry on.' There must be some sympathy with staff in these circumstances. They have to make a judgement as to whether a bullying incident has taken place in the context of a high level of petty violence and with the possibility that the complaint is a joke or a way of getting at another student. On the other hand, if the general response is to dismiss such complaints, then serious incidents will almost certainly be missed: 'Sometimes I think they don't take it seriously, half the time teachers don't hardly believe you.'

Student accounts of bullying

If we examine student accounts of bullying we do not find a commonality of definition. Rather, we find common themes. It is not the actions of others *per se* but the contexts and social relations within which they are set that mark out some acts as bullying. Compare the following accounts:

When they call you names and everything and hit you for nothing ... there's locking in rooms and stuff like that, sometimes they smack their hands like this and it means you're dead and, like, they come over to you and kick your chair. There's one person that does it all the time.

They wind me up for the next lesson and then someone just jumps on you and you're not doing anything to them. When you come into the lesson they jump on you and say, why are you calling me?

Going about battering people, picking on people that you know you can batter like first years. There's little ones like Greg (in the fifth year), and all the fourth years and even the first years call him 'cos he's that small they don't think he can do anything.

They started pushing him and then he pushed back and they all just battered him ... There was nothing he could do about it; three of 'em battered him.

The quotes illustrate three themes which run through the students' accounts and which they seem to use to distinguish bullying from other forms of aggressive action: the action is unprovoked; the action happens more than once; and, the victim is seen as relatively powerless. Finally, there is evidence in interviews of the way bullying restricts life for the victims even at times when they are not being bullied. Thus, 'Canteen is safe 'cos if you go down to the far corner and no-one can see you and at the back of the school there's like dents in it where you can hide and avoid people', and 'When I come over from the other building I try and walk all the way around so no-one can get me.'

Responding to the evidence

On the evidence gathered it is neither the teachers' perceptions nor the abstracted survey definition which gives the clearest guide in identifying bullying in this school but rather the responses of the students themselves. They consistently referred to three indicators which might alert staff to serious situations:

- There is an apparent power difference between the individuals or groups involved.
- The violence appears to be unprovoked.
- The victim has been attacked more than once.

If the staff are to respond to this information then the task shifts from agreeing on a common definition to agreeing on a common procedure, one based on the indicators, rather than absolute definitions of bullying behaviour. For example, using these indicators, incident 2 and incident 5, described above, require investigation, while incidents 3 and 4, though involving behaviour which the school might wish to change, would not be investigated as potential bullying. This investigation – the evidence gathering – has provided a possible starting point for action.

Conclusions

This research does not claim to advance an understanding of bullying or its causes. Its purpose was to illustrate the value of a systematic investigation into such an issue in order to ground the problem in the context of the particular school. Such a focus on one issue in the school runs the danger of distorting the whole picture of how the school operates. Only certain sorts of behaviours are being investigated and reported. There are no reports of lessons running smoothly and of breaks and lunch times passing without incident. However, it is clear that the specific context of this school is one in which the scale of aggression runs from that which is regarded as purely entertainment to serious, damaging physical and verbal attacks. The school has a major problem in trying to create quality teaching and learning time

in such a context. The research illustrates that, with some exceptions, bullying for the majority of students is the unacceptable face of that aggression.
Perhaps this focus and developing agreed indicators with follow-up action
could provide a step in reducing the overall level of aggression with consequent improved classroom conditions and reduced stress for all.

Of the methods used in this chapter, the participant observation and the
informal interviews were by far the most revealing of the social context in
which the school is trying to operate but the survey and the formal interviews provided specific information about their scale and the nature of the
problem. It is possible that some of this information could only have been
gathered by an outsider and this may be a luxury that schools cannot always
afford. On the other hand, as a principle, gathering evidence from more
than one perspective could be a significant way in which schools can shift
their understanding of the situation and therefore begin to take action to
improve it.

As proposed at the beginning of the chapter, the basic principles illustrated
here can be applied to other areas for improvement. In general, the more
complex the issue the more important it is to see it from different perspectives. Reliance on one source of evidence or information could lead at best
to a great waste of time and at worst to serious damage in the very area one
wishes to improve. Chapter 5 provides a summary of sources of information
and methods of inquiry. This chapter shows how applying some of those
methods in a particular school can lead to a much deeper understanding
of the issues and, hopefully, more effective action.

7

52 absentees: a case study of one school's attempt to improve attendance

Mike Cockett, Mary Connery and Kevin Brain

This is a case study of one school's attempt to improve attendance. Its purpose is both to illustrate the complexity of attendance related issues and to provide an example of evolutionary planning and action. The school is a comprehensive school serving a large estate in the south of Manchester. It is regarded as a successful school in that context but, like all schools in the area, it has significant attendance problems. This study illustrates some of the issues which arose in attempting to improve attendance and in attempting to research the effects of intervention programmes. The innovation programme was funded by the then Department for Education (DfE) under the Grants for Education Support and Training (GEST) programme and was also researched by the Manchester Metropolitan University's Didsbury School of Education. This chapter has been written by the researchers in cooperation with the school.

The background is significant because the starting point for the school was an opportunity presented by external funding. In the usual way it put in a bid to the local education authority (LEA) to participate in the programme and was one of five successful schools. The GEST criteria and the LEA response to these imply a model of school improvement based on some level of social engineering in which a social problem is specified, a cause identified and a remedy then implemented to achieve specified effects. In this case the purpose of the approach was to identify the causes of truancy and by taking action reduce its occurrence. That action, it was intended, should become a model for other schools through a traditional process of dissemination. As was proposed in chapter 3 there are serious problems with this model. It underestimates the problems facing schools in recognizing truancy, in understanding the factors which influence attendance behaviour and in taking action which has a lasting effect on attendance.

Explaining absence: a brief review of the literature

Truancy is a complex and hotly debated issue. The term itself is ambiguous. None of the Education Acts define truancy and researchers themselves use different definitions. For instance, Galloway (1985) uses the term to identify students who are absent purely on their own initiative, while Pack (1977) includes parentally condoned absence. The term truant has strong emotive resonance, particularly with crime and juvenile delinquency. As Carroll (1977) points out, the term absentee is much better since this directs our attention away from individual truants viewed in a pejorative light and more towards the interplay between non-attendance, home, school and wider society. There is now a wide body of research on school absenteeism. As explored by Carlen *et al.* (1992), explanations of absenteeism tend to focus on four general areas: the individual, the family, the locality and the school. The first three of these associate or attempt to explain truancy in terms of, for example, unhappiness and unsociability (Tyerman 1968); disrupted home lives and families where parents tend not to care about attendance, homework and punctuality (Reid 1986); homes that are overcrowded (Steedman and Fogelman 1980); poverty (May 1975); and the prevalence of anti social attitudes, particularly in working-class communities (Galloway 1976).

Studies that considered the effect of the school in generating truancy were virtually non-existent until the mid-1970s. Of critical importance here was the work of Rutter *et al.* (1979). This study found that factors such as teacher actions in lessons, good conditions for students and the extent to which they were given responsibility all affected attendance rates. Since the late 1970s the school effect has become the dominant framework for explaining truancy. Publications such as the *Elton Report* (DES 1989a) and *Education Observed* (DES 1989b) have given official backing to this view. More recently, attention has been focused on the curriculum in generating truancy. The latest research project undertaken for the DfE surveyed 33,000 students and argues that non-attendance is principally a curricular issue (O'Keefe 1994). There are also studies that argue that non-attendance is part of the way in which working-class children, in particular, resist the institutional control of schooling by drawing upon cultural resources from outside the school to reject the imposition of a schooling perceived as irrelevant (Willis 1977); resisting the hidden curriculum of schooling (Ramsay 1983) which is designed to keep them in their place; or engaging in a process of resistance to the social control functions of school (Carlen *et al.* 1992).

School	*Curriculum*
Boring	Too much writing
Too many rules	Too much work
Treated like a young child	Too much homework
Boys are immature	Too difficult
Don't get on with teachers	Don't teach what you need for a job
Bullying	
	Home
Friends	Look after young children
Older friends who don't work	Look after sick relatives
Gang culture	Family break up
Not 'cool' to come to school	Extended family argument
Should not be seen to do homework/carry	Moving between one house and another
books, etc.	Trouble with police
Want to keep their friends	Holidays
Health	
Weight	
Low grade infections, e.g. throat, chest	
Allergies – asthma, eczema	
Epilepsy	
Surgery	
Broken limbs	

Figure 7.1   Reasons for absence

Any particular school looking through the literature, then, is faced with a bewildering variety of frameworks, each of which contains sub-frameworks of equal complexity. This poses enormous problems for schools because, given the variety of factors influencing attendance, it is impossible to develop a single 'remedy'. How, then, is action to be taken which improves attendance which it is within the competence and the resources of the school to carry out?

The Phase One plan of action

The GEST bidding process demanded identification of a range of strategies to be tested against performance indicators. The school, while ready to keep its part of the bargain and try out the various strategies, actually intended to invest most effort in a much simpler starting point. They decided to interview all Year 10 students whose Year 9 attendance was less than 80 per cent. These were chosen because this was seen as a crucial time for many of them. They were then starting their GCSE public examination courses and attendance figures from the past had shown that Year 10 attendance tends to slip after a relatively high start. The aim of the interviewing at this stage was to identify problems and advise strategies to help the students. In total 52 students were interviewed. Figure 7.1 lists their reasons for absence (with most students giving more than one reason).

For comparison purposes, in addition to the target group a random selection of 24 students with year 9 attendance over 80 per cent was also interviewed and their reasons for absence recorded. Other data collected on both groups included whether they were on free school meals and which ability band they were in for maths and English.

Analysis of the data revealed not just a complexity of factors contributing to absence, but a complexity of constellations of factors. This suggested that there was no obvious, single strategy to adopt as a way forward. The project coordinator decided, therefore, to take action tailored to the perceived needs of individuals though, for some, this involved forming a support group for students with similar needs. By the end of phase one it was clear that attendance had improved for the target group. There were more students with improved attendance in the target group than in the comparison group. Decisions had to be made about what had been learnt in the process about what could and should be carried over into the next phase.

What had been learnt

Phase two of the programme had to be developed without external funding. The school decided to continue to fund the work of the coordinator but some external support was lost including that of the Education Welfare Officer who had run the girls' support group. It was accepted that year 10 was too late to start. Even before the end of phase one a new target group had been identified in year 9 and a similar process of interviews with follow up action instituted. With experience the coordinator began to observe both positive and negative effects of her work. The following issues are taken from the coordinator's commentary on the first eighteen months of her work. They are presented here to illustrate the sort of learning that was taking place.

A non-punitive role

The initial interviews and the follow-up action were not aimed at catching and punishing truants. The purpose, which was understood by both students and parents, was to treat absence as a problem which could be alleviated or solved by working together. It was the coordinator's role to ensure that the school responded as far as it could to legitimate problems which the absentees faced. This non-punitive role was considered by the coordinator to be highly significant.

Gender

There seemed to be differences of response between boys and girls. The girls seemed to take a more realistic attitude to attendance targets, recognizing

that there were some things they were unlikely to achieve even if they promised to do so. The boys, on the other hand, would promise the earth and
make big efforts to begin with, which they failed to sustain. Eventually the
girls used the coordinator as a mentor and shared concerns not just about
themselves but about other girls, alerting the school to potentially danger-
ous situations. This raised questions about whether a male mentor would be
valuable to the boys.

Support

The two support groups established in the pilot phase, for those with the
most severe attendance problems, could not be continued beyond the end
of external funding. They were both successful in that the attendance of
the students improved considerably. However, when attempts were made to
reintegrate them into normal tutor groups attendance fell. The school has
serious doubts about whether there are cost-effective ways of improving
attendance once it has dropped below, say, 60 per cent.

Parents

As the programme progressed there was an increasing emphasis on contact
with parents. Once again, this was on a non-punitive basis. For many parents this has been their first direct contact with the school. The vast majority were very supportive and grateful that a problem they were having with
their child was being shared.

Reintegration

A major task for the coordinator was negotiation with teaching staff about
the treatment of absentees on their return. This ranged from discussions
with individual staff whose poor relationships with particular students are
seen to be part of the problem, to negotiating reduced workload and academic support for students with major responsibilities at home. These nego-
tiations proved to be as important for students returning after illness as for
those absent for other reasons. Indeed lack of such a programme can, in
some cases, lead to truancy following illness.

The curriculum

It was recognized that a major problem remained with the curriculum itself.
The school had been part of the Alternative Curriculum Strategies project
described in Chapter 3 but a combination of doubts about the effectiveness
of that programme and the advent of the National Curriculum had swept

that aside. The school recognizes that something should be done but it is not, as yet, clear what that should be.

The ecology of absence

Because of the complexity both of the problems as they presented themselves and the remedial action taken by the school and others it was clear that a new model which might aid the understanding of this complexity was required. While few would argue that there is no link between the social and economic circumstances of students and their school achievement, for example, the nature of that link remains problematic: it is not a simple cause and effect. What is needed is a model for understanding that relationship and a model for understanding what schools might do about it. The GEST model might be called a 'getting it right' model, a sort of social engineering or technical rational approach and it does not cope well with complexity. Schools and LEAs asked to evaluate the effects of the actions they have taken often do not know because effects are augmented or masked by other factors and events often outside their control. The figures for the attendance rates of the students in this school are not proof of the success or failure of the school's strategies because we cannot be sure the attendance rates were not produced by some other factors. What is needed is a model which both incorporates all possible factors and which shows their interrelationships. It is not the individual factors but the way in which they interact in particular circumstances which leads to particular sorts of attendance behaviour. Gleeson (1994) argues:

> another way of viewing truancy is as a form of social exclusion, not solely or functionally linked with school but with the ecology of an area, catchment or neighbourhood, involving an intricate balance between family, housing, welfare agencies, health, recreational and leisure market forces.
>
> (p. 16)

It is this notion of an ecology which we wish to develop and apply. The school coordinator described some of the issues in this way:

> We have problems with children working on the markets early in the morning. They have to do those jobs to bring the money in ... Girls are kept at home and accept this ... We have kids who constantly seem to have minor ailments ... For some of our kids the problem is the curriculum. It's completely irrelevant.

What is interesting in this commentary is the way in which general factors merge with a particular local context. In areas of poverty and unemployment children have to work to bring in extra money. In this particular locality one opportunity to earn that money comes from helping to set up and run market stalls. Likewise, girls being kept at home illustrates both the influence of gender roles and the nature of support available for a particular family. Families may be faced with a choice between using an older school-girl as a carer and a parent staying off work and thus losing money. For other students the disaffection with the curriculum arises out of a combination of an assessment of their own abilities and a belief that whatever they achieve in school, because of the local labour market, it is unlikely to improve their job prospects.

The image of an ecology of an area helps us to recognize the inter-dependence of factors and, therefore, to imagine ways in which we might approach the problem. We are familiar with environmental arguments which show how changes in one aspect of the environment can have unforeseen and possibly disastrous consequences elsewhere. The erosion in one area is seen as a consequence of flood control and land reclamation in another. Efficient use of farm machinery leads to loss of hedgerows and soil erosion. This is the notion that can be applied to action to alter the ecology of absence. We may be able to map the general picture but how that will affect individual students we cannot tell. The ecology metaphor provides us with a way of linking individual circumstances to general factors such as class and poverty and including the varied factors that affect any individual's attendance pattern. Two studies of individuals from the school will develop this argument.

Sheila

Sheila's attendance throughout Year 9 had been sporadic. Over the year her attendance rate averaged 50 per cent. The school was aware that Sheila had many responsibilities at home and that this was leading to attendance difficulties. Sheila was, at 15, the second eldest of four children. At the time of the interview her older sister also lived at home with her 5-week-old baby. Sheila's brother was 8 years old and suffered from hyperactivity and Sheila's mother had recently given birth to another daughter. The problems of coping with an hyperactive child had created tension between the parents who had consequently separated. The father lived nearby but could not cope with living with the family. Sheila herself when interviewed said that she actually liked coming to school. This was confirmed by her teachers who all felt that she worked well when in lessons. However, Sheila also confirmed that being needed at home made her feel important and in many ways grown up. As Sheila entered Year 10 her attendance appeared to improve but then her mother became ill and she was required to stay at home to look after the children.

Mark

Mark was 14 at the time of the interview and since Year 8 had a pattern of irregular attendance. Mark was the youngest of four children. His parents were divorced and his mother had recently remarried. He lived with his father and two older sisters, visiting his mother at the weekends. In addition, his father's new partner lived in the house with her 5-year-old daughter and 5-month-old baby. Mark had special needs in English and selectively missed certain lessons as well as whole days. He found school uninteresting and often absented himself with friends. At the start of Year 10 Mark started to attend regularly due to the fact that one of his options allowed him to study Motor Vehicle Maintenance and he wanted to be a mechanic. However, after a month, he started to truant with his friends spending time in a deserted flat smoking cannabis to alleviate boredom.

We can see that the ecological context in which Mark and Sheila make their decisions is formed by major social forces such as class; by factors distinctive to the particular area such as the quality of schooling and the availability of services; by the nature of the local labour market; and by individual circumstances such as family relationships. Schools are part of, and operate within this ecology. What they do shifts the ecological balance, sometimes to good effect but also possibly with unforeseen and negative consequences. If we refer back to the list of factors to which students attributed absence (Figure 7.1), it can now be seen not just as a list of individual reasons, but as an outline map of the ecology of the school and its neighbourhood.

Choices and values

So far, it might be suggested, we may have developed a more complex model but we are still saying that absenteeism is caused entirely by circumstances. The individual is still seen as a victim of circumstances rather than an active agent. This is not our argument. Truancy is not 'caused' by the ecology of an area any more than it is caused by a single factor. On the other hand, it cannot be concluded that attendance at school is entirely a matter of individual choice, as some would want to argue. Since it is possible to point to individuals in apparently similar circumstances who do not truant, then, the argument runs, the deviant must have chosen that behaviour and is therefore personally responsible. The case studies illustrate a more complex picture. The ecology argument is not a deterministic one. Individual choices are important but some choices are more conscious than others and some ecologies present dilemmas to individual students which do not affect others. For example, the particular circumstances of Sheila's home life and their consequences are unique to her. She is not powerless to choose but she does have a particular sort of choice to make. Because of the relative poverty of her circumstances, she must choose between caring in the family and school attendance. In other circumstances such commitment to the family and such a sense of achievement in a caring role would bring praise rather than blame. Mark presents a different picture. He does not seem to have any positive options. This does not mean that being working class or facing those life circumstances determines that he will truant, but it does mean that the nature of the dilemmas he faces and the range of options open to him are different. The local ecology influences but does not determine behaviour, though it is necessary to recognize circumstances in which individuals are swamped by a whole range of problems and in which they are swept along by events rather than pursue a direction they have chosen.

Strategic learning: lasting effects

If we are to take the notion of an ecology of absence seriously then two key points follow. Schools need to develop an intimate knowledge of their own local ecology. In doing this they can formulate general ideas about the factors influencing absence linked to a specific knowledge of the way in which those factors work in their particular context. Schools need to accept the idea of partial success and indeterminacy. Given the complex nature of the problem, schools will never be able to determine just exactly what it is about one strategy that has an effect.

Partly because of foresight and partly because of the way opportunities emerged, this school learnt a great deal about attendance behaviour and a plan emerged from the initial action. After two years, the school coordinator was seconded to work outside the school. Her work was allocated to assistant year heads charged with maintaining the interviewing programme and the follow-up action which she had instituted. Twelve months on from her departure the assistant year head programme is working well, particularly in relation to contact with parents. Some form tutors are also beginning to take on this role. In only one year group was it not possible to implement this programme, for a variety of reasons. This year group was the only one in which attendance was not improving. This accident of circumstances has confirmed the school's opinion of the success of the programme. The simple decision, right at the beginning of the exercise, to interview students has led to a greater understanding of the complex of circumstances local to the school, of the complex of factors influencing individual behaviour and to a complex response in attempting to address those individual circumstances. The school still has no sure fire remedy for truancy but it is beginning to improve attendance.

Learning from case studies

This case study illustrates a process of change in a complex organization, a complexity governed by those forces and conditions described in Chapter 3. Even in a detailed analysis of this sort, it is impossible to capture all that has actually happened. It may be that significant factors have gone completely unreported, since we have missed the fact that they were significant or that we have simply forgotten. So, no formula has emerged which can be applied to all schools. This does not mean, however, that, faced with the sort of complexity described here, it is impossible to take action. The evidence of this study suggests that the best sort of action is often quite simple. Interviewing students is a starting point open to all schools. What we cannot say is that such an interviewing process will lead to the same consequences in all schools. There will be consequences but what they are will depend on particular circumstances the details of which it is impossible to know in their entirety. One essential condition will be the willingness of the school to learn from the action, whatever it is. In this school, at the time of writing, there is still a reluctance to face some of the issues which have emerged. The ambivalence around the reintegration of long-term absentees has not been resolved. Staff, at one and the same time, both agree that students should be reintegrated and yet find it difficult to take positive action to achieve this. One reason is that such action arouses cultural sensitivities about the fairness of spending time on the matter and about apparently rewarding rather than punishing deviant behaviour.

Setting measures or performance indicators against any one strategy is of little value but this does not mean that measures are not important. In this case the measure remained the relatively simple one of improved attendance. What could not be measured was the effect of all the separate ingredients both public and hidden which went to make up the successful prescription for this particular school. Measures are also important in the process of continually monitoring what is going on. The fact that we cannot be sure of the effects of our action means that such monitoring is of vital importance if we are to notice, soon enough, deviations from the desired consequences.

Of the great range of strategies tried out in the five schools in this GEST programme, very few survived the ending of external funding. In a few cases they sank without trace, the schools apparently having learnt little from the programme. What distinguished the strategy in this school from that in others was the way it was set up in the first place. It was set up as a learning strategy. It was not set up as a solution to the problem. This is an important distinction. It was not so much the action itself which was taken but the processes surrounding the action which allowed the school to learn. In another school a 'half-way house' experiment aimed at returning absentees, first to school in a special unit and then to the normal classroom, failed because the process of returning those students to the normal classroom was resisted by both teachers and students. The school virtually sealed itself off. To put it mildly, the staff of the school did not want to learn how to reintegrate those students into their classrooms.

This case study is not a study of how to improve attendance. It is a study of how one school began to learn how to improve attendance, was partially successful and is continuing to learn. That is probably about as good as it gets.

8

'No problem here': action research against racism in a mainly white area

Patricia Donald, Susan Gosling, Jean Hamilton and **Ian Stronach**

This is the account of an action research initiative supported by the University of Stirling and Central Regional Council, Scotland. It concerns a one-year project in which three primary school teachers researched aspects of multiculturalism and anti-racism in local schools, largely in their own time. Our purpose is to communicate our research findings, tell how these findings were created and used, and consider the implications for future initiatives of this kind. It is a practical account. We want to start by briefly explaining the policy context which gave birth to the initiative, and how we came together as a small group of primary teachers and an academic researcher. We tell that contextual story not because of its intrinsic interest (it has none) but because others may find it possible to create similar forms of cooperation, and start action research targeted at specific and relatively neglected policy areas. This, then, is action research directed at the kinds of problems that get denied or deflected in schools, that carry no policy headline, and for which financial support is hard to obtain.

Why was the University interested? Well, it wasn't really. In a first referral of the original proposal the word came back, 'Surely such research isn't a priority in a part of the country like this where . . .' It was not the last time we were to get the 'no problem here' message. The Central Regional Council (which we refer to as the 'Region') was more interested. New national guidelines for educational curricula in the primary and lower seondary levels stressed the need to create 'awareness of bias and prejudice' (Scottish Education Department 1990). On the basis of such national policy, the Region had produced multicultural and anti-racist guidelines (MCARE) in 1990 (Central Regional Council 1990). In the guidelines the

Region stressed the need for 'effective action', while acknowledging that issues were 'sensitive and complex'. In a very Scottish twist to the argument, anti-racism was presented as an 'extension of current outlooks' (Central Regional Council 1990: 4), an integration of MCARE under an older Scottish tradition/myth of egalitarianism in education and culture (Stronach 1992). Nevertheless, this interest in MCARE was tempered in practice by the knowledge that minority ethnic communities were 'relatively small and scattered'. Funding was likely to be similarly distributed. As a result there were educational staff in the Region who wanted to do a lot, but had money for only a little. Why were the teachers interested? Mostly they were not. When the Region and the University advertised for action researchers (with or without experience), there were no takers from the secondary sector at all. But three applicants from the primary sector were selected and they formed the nucleus of the action research initiative. The team had about £2000 from the University at its disposal, and six supply cover days from the Region.

The next step was to work out a research agenda for the group. The Region had a shopping list of concerns in this area. They concerned the dilemmas of 'embedding' policy in school practice, of encouraging schools to be 'proactive'. They were interested in looking at how MCARE could be integrated into school development, and assessed through audit or in-school evaluation. In addition, the regional guidelines suggested that schools 'should provide opportunities for all children . . . to develop the motivation and skill to question and analyse the reasons for discrimination, prejudice and injustice within their school' (Central Regional Council 1990: 8). We did not need to assume that there were MCARE issues that needed to be addressed in the Region's schools: a recent local report had suggested that incidents of officially reported racial abuse in the area had more than doubled in the past year. There was also evidence from a recent Commission for Racial Equality conference in Scotland that the myth of the non-racist Scot was wearing thin: 'the rate of complaint in Scotland equals that of the UK as a whole, therefore the claim that racial discrimination does not happen in Scotland is a false one' (Roger Kent, reported by Lopinska, 1991).

These concerns, united with a desire to see how the Region's MCARE policy was working out in detail, led us in two directions: (1) an investigation of MCARE implementation in one primary school; and (2) an exploration of the prevalence and nature of racism in two primary schools in the Region. The result was three case studies, the outcomes of which were fed back to the Region and to the schools concerned (Donald 1993a, Gosling 1993, Hamilton 1993a, b). The research process and early findings were discussed at periodic meetings of the group which took place after school. We intend to examine these cases in turn, and to discuss the impact of the strategies which were adopted.

Case I: Evaluation of MCARE implementation in a primary school

Susan Gosling undertook an ambitious and comprehensive evaluation of MCARE in her primary school (Gosling 1993). The overarching research question was: 'To what extent and how effectively has the school implemented the Region's MCARE guidelines?' The research method involved first of all a process of 'climate mapping', in which the physical environment of the school was observed and examined in relation to MCARE issues, considering such indicators as evidence of graffiti, the nature of display materials, an inventory of MCARE resources available and in use, and school documentation. Secondly, a series of semi-structured interviews was carried out with the head, teachers, ancillary staff, a small group of parents, and several groups of children – one of which comprised ethnic minority children.

What were the results of the audit? It was clear that the Region's MCARE policy was having an effect on the school. The school had an equal opportunities policy that addressed MCARE concerns. An assistant headteacher had responsibility for equal opportunities, and there were signs that teachers were addressing MCARE issues (e.g. a display of Edinburgh Castle had a black piper). There were 'welcome' signs in different languages, including minority ethnic ones. Curricula dealt with a variety of cultures and religions. The resource inventory showed that there were MCARE materials available, although there was a dearth of fiction by or about minority groups. On the whole, interviews with the head and teachers tended to confirm this position. Relationships within the school were felt to be good, there were a lot of positive attitudes around, and an awareness of MCARE. Or at least, there was enthusiasm for the first two letters of that acronym, and a bit of concern about the 'negative' and 'emotional' implications of anti-racism. The picture looked rather less positive when the parents' data were examined. The group was too small to be representative, but the responses were worrying. Their theme was assimilation, the need for those who were different 'to blend in' (see Case 3 and the notion of 'difference'): 'If people come to our country . . . they should live by the same rules as we do.'

Ancillary staff were at first unlikely to define trouble in the playground in racial terms, although they had overheard some name-calling. Their explanation of fights in the playground covered a multitude of sources – physical insults ('fatty', 'shorty', etc.), spillovers from emotional games of football, family feuds where older brothers and sisters attacked or defended on behalf of their younger brothers and sisters, and so on. Fights were what some children do, or have done to them, and they could name a few bullies among them. The following transcripts, however, show an interesting 'denial' of racism:

Ranji's just a toerag [slang: non-racist and general term of abuse current in Central Scotland]. I've had Ranji coming up to me and saying 'I'm getting picked on because that one there's calling me a black … whatever.' … But when you stand back, it's Ranji who's running around kicking lumps out of all the other ones. But the minute they retaliate he's got this, 'Oh they're picking on me because of my colour'. To me it's all in Ranji's head.

On the whole there's no racist problems … There's never been.

So the ancillary staff initially felt (although one is less sure) that racism was not a problem in what they saw around them in the playground. Yet a group of majority ethnic Scottish children from the same playground were adamant: 'Ranji, Bobby, Helen get called names a lot'; 'Black bastard … Most people in Mrs Smith's class call him that. Mostly Ranji gets picked on. Ranji, and that, just walk away.'

The problem emerges. In general, the adults do not see a racial problem; but the children do, and for all the usual reasons they often choose to say nothing ('grassing', teachers don't believe you, or if they do, you get bashed later at home time). So much of this behaviour remains invisible to the adults in the situation. And, of course, reality is not always a simple division into good and bad – especially in the playground. The name-calling and threats directed at the group of children with learning difficulties were even more intense: 'They call you F word, B word, C word. Arsehole'; 'It's horrible. You're scared to tell your parents.'

Such evidence, of course, may not be typical of what happens in playgrounds, in this school or in most others. But it does tell us something about what can sometimes happen, and how it might go unnoticed by the adults in the situation. The central problem unearthed by this case study concerned the 'implementation' issue identified by the Region. It was clear that the school was implementing MCARE policy; there were policies, teachers were aware, resources and curricula reflected such an emphasis. But the school had not yet touched anti-racist behaviour. There were elements of denial – the 'no problem here' syndrome – and teachers were not fully aware of, or responsive to, the racist behaviour and attitudes of the children, and the possible problems arising with parents. The teacher-researcher concluded that the overall MCARE situation was a patchwork of success and failure (see Figure 8.1). Her recommendations were as follows:

- A specific MCARE school policy document should be written expressing clearly the school's stance.
- Guidelines are needed in order to identify and deal with racist incidents, including advice on how to counsel perpetrators and support victims.
- School development planners should note deficiencies in MCARE provision and plan to improve the situation.

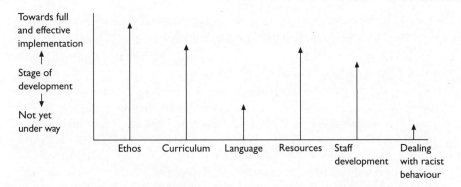

Figure 8.1 Aspects of MCARE evaluated

- Assertiveness training should be brought into the curriculum and made available to all children, but especially those who have been victimized, bullied or abused.

The researcher later concluded that the school had responded to the case study. Policies were revised, and awareness had risen. Nevertheless, the school was little different in its response to racist incidents, and remained reluctant to try an anti-racist approach.

Case 2: Racism in Littletown Primary

Patricia Donald conducted ethnographic research into the prevalence and nature of racism in another primary school (Donald 1993a). Her research plan was an inverted version of the method adopted in Case 1, that is, she started with Asian children's experiences, and their perspectives of life in the village. She then collected data from the majority of ethnic children through questionnaire and interview. In a third stage of the action research, she created a detailed account of a racist incident, but disguised the ethnic identity of the victim (see Appendix to this chapter, 'Beth's story – the party') and fed it back to children in the first three years of primary school, gathering their reactions to the incident first as a non-racist, then as a racist story (Donald 1993b). Next she investigated racism in Primary 6 (P6) (sixth year of primary education) via a study of friendship groups. Finally, she considered the implications of her research for MCARE policy in the school.

Littletown's ethnic population consisted of four Asian families, one Pakistani and three Indian. Each family had three children, and all the families had suffered racial abuse or harassment of some kind during their stay in the village. They all eventually moved out of the village, although some of the children remained at the village school. One of the P6 Asian children (age 10/11) had a particularly vivid story to tell:

> I was at Laura's party once and I was standing beside B, C and Laura. And Vicky and Alison were doing . . . were laughing at me and started kicking me and everything and they started calling me names and they were laughing at my dress and everything and they were kicking me and it was sore and I had bruises all over my legs and everything like that. And then I said, 'Laura, Where's my jacket? Can I get my jacket please?' and she goes, 'Yes, it's in the kitchen', and I got my jacket and I ran home and I was crying and my dad asked what happened and then Vicky's gran came up and my dad told Vicky's gran and she's not said anything since.

Some of the other girls (they were all from the same class) had been calling her 'Paki', saying things like 'Oh god, look at your colour'. Eventually she could stand it no longer:

> I felt angry and upset as well, but they kept on saying it, but I couldn't keep up with it, so I just ran home with my jacket and I said 'sorry' to Laura and I just ran home and that was it. [Why did you apologise to Laura?] For spoiling her birthday and going home because she wanted everybody to be there.

Interviews with other P6 Asian children confirmed this picture. Looking back on her years in Littletown, B told how she had:

> really really liked Littletown when my dad got a shop and I thought that this was going to be very good, that we were going to stay [stay = live] in Littletown, and I've got friends and my dad's working and soon I was going to get another wee brother . . .

But the story turned sour:

> The trouble with staying in Littletown was that people threw bricks and everything, people weren't nice to us . . . They used to hit and bang the doors and break the window . . . It was teenage boys who just come about . . . My mum and dad think it was because we were brown, brown, a horrible, we were . . . not very, just because of our colour, it's because of our colour. That's like if we're somewhere else, people just call us names . . . at the park . . . at the shops.

It was clear that racism was a problem in Littletown. But what would the majority ethnic children make of it in primary school? In order to find out, the racist incident was converted into a story, 'Beth's story – the party', simplifying the language, and not identifying Beth in ethnic terms. The groups discussed the story as a general tale of unfairness, and were then told that Beth was Asian, and asked what difference that made to the account. A total

'White Beth' responses	'Black Beth' responses
P1 Hair-related names; idiot; stupid; fizz off; beat it; 'bad words'; shut up	Responses similar
P2 Hair-related names; pig; cow; bitch	Horrible face; bitch; stink face; blackie; brownie; Japanese; Spanish; Chinabrain
P3 Hair-related names; stupid; dummy; baby/ crybaby; pig; chicken face; shit; 'swear words'; flat nose; freckle face; mudpie; bugsy; ugly; scaredy-cat; Betty instead of Beth; smelly; frockie (dress)	Ugly dress; ugly face; horrible; blacknose; flat head; Pakistani; brown face; bam; specky; c---t; blackie (dog)

Figure 8.2 'White Beth' and 'black Beth' responses

of 48 children from P1-P3 were interviewed in class in small groups, during the course of normal class work. It was clear that their racial awareness and repertoire of names increased with age, and that they thought that Beth had been unfairly treated in both versions of the story (on being shown a photograph of a 'white' Beth, and then a 'black' Beth – see Figure 8.2). P1 children did not differentiate between the two photographs and did not seem to be aware of racist names in use. P2 children gave instances of name-calling they had overheard, but it may be significant that when a P3 boy who had been identified by another child as a racist name-caller was involved in the research, he did not offer any racist names. Some responses were clearly guarded.

A further attempt was made to understand the extent of racism amongst the older children. The subject was approached obliquely via a study of 'friendships' through a sociogram approach, asking each child to write down the names of three friends. The most isolated children, who included Asian girls, were interviewed individually to see if they felt subject to verbal abuse. The findings showed that there was evidence of racist and general name-calling in the classroom, the playground and the village. Boys were more guilty than girls, and Asian children received more abuse. One Asian girl was isolated, while the other was the most popular child in her class – but still received the worst of the abuse. Many of the white children con-sidered colour-related abuse, like 'Paki' or 'Darkie', to be the worst names that anybody can be called. Most majority ethnic children considered that minority ethnic children were treated unfairly in this respect.

What were the conclusions of this study? First, it was clear that more racist incidents were happening than were being reported to the teachers. Secondly, the need for an anti-bullying policy was evident, as was the need to address these issues in personal and social development classes. Third, staff development seemed essential, and time was set aside in the following term to discuss what had been learned with the staff. Finally, it seemed that some of the stories in the data could be adapted as research instruments in themselves, and might be capable of being used more generally.

Case 3: Black children are fair game for the school bullies

This school had an equal opportunities policy but unlike the school in Case 1, there had been no conscious attempt to address MCARE concerns through the curriculum or to provide resources. This school typified the 'no problem here' viewpoint. In over 500 children, there were two Chinese families, four children in all. No racist incidents had been reported since they came to the school.

The method in this instance was to discuss Beth's story (see Appendix to this chapter) with 52 students in P7. The children were told that the story was true, and that the event had happened to someone of their own age who lived not very far away. The girl's actual words were incorporated into the story as far as possible. The discussions were held in groups of four to six, two of the groups being all-boy, and two all-girl. The children's remarks were recorded on a flipchart in summary form so that they could all see that their contributions were being used. (For technical and accommodation reasons it was not practicable to tape-record the discussions.) The technique also helped when it came to identifying patterns of response and analysing the results.

After reading the story to the group the researcher asked for initial reactions to the incident. Without exception, all of the children identified the two girls, Vicky and Alison, as 'bullies' and agreed that their behaviour was 'unfair', 'unfriendly', 'nasty', 'rude', 'cruel', 'terrible' and 'a shame'. Only one group, of five girls and one boy, looked at the researcher in surprise when asked what they thought of the incident, saying, 'It's natural! A lot of people do this.' They went on to explain that name calling and fighting was part of their everyday experience. This response was not typical, as most of the children appeared to be moved by the story. They said that they felt sad for the 'author' and that it was a shame that such a rotten thing had happened to her. Regarding gender, there was no appreciable difference in the children's reception of the story, although the 'author' was clearly a girl. (The groups had no opportunity to discuss with each other their reactions and so it can be claimed that their first responses were uncontaminated.)

The children were then asked why such an unpleasant thing should happen to the girl in the story. The groups had little difficulty in labelling the prime motive as 'jealousy'. It was unanimously agreed that the two bullies were jealous of either the dress the girl was wearing (which was a key issue in the story), or the girl's friendship with Laura. Another motive, mentioned by one group, was that the girls were showing off and had attacked her 'for fun'. This was the way bullies were perceived to behave. The children all agreed that Beth was justified in feeling 'upset and angry' about the incident. They were also quite indignant that she had apologized to Laura for spoiling her party. It was Vicky and Alison who should have apologised. The children felt that Laura could have done something to help her friend, for example, by telling the two bullies to get out, although they acknowledged the possibility that she herself might have become a victim if they decided to retaliate.

At this point the group was shown a photograph of an Asian girl in her ethnic clothes and told that the girl in the story looked much like this. They were asked if they still thought that the bullies were motivated by 'jealousy' of the 'author's' dress or friendship. Without exception, the children changed their theory about the motivation for the attack. The jealousy theory was discarded. 'Oh', they now said, 'it's because she's black!' One group, to clarify this point, asked if all the others at the party were also Asian. When told that they were white, there was no doubt in the group's mind that she was the target for the bullies because of her colour. They suggested that the other guests would 'resent Indian people'. The children clearly indicated that the racial issue set this incident apart as a different kind of bullying. Even the group who considered bullying to be 'natural' among their peers, changed their tune now and said that treating a black person in this way was 'not natural now'.

On analysing the children's responses, it seemed in general that black people were perceived as 'different' and so were bullied. Only one child said that a white girl would have been treated in the same way at the party. It was remarkable how many times the word 'different' occurred during this part of the conversation. Black people had different skin colour, wore different clothes, had a different religion and spoke a different language. More significantly, the children perceived black people as belonging to a different country from themselves. They had not considered the possibility that the Asian girl might have been born in Scotland and speak with a local accent. 'She's different, she doesn't come from Britain.' One girl said that some people might think that 'coloured people are intruding in this country'. The differences mentioned above were clearly not valued by the white children. Instead, they marked out the black children as being of low status and, therefore, potential victims for ill-treatment and bullying.

The children were asked to identify any names that, in their experience, black people were called. The insulting terms most commonly used in this area were: darkie, blackie, nigger, paki and pakistani. One group said that the 'author' would be accused of being dirty, of not washing because she was black. On the other side of the coin, one group was adamant that coloured people did not call white people names, although one boy said, with much mirth, that a black child in the school had once called him 'whitie'. This

boy did not feel at all threatened by this name calling and treated the incident as being rather ridiculous. The message was that black children had no
power. The majority of the children felt that the Asian girl should have
ignored the bullies and walked away from them. On a more optimistic note,
all of the children agreed that the Asian 'author' was still right to feel angry
and upset about what had happened to her – Vicky and Alison were still
bullies who were showing off. There was evidence that some of the children
had started to question the reasons for discrimination and said that real
friends would not care about a difference in skin colour.

It was disappointing that there was such a general acceptance among
white children that black children were of such low status that they were
likely victims for the school bully. The key concept was that children who
were considered to be different from the perceived norm were treated with
suspicion or disregard. What are the implications of these findings for
MCARE in a school which has few minority ethnic children?

- It may be that the problem of racist abuse should be tackled, in part,
  by addressing the wider issue of school bullies. The majority of children
  knew that the incident at the party was wrong but were poorly equipped to
  challenge the bullies and, like the children who attended the real party,
  would probably have done nothing to protect and support the Asian girl.
- Attention ought to be given to the problem of school-based bullying
  generally, especially in the early years. It is, sadly, sometimes only too easy
  to identify the child whose aggressive behaviour to others persists throughout their school career.
- Children need also to be educated to accept and value the differences
  between them, and these factors should permeate the school curriculum.
  It is also important that they should be encouraged to challenge racist
  incidents when they arise and make it clear that this is not socially acceptable. But that is easier to say than to do – we come back to the Region's
  initial concerns about awareness raising and implementation.

Conclusions and issues

Can we evaluate how effective were these action research strategies? There
are a number of ways of addressing that question. The first of these concerns the political context of educational development in Scotland. Action
research is cheap on money, but expensive on time. It follows that teachers
and researchers can choose to explore policy and practice areas that national
government refuses to prioritize. In the Scottish case, there was no prospect
at a national level of large scale funding to address MCARE issues. Regionally,
there was less money than there was commitment. And the local authority
failed to support further MCARE related research, preferring to pursue the

'safer' topic of gender equality. The major investment, therefore, came at the professional level – teachers and researchers had to decide for themselves that it was worth doing.

That takes us to the professional context of the action research initiative. We would explain the difficulty in attracting any secondary teachers to the project, or many primary teachers, partly in terms of the current innovation overload in schools. This kind of action research involvement is based on professionals making an 'extended' rather than a 'restricted' definition of their role (in the old language), or a 'socially critical' rather than 'technical' one (in contemporary language). The pressures of carrying out this kind of research initiative 'after hours' were considerable for the group.

Both these contexts suggest that action research strategies need heavy professional and political investment by the teachers/researchers, and that the current climate in education is generally unfavourable. In particular, it is easy to see how managerial and contractual relationships, enshrined in contact hours, performance indicators, and other forms of hierarchical accountability, may undermine the kind of professional commitment that action research relies on. It is also necessary to consider that the 'no problem here' syndrome was as likely to influence responses to this initiative by professional teachers. All in all, it does seem that action research in the context of Scottish schools is a strategy for the margins, more a tactic of resistance than of 'transformation', a way of giving voice to the policy silences that exist at the national level, and perhaps amplifying the policy whispers at the local level.[1]

But these are considerations of possibility rather than effectiveness. How effective was the action research strategy of the team? Again, it depends on what is meant by 'effective'. One version of 'effectiveness' relates to the validity of the process, and raises questions about the nature of the new knowledge created. It is certainly true that the researchers did not create new knowledge about racial prejudice: these patterns of conflict and discrimination are common in the specialist literature. So clearly we reinvented the wheel. But that misses the point: the purpose of the action research was to generate personal knowledge (to which commitment could be bound) and local knowledge (from which undeniability could be extracted) – we are like that, our kids do these things. Action research of this kind is about generating personal and local knowledge that can be translated into the leverage of power. Or, to put it in a more sophisticated kind of way, it is about the power already inherent in those kinds of new knowledge, in that kind of redefinition of the problem, in that changed recognition of ourselves as professionals. If these are the criteria for judgement, how did we do?

The research findings received national coverage from the newspapers, and the researchers were interviewed on local radio; the account was extensively covered in local papers. As a result, local politicians and education officials were well aware of the research. Six months after the research was completed, the teacher-researchers were certain that they had made an impact on the schools themselves, and on regional inservice provision. One commented that 'promoted staff and teachers who read my findings were shocked that their students had such strong views about black children'. The schools concerned revised policies, debated issues. The power of local knowledge was stressed, and there were some signs that anti-racist issues might now be addressed. It was also clear that those in the Region concerned with MCARE had been supplied with powerful evidence: the issue of turning MCARE policy into practice was more central. And, of course, we hope that dissemination such as this can add to that pressure.

In personal terms, the teacher-researchers felt a greater commitment to MCARE and a deeper awareness of their own prejudices. Over the following year, they tended to back away from their initial decision that they had done enough, and to consider further steps. As one of them said, 'Some of them [my prejudices] at one time I would have considered constituted a sense of national pride ("there's no problem here" syndrome) but that I now consider racist.' All remained involved in MCARE activities and intended to develop further materials, or take part in in-service education.

In conclusion, it might be argued that action research can have a number of impacts: none (ignored); conformative[2] (fails to engage critically in substantive focus); ameliorative (more effective procedures); self-transformative (big impact on professional/personal self-definition of those involved); confrontational (provokes reaction rather than change in the policy context); and transformative (socially critical effects in the context, or elsewhere). It is always difficult to estimate the impact of research on the longer term development of professional practice, but it seems reasonable to claim that there is good evidence of 'ameliorative' and 'self-transformative' change, and that such changes will ripple out through inservice work in the Region for some time – Beth's story may prove to be an enduring bridge between data and development. It is quite likely that some 'confrontation' will result: we have evidence enough that anti-racist strategies will meet resistance. Of course, we would like to make still bolder claims, but £2000, after all, is a small investment in social justice. Far larger investments – in every region of Scotland – will be necessary if we are to begin to uproot the racism in Scottish culture that nourishes the 'no problem here' response.

Appendix: Beth's story – the party

I want to tell you a true story about a girl called Beth. Beth had a friend called Kate. Beth and Kate were in the same class at school. It was Kate's birthday and she asked Beth to her party that night at the community centre. Beth was excited because her mum had made her a beautiful new dress to wear.

That night, Beth was getting ready for the party. She had a bath and washed her hair. When her hair was dry, her mum helped her to plait it. Then, Beth put on her new dress. She was really looking forward to Kate's party.

'You look lovely,' said Beth's mum. 'Now, get your jacket and dad will drive you to the community centre. Have a nice time dear.' 'OK mum. 'Bye', said Beth. When Beth got to the centre, she put her jacket down and walked into the hall. All the other girls were already there. Beth saw Kate and went up to her. 'Happy birthday Kate', said Beth as she gave Kate her present. 'Oh thanks Beth', said Kate.

Kate went to the kitchen to show her mum the present. Beth looked around at the other girls. Suddenly, she heard somebody behind her giggle and say her name. Two girls started to laugh at her.

'Oh look at your horrible hair', said one.

'Look at your horrible dress', said the other.

They both went on making fun of Beth until Beth began to feel very upset. Then the two girls came nearer to Beth and started to kick her. They kicked her again and again until her legs were really sore. Beth ran out of the hall to try to find Kate and her mum but she could not find them in the kitchen. Beth went back into the hall to get a drink of cola. She thought that the two girls would leave her alone but they didn't. They called her names and started kicking her again. Beth started to cry and ran out of the hall. She found her jacket and ran home crying.

When she got home, she told her mum and dad what had happened. They gave her a big hug and tried to make her feel better, but Beth was angry and upset. She had missed most of Kate's party and the other girls had all enjoyed themselves.

Questions

1 What do you think of that story?
2 Why do you think those girls were picking on Beth?
3 Should Beth have felt angry and upset?
4 (Show Photograph 1 of white girl.) Here is a photo of someone who looks like Beth. What names do you think the two girls might have called Beth?
5 (Show Photograph 2 of Asian girl.) If this was Beth, what names do you think the girls might have called her?
6 Was what happened to Beth fair?

Notes

1 For a slightly longer plea for such advocacy, see I. Stronach, 'Helping teacher researchers help themselves', *Observations* 9, SCRE, Edinburgh, Autumn 1996,

p. 6. The teacher researchers involved in this research won the SCRE Practitioner Research Award for 1994.

2 'Conformative' research and evaluation is increasingly common in competitive research situations where the need to please the sponsor can inhibit the critical and independent spirit to which university research in the UK is so heavily committed (rhetorically). For cases of 'conformative' research, see an analysis of SCRE and NFER reports in I. Stronach and B. Morris, 'Polemical notes on Educational Evaluation in the age of "policy hysteria"', *Evaluation and Research in Education* 8(1/2), 1994: 5–19.

9

Researching knowledge of, and communicating about, student progress: a case study of collaborative research

Rob Halsall

In common with a number of other case studies in this book, the main purpose here is not to report the findings of the school based research that was undertaken, though there is some attention to this. Rather, the concern is to present an example of the research process and to discuss some of its outcomes. The chapter aims to show, in particular, how a collaborative approach to research was established in order to:

- make the activity more manageable, given the time constraints there are on different people (an issue consistently identified as problematic for teacher research; e.g. Elliott 1991, Dadds 1996);
- increase the likelihood that a wider group of staff beyond senior managers would develop a sense of ownership of, and commitment to, the research focus.

The context

The school is an 11–16 high school of some 1200 students. It is situated in a moderately affluent urban suburb in Greater Manchester, though a fairly high proportion of the intake is drawn from lower socioeconomic neighbourhoods. Key features of the background to the study are:

- An Ofsted inspection in autumn 1994 which informed the school action plan produced in the following spring term. This drew on the five key issues for action which had been identified by the registered inspector. One of these was to 'extend the process of monitoring and evaluation from their existing sound base'.

- The emergence of a revised and comprehensive whole school policy on the assessment, recording and reporting of achievement.
- The 1995 public examination results which revealed that 46.4 per cent of the students gained five or more A–C GCSE grades, with 93.5 per cent being awarded five A–G grades. The former figure compared with an average of 47.5 per cent for all state schools in the borough, the latter with an average of 89.6 per cent. The Year 11 Information System (YELLIS) value added analysis suggested that these results were broadly as might have been expected, but there was a growing desire within the school – and on the part of many parents who perceived only the 'raw' results – to improve the position.

Getting the research underway

The initial thinking

The idea to engage in a research project arose out of discussions between the head and the member of staff responsible for assessment (who also had a role concerning able students, as captured in the school's policy on the assessment, recording and reporting of achievement). These centred around what to do about students who were thought to be able but underachieving. Their feeling was that the introduction of some new monitoring of student progress activity, perhaps an enhancement of one-to-one reviewing, and research into the practice and impact of this, might lead to valuable insights into the causes of underachievement. The head proposed that, as someone with close links with the school and experience of educational research, I be invited to advise on, and be involved in, such a project. Additionally, because of this link with higher education, and because the school was very active in university–school partnership work in initial teacher training, it was decided to invite the school's central mentor for student teachers to join the group. Indeed, the head envisaged that the student teachers themselves could become involved in the project as a form of training enhancement. Subsequently, the four of us met on two occasions to discuss the idea and to clarify my role.

Clarifying the focus

Our discussions raised a number of points concerning the initial idea:

- Although there was a particular concern for underachieving able students, monitoring student progress was a generic issue; the conduct of any project, or at least any recommendations arising from it, needed to bear this in mind.

- While there was a particular interest in underachievement, it was recognized that there were difficulties in identifying this, as indeed there were in identifying who was able.
- The school already had several means of monitoring progress; rather than add another and research its operation and effects, perhaps it made more sense, at least to begin with, to research the effectiveness of existing practice.
- Gaining knowledge of student progress was important, but so too was the matter of what to do with the knowledge.

The decision finally taken was that the project would be research into the effectiveness of the school's existing practices in monitoring student progress, in identifying underachievement, in identifying able students, and in communicating knowledge about progress to the three groups that would be in a position to address this: students, their parents and the staff.

Setting up the research

The initial idea that was floated in our discussions was that the research would be undertaken by the 'group of four' and volunteer student teachers. The notion of involving this last group had its merits. Apart from the training enhancement possibility, it would help to make the project more manageable – a key issue given our already emerging view that time-consuming interviewing would probably be a central activity. However, although such students *might* have had the maturity to interview parents and teachers, a view emerged that their involvement might not lead those groups to afford to the project the sort of status we wished it to have. It was decided, therefore, not to bring them on board. However, the manageability issue remained. This was then discussed in relation to another issue: the matter of the staff's 'receptivity' to any eventual findings, in the context of the importance of having as wide a body of staff as possible feeling that they had ownership of, and commitment to, the project and its concerns. We decided to explain its purposes at a staff meeting at which we would also invite the teachers to become involved as members of the research team.

The head asked me if I would draft a research design and the data collection instruments. I agreed to this on the understanding that the rest of the team agreed to review these, which – when they were finally assembled – they did. The group comprised the 'original four' and six other teachers. We first met to discuss the draft materials. My new colleagues agreed that the best way forward, initially at least, was to collect data from all three 'knowledge user' groups by way of interviews. However, some people expressed a lack of confidence in pursuing a number of the interview schedule items unless they were turned into more closed questions, so I agreed to rephrase them. Additionally, the staff pointed out gaps and inaccuracies occasioned by my sketchy knowledge of the school's existing practices regarding the research foci. We met once more to go over the revised schedules, to discuss how we would achieve consistency in recording data, and for an input from myself on the 'art' of interviewing. We also agreed on who would be responsible for identifying interviewees and for coordinating the interviewing arrangements.

The research design

What questions did we need to answer?

Clearly, the questions we needed answers to were largely grouped around the four major research foci, though we felt a need to add a fifth broad area. Thus:

(a) How effective were the school's existing practices in monitoring student progress?
(b) How effective were they in identifying underachievement?
(c) How effective were they in identifying able students?
(d) How effective were they in communicating knowledge of student progress to students, parents and relevant staff?
(e) What knowledge did parents have of the school's practices in monitoring student progress?

The emphasis in the student schedule was on (a) and (d) above; in the parent schedule on (d) and (e); and in the teacher schedule on (a)–(d). Now, it is not the purpose of this chapter to present the complete findings and, in line with this, I do not feel it appropriate to present the detailed schedules. However, I do present below the *gist* of most of the questions as this might help readers make more sense of the later section on findings.

The students' questions

- How much do you think your teachers know about your progress, strengths, weaknesses, problems?
- How clear are you yourself about your progress, etc.?
- How helpful are each of (teachers written comments on your work, target setting, progress interviews, etc. – that is the various school practices) in giving you a good idea of how well you are doing? How are each of these helpful or not?
- How much do each of (the various school practices) really encourage you to do better in your work or to keep working hard?

- Do you feel that your work is marked and returned to you quite quickly in most subjects?
- Do you feel that the written comments on your work are full enough for you to understand why you have done well or to understand how you could have done better? When you get marked work back do you take much notice of the the written comments?
- How often do you show your parents your marked work? How often do you discuss with parents the work that has been set for you?

The parents' questions

- How much do you feel you know about your child's progress at school? Do you feel you know enough about his/her strengths . . . and about the areas in which s/he can improve?
- Do you feel there is sufficient reporting and other feedback from the school?
- What things do you find most helpful re being made aware of the child's progress and needs?
- How much do you know about (target setting, records of achievement, form tutor reviews, etc. – that is the various school practices)?
- Do you feel that your child receives sufficient work to do in school/at home? Is it sufficiently challenging?
- Do you feel that you have sufficient access to your child's work to decide how s/he is progressing?

The teachers' questions

- As a subject teacher/form tutor do you feel you know enough about the progress, strengths and weaknesses of individual students in your subject/across subjects?
- Do you feel you have a clear idea of each student's potential so as to be able to make a judgement with regard to possible underachievement?
- What methods do you employ to identify the most able students/underachieving students? Which of these do you think are the most effective? What other methods do you think might be helpful?
- Where underachievement is identified, what action is taken within the subject area, and what is the nature of the ensuing communication – if any – to other staff, to the student and to the parents?
- How do you/your department plan programmes, and generally cater, for more able students?
- Has there been sufficient, useful inservice work in relation to providing for able students, including those who are underachieving? What has been – and what could be – the most useful form of inservice activity?

How to collect the data, and from whom?

I have indicated earlier that the decision was taken to collect the data by means of interviewing students, their parents and their teachers. Coverage of everyone, or at least very large numbers, could have been attempted through the use of questionnaires. However, this would have posed a number of problems, especially given the involvement of students and parents. For example, some might have had difficulty in fully understanding some of the questionnaire items, and interpretations of what items meant could have varied. Additionally, we were mindful of the fact that questionnaire responses tend to be constrained by the format of the questions. We felt that fuller and more meaningful replies would come out of interviews.

However, the decision to utilize face-to-face interviews raised once more the issue of manageability. Consequently, we chose to focus only on Year 8 students together with their parents and teachers and, moreover, on just a small sample of these. This year group was chosen because:

- in comparison with Year 7, these students had become fully settled into the school and were well known to staff;
- more extensive primary school records were available for Year 8 than for older students;
- cognitive ability testing had only just been introduced by the school, starting with Year 8.

As for the sample of students, because of the school's specific interest in raising the achievement level of able students, especially those who were underachieving, it was decided to randomly sample, in equal numbers, from among those deemed to be able achieving and able underachieving. The students were selected by the head of year on the basis of all the information available on the students. In the end, interviews were held with 16 parents or sets of parents, 18 students and 14 teachers. The interviewing was shared equally among the research team, with whoever interviewed a student also interviewing his/her parent(s). All student and teacher interviews were conducted on school premises, in private, while most parents opted to be seen in their homes.

The findings

There is not the space in this chapter to present all the data and, in any case, this is not necessary for its purpose. The focus is on just those findings which revealed a considerable degree of consensus, produced here in summary form. First, there was much in the way of existing good and productive practice that should be a cause for satisfaction within the school. In particular:

- The students generally felt that both teachers and themselves are well aware of their progress, strengths and weaknesses; they particularly valued the role of annual reports, effort grades, subject target setting and teachers' discussions with them, in assisting self-awareness.
- Annual reports, effort and achievement grades and parents' evenings were seen by the students as especially motivating.
- The teachers were confident that, in their subject role, they knew sufficient about student progress, strengths and weaknesses.
- The teachers employed a range of means to identify able students and adopted a range of appropriate actions in teaching them.

There were also findings that were less 'reassuring', though often they corresponded to what many teachers expected. Certainly, they would not be unique to this school. In particular:

- Parents felt that they knew relatively little about their children's progress, strengths and possible areas for improvement.
- Parents were not satisfied that sufficient homework was set, nor that the challenge and stimulation it provided was always adequate.
- Students did not value certain practices as contributing to self-awareness about progress. These were form tutor progress interviews, subject records of achievement and written comments on their work.
- A number of teachers felt that the present functioning of the responsibilities of, and communication flow into and out of, form tutors and head of years could be improved. This was particularly so in relation to:
  - knowledge of progress across subject areas;
  - the ability level or potential of students across the board or in specific subjects;
  - contact with parents.
- While teachers had welcomed the inservice provision hitherto, regarding able students and underachievement, there had not been enough of it, nor had it been sufficiently practical or subject specific.
- The teachers felt that they were more confident in identifying able students than in identifying underachievers.

The aftermath

The 'original four' discussed what should be done with the findings. We agreed that a report should be produced for discussion by the whole staff. I was asked to draft this, for comments and reworking by the rest of the research team. The final report was structured thus:

- *Introduction:* the context of the study, much as in this chapter, together with an explanation of how the research had been undertaken and how the report had been written.
- *Recommendations:* these were prefaced with a summary of the more positive findings, a 'disclaimer' concerning the small sample, a statement that the recommendations were intended to stimulate debate, and a recognition that resource constraints might be too problematic for the implementation of some of the recommendations. Some of the recommendations pointed to the need to 'tighten up' existing practices, while others suggested that consideration be given to new practices or the cessation of existing ones.
- *Methodology.*
- *Findings:* full details of the responses to all items on the three schedules.

The report was then discussed at a meeting of all staff, at which it provoked a lively debate. As we anticipated, some teachers aired strong views in opposition to a number of the recommendations, especially those involving the possibility of new practices and, indeed, they focused only on these. Others were more open to the possibilities, but more important, moved the debate on by extending the focus to other recommendations that were less contentious. Following this meeting, and having digested the positions taken, the head and senior management colleagues came to a view concerning the recommendations that might be further explored and acted on. These were then discussed by the governing body. They were to do with:

- developing more consistent implementation of certain, existing practices, especially form tutor progress reviews, subject records of achievement and the marking of work;
- improving the information that went to parents and redefining relationships with, and responsibilities to, parents;
- refining the monitoring of achievement process, with a particular concern for communications regarding achievement (and underachievement) to all relevant parties;
- including achievement as well as effort in the twice yearly reporting of grades to parents.

All of these subsequently appeared as priorities for the school development plan for 1997–2000. The experience of the research activity itself also prompted the school to include as a priority the planning of opportunities for reflection and evaluation, at the levels of whole school, departments and individual classrooms. Finally, the research and ensuing debate served to raise the school's self-awareness of the uncertainty that existed about being able to identify with confidence underachievement. This has led to recognition of the need for further thought concerning how the school might move forward on this.

Reflections

I feel that the research activity succeeded in its main purpose to more clearly identify what was and what was not working well regarding the school's practices in monitoring achievement, in identifying both able and under-achieving students, and in communicating progress to interested parties. It has had practical outcomes as outlined above, at least in the sense of informing future priorities and ongoing debate, though it is too early to know whether there will be any impact on actual student progress.

We did wonder if we had adopted the most appropriate methodology. In particular, we had some worries about the small samples and the decision to focus the student sample solely on a mix of able achieving and able under-achieving students. On reflection, we do not think that any additional issues would have arisen from a different sampling procedure, nor that the ensuing debate and decisions would have been very much different. Of course, we cannot be sure of this.

Certainly, we were pleased with the decision to go down the research route and to adopt a team approach to the research. It did seem to make an impact on the ensuing debate. For example, many staff did feel that hav-ing 'hard data' rather than hunches meant that the issues we raised should be discussed seriously. Even when the data served simply to help confirm hunches, this too was seen as helpful as it sharpened up the need to take action. A number of teachers also welcomed the fact that the data was coming from a wider group of staff rather than from the 'hierarchy' alone and, because of their involvement in the research, either as interviewers or interviewees, there were some teachers who were more proactive than usual in engaging in the debate.

Very importantly, there was little sense of time misspent. Here, the use of a team, including myself as external critical friend, was seen as crucial because of the relatively little time that had to be devoted to the exercise by any one member of staff. Theoretically, of course, the whole exercise could have been undertaken by myself alone but in practice I would not have been able to find the time to undertake all the interviewing. Moreover, the interview schedules and data analysis would have been that much less informed and, most importantly, the research might well have been per-ceived by the staff as an academic exercise and/or as a piece of top-down management.

Not only were members of the research team more involved than usual in the ensuing debate, but more generally the exercise served to make them aware that, although they initially needed support from myself, they were actually capable of engaging in research activity. Certainly, they appreciated the experiential learning opportunity, in respect of the research skills they had begun to develop, and the insights they had gained about some of the issues to do with undertaking research: for example, to do with sampling, the framing of schedules, gaining access to data providers and constructing a report.

In conclusion, what I believe has begun to emerge among a wider body of staff – and I would not claim more than that – is a growing belief in the potential value of research to a school in its deliberations about its priorities and the actions it needs to take, and in the fact that the staff themselves can fruitfully engage in that research. I do not know whether what we did will help to shift the school culture, or whether it happened *because* of the existing culture. Certainly, as indicated at the beginning of the chapter, there was already a commitment on the part of the school to be a learning organization, and a determination to serve the students even better than had already been the case. Indeed, the public examination results for summer 1996 represent one outcome of this. Whereas 46.4 per cent of students had gained five or more A–C GCSE grades in 1995, the figure for 1996 was 55.6 per cent, with no deterioration in the numbers gaining five or more A–G grades or leaving without at least one grade G. Furthermore, not only had the raw results improved but so too had the value added scores. The obvious point, I suppose, is that the culture of the school had already been impacted on through the ways in which the head and her senior colleagues, with the support of the governors, had worked on the internal conditions of the school. However, the experience of the research study might well reinforce that shift and perhaps take it further. If so, then it will have been a worthwhile, and cost-effective, activity.

10

Using structured play to promote language development in the early years

Rosemary Rodger

This chapter describes and analyses the progress of a school improvement initiative identified by an infant school in an inner city area with a very high proportion of children whose first language is not English. The initiative was supported by the North West Consortium for the Study of Effectiveness in Urban Schools (NWCSEUS, see note at the end of Chapter 1). My role was that of external critical friend and project facilitator, as negotiated with the consortium.

The school was very much in agreement with the aims for teaching English as an additional language (EAL) outlined by the School Curriculum and Assessment Authority (SCAA 1996a) that children should be able to use English confidently and competently, and as a means of learning across the curriculum. The priority for improvement within the school lay in the school's development plan (SDP) and was initially to raise the standards of speaking and listening throughout the school and to find an appropriate baseline assessment to measure the progress made by the children with EAL. There were several reasons for this particular focus: the high number of EAL children in the school; the local authority focus on support for such children; and perhaps most important of all a school-wide concern to raise standards. Discussions were held within the senior management team to consider the ways in which priorities could be identified for the focus on raising standards in speaking, particularly work-related talk, and the range of ways in which this was likely to be most effective within the day-to-day work of the school. Perhaps most important of all were discussions which focused on the ways in which the school could be successful in this venture without appearing to make extra demands of the staff. The staff were kept well informed about these discussions and, in fact, they were the instigators of what was to emerge as the main strategy within the initiative: the videoing of current practices.

Clarifying the focus and my role

The project developed slowly over the first term with three meetings taking place early in the project between the senior management team and myself. The initial meeting led to the production of an action plan. The need to audit current practices within the school regarding speaking and listening was identified as a major task as was the use of an appropriate baseline assessment to establish the extent of the children's language delay. A major problem for the school was the high transient school population. About 50 per cent of the children either leave the school throughout the year or are absent due to their return to Pakistan for long periods of time. Baseline assessment was an on-going process as the children re-entered the school at various points throughout the year. The school piloted the local education authority (LEA) baseline scheme and support was provided by the Section 11 teacher who made extensive use of the Standards of English Language Acquisition Scale (SELA) to monitor the children's developing competence in English. The English coordinator, who was also the reception class teacher, attended an LEA course on the training of people in primary schools to fulfil the role of Section 11 teaching in the future. The school disseminated this training at the beginning of the second term into the project, although aspects of other training had already begun to change practices within the school. This focused on the ways in which classrooms can become talk rich environments through the carefully planned introduction and development of structured play.

Early on, there were issues, certainly in my own mind, about the nature and extent of my role once the improvement initiative was underway. The need for mutual trust and openness in our discussions to ensure the success of the partnership was immediately evident. Was there clarification of our respective roles within the project? How could I, as an outsider, support the initiative? Was the focus for the improvement realistic? Did we all have the same understanding of this initiative? It was fortunate that through earlier work with the school, to do with the training of student teachers, relationships were well established. What eventually transpired was that while the school was the chief instigator of the action plan, subsequent development of this became a focus for my role and it was established that I was not to be seen as an imposer of external change, but more of a facilitator enabling the school to 'adapt external change to internal purpose'. Discussions focused on the manageability of the priorities, the coherence to help achieve successful implementation and the consonance with external evidence in relation to improving oracy within the English curriculum in particular.

The focus on language acquisition for children with EAL in the LEA's Baseline Assessment scheme was not very explicit. However, within the overall scheme there were elements which overlapped with our early ideas about the project. In relation to speaking and listening the profile identified four levels of performance. The speaking and listening criteria were:

C Competence typical at level 1 of the National Curriculum.
E Emerging competence.
D Developing competence.
B Barely competent.
N No observable evidence of competence in this area.

Upon applying these in the nursery it was evident that there was a high proportion of children who were functioning at levels B and N, thus adding to the school's concern that this was indeed an issue which needed to be focused upon. An additional catalyst in clarifying the project's focus and in moving it along was the inaugural conference of the NWCSEUS, attended by the head, deputy head and myself. At different times during the day each of us attended the workshop which was examining value added indicators. It prompted us to ask ourselves a number of questions. Was value added too intangible a concept to include in the early years and Key Stage 1 curriculum? Were there too many other factors to be taken into account in reaching a judgement that x amount of value is added to the learning of young children? Perhaps ambitions to introduce a baseline assessment scheme would not after all lead to the improvements intended. These considerations led to a decision in a subsequent meeting in school not to engage in a value-added project, though this was perceived to be something which could be implemented at a later stage. Discussion moved towards the possibility of focusing on the value of structured play. This was pursued further in following meetings in which it was agreed that the project should have a classroom focus, that teachers needed to talk about and share their teaching practices, and that the focus would be the role of structured play in developing speaking skills. This decision was especially well received by the school's English coordinator who was undertaking training to do with making greater use of the value of structured play. I was also encouraged by it, as previous personal research (Rodger 1995) with young children in a neighbouring LEA, along with other research findings (Meadows 1988) provided strong evidence that high quality talk often occurred in situations where there was no adult present.

The project had now reached the stage where we were able to pose the question: What were the most effective ways of improving the quality of talk throughout the school, especially for the youngest children who already demonstrated a low level of competence in speaking and listening as evidenced by the baseline assessments? Following the final preparation meeting strategies for carrying out the research in the school and for involving staff were decided. They included:

- the provision of experiences/activities which have the potential to improve language acquisition;
- the development of an effective system of monitoring talk through the use of a tracking sheet (see Appendix to this Chapter);
- the identification of a series of sessions in which the children were to be videoed in the structured play areas in four classrooms to cover all four age groups from nursery to year 2. The purpose of the videoing was to record classroom talk in the structured play area for whole staff discussion to provide a basis on which to answer the question above.

Two research methods emerged from discussions within the school: the use of a monitoring sheet to provide data about the location of high quality talk and, in order to counteract the limitations of such an individual approach, a more reflexive approach in the use of videotape to stimulate the production of a dialogically structured text, that is the telling and retelling of the same event from different perspectives (Tobin 1989). Staff in the school were also very keen to use this as a method of finding out where the high quality talk occurs. These *visual ethnographies* were to provide the most useful data in the school's quest for quality talk. The staff compared the technique of videoing with their own assessment by observation strategies as an important and valuable way of getting an accurate picture of the children in their classes.

The 'action'

All classes in the school considered the ways in which structured play contributed to an improvement in communication for EAL children. However, for the purposes of this chapter the focus will be on the nursery and reception class where baseline evidence was showing a low level of competence in speaking and listening. The approach to structured play in the nursery and reception class was very different. In the nursery one of the rooms was designated the structured play room and at specific times in the day children from each of the two classes in the nursery unit were allowed to use this area. Videoing of the structured play took place in the afternoon when the area was set up as a hairdresser's salon. The children were allowed free choice as to whether they played there or not. Consequently, during the video about twelve or more children were recorded struggling to be either the hairdresser or the client. A large number of the children had EAL but interestingly the video highlighted the way in which an English-speaking child, because of her shyness, was excluded from the play until intervention by the class teacher enabled her to participate.

In the reception class the structured play area was developed to provide opportunities to extend the topic 'Light and Dark' by setting it up as a bear's cave. The space to do this in the classroom was very restricted, consequently the cave was very small and had room for only two children at a time. Ingeniously designed walls and flaps over the entrance ensured that there was a high degree of authenticity and privacy for the children. The stimulus for the cave was the story 'Do Little Bears Sleep?', copies of which were displayed inside the cave along with other stories already familiar to the children. Creatures were suspended from the ceiling and cushions on the floor provided a comfortable, concealed environment away from the hustle and bustle of the classroom. Torches of various sizes and colours were available to see the pictures in the books. A clipboard with outlines of 'Mr Blobbie' was readily available to the children. The class teacher routinely targeted pairs of children with EAL to explore and work in the cave. Her intentions went beyond allowing the children to construct their own literacy and play experiences. Her curriculum plans identified the ways in which this environment was planned to support the children's learning. For example, she encouraged the children to share a story, always pairing a more linguistically capable child with a less confident child. If practical, children who spoke the same home language were encouraged to work together with the aim that when the adult-directed learning lost its momentum the children could communicate in their home language in their self-initiated learning.

The videoing in the nursery and the reception classes captured the way in which the emphasis given to structured play within the teacher's planning determined the extent to which the play was supporting the children's language development. In the nursery class there was no explicit reference to structured play in the planning, whereas in the reception class the planning made references to the way in which the children's learning was to be developed in the structured play area. This was an important element within the discussions in the staff meeting at the beginning of the following term. The characteristics which determined the structured play in the classes of older children followed the same pattern as the reception class: the structured play was very much linked to the topic for the half term, although not always included so explicitly in the teacher's planning for speaking and listening. The Section 11 support assistant throughout the school made no use of structured play at this time to support her work with the EAL children.

The use of the monitoring sheet to track the whereabouts of high quality talk in the classroom was unsuccessful as a research method due to its time consuming nature and some misunderstandings by the staff as to its purpose. The monitoring sheet was not discussed with staff prior to implementation, which is a likely explanation for its failure in the classroom. Consequently there is little to discuss in the way of findings as to the whereabouts of the high quality talk.

Reflection

This section focuses on the use made of the videoed material in a staff meeting and the strategies identified by the school to ensure the improvement initiative is sustained. The targeted priority to implement a systematic programme of structured play throughout the school was achieved as a result of the staff meeting. The videos acted as a catalyst in that they provided endorsement for the staff's opinion that it was indeed important to provide children with the opportunity to engage in it, and in that they demonstrated that the children with EAL applied their knowledge of language in more naturalistic settings when given the opportunity to do so. The videos were viewed again by the staff in year groups. The goal to implement a programme of structured play throughout the school was lacking in specific objectives and, according to Joyce *et al.* (1993: 72), needed to become more closely focused on 'specific pupil-learning goals'. The provision for structured play in the nursery was reviewed by all the staff to consider strategies to integrate structured play within the provision overall, in place of the existing system of having it as an additional experience for the children. In the first phase of the project the school worked towards adopting strategies tailored to the goal of improving oracy for EAL children through the introduction of structured play in classrooms available to them on a regular basis. What was lacking at that stage was evidence from the teachers' own experience that this would indeed improve the quality of talk in the classroom overall and thus contribute to improved competence overall in language and literacy development. The discussions held with the staff to disseminate the videos, which by that time were compiled into a sequence of structured play activities in the nursery and reception class, were important in the way in which practices were compared and analysed. Discussion of the range of competences demonstrated by the children gave strong support for the use of structured play. Those which surprised the staff most strongly were that:

- Children, especially when working in pairs, frequently demonstrated higher levels of proficiency in English than expected.
- Smaller numbers of children playing together were more effective in generating high quality talk than larger numbers of children whether it was structured play or not.

The staff discussed the lack of attention given by themselves to structured play both within their planning and in the organization and management of their time on an everyday basis. It was suggested that stronger links to the potential of structured play needed to be made in their short term (weekly) planning. Staff already indicated the way in which they provided for structured play within their long term planning, but did not regularly identify specific learning targets as they did for other activities planned to meet the requirements of the National Curriculum. At that time the school followed the National Curriculum and not the Areas of Learning as identified by SCAA (1996b). The staff were fascinated by the videos and focused on the abilities of specific children and their relationships with each other. A major factor they identified as significant was the increase in the amount and quality of talk where children were paired. The pairing of two children with EAL generated much talk in the home language, as one might expect, but was less successful in developing talk in English without the presence of an adult. There was a high level of talk between pairs of girls, particularly in the reception class, with a good balance between the contributions. Where the teacher provided a stimulus for the children, such as the torches in the bear's cave, the talk was of a higher quality. Too many children had the effect of limiting the talk, as for example in the hairdresser's salon in the nursery where children pushed to be the client or the hairdresser. What was also evident in this extract was the lack of key language in the whole domain of hairdressing. Did this raise the issue of preparation for structured play for children with EAL? The reception class children were familiar with words to describe the cave and were provided with the stimulus of books, writing materials and objects to touch and observe, thus providing many objects to talk about.

Discussion following watching the videos identified the following key areas on which to focus for future improvement within the nursery and reception class:

- limit the number of children in the structured play area;
- identify the role of the adult;
- prepare the children via a story or discussions about the roles in the structured play area;
- ensure all children have access to the structured play area by making it available to children on a rotational basis most of the time;
- include leaning intentions for structured play in short-term planning;
- monitor the development of language acquisition for those children with little or no English.

The relevance of the performance descriptions for language development (speaking and listening) were considered in the staff meeting for children with EAL. These are:

C Children talk about matters of immediate interest. They listen to others and usually respond appropriately. They convey simple meanings to a range of listeners speaking audibly and begin to extend their ideas or accounts by providing some detail.

E Children listen attentively in one to one and group situations, respond appropriately and know some stories, songs and rhymes by heart.

D Children listen attentively and talk about their experiences using sentences.

B Children listen and respond using single words and actions.
N No observable evidence.

The usefulness of this in assessing the children's developing competence in English language would, one is led to believe, tend to focus on the D, B and N categories. In direct instruction which tends to be the nature of the support for children with EAL there is often little opportunity for children to respond to matters of immediate interest. The videos are interesting in the way they reveal children doing just this, such as the exploration of the torches in the Bear's Cave. What is this telling us about the most successful way in which to develop language in EAL children? With support many of the children become bilingual, but this tends not to be the picture emerging in the nursery where children were observed using single words with prompting and actions much of the time. The SELA scale provides additional support for the child relatively new to English. Several children on the video were observed demonstrating good familiarity with English, through the interest in story books in the cave in reception class. Children in the hairdresser's in the nursery were watching, imitating and listening, although whether they were able to understand what the teacher was saying in English is unclear from the video. A child sharing a book with a parent in the book corner was observed repeating English words from an everyday objects picture book. All of this evidence points to the learning characteristics of the children new to English without need to resort to any other baseline system.

Finally, what about staff development? The role of staff in supporting children's talk in the structured play was evident from the video of practices in the reception class. Younger staff members valued the opportunity to see the way in which more experienced colleagues managed this in the context of all the other responsibilities in organizing and managing a class of thirty children. The experience was felt to be less threatening than classroom observation and particularly useful to subsequent discussion as the main focus of the video was the factors contributing to high quality talk. The staff meeting provided an opportunity for team building and team work, and development of a common purpose and a shared language. The most significant feature from an outsider's viewpoint was the sharing of something which at the outset was exclusively within the remit of the head and deputy head and had not formed the basis of staff discussions.

Discussion

The suggestion introduced by me was to keep a tracking record of targeted children to involve the staff in the project. The aim was to feed in the findings to staff meetings and share the similarities and differences in the outcomes identified on the video with teachers' observations in school. This record was implemented hastily, had little involvement of the staff in its inception and was consequently viewed with some distrust by staff who were unclear as to its purpose. As was referred to earlier, the idea of keeping a tracking record was not welcomed and was not part of the evidence base in helping raise staff awareness of speaking and listening opportunities.

Following the staff meeting the implementation stage of the project was assured through the involvement of a wider group of people, developed and sustained commitment, collaboration in implementing action plans and further staff development. The identification of success criteria was not at this stage overtly referred to in the staff meeting. However, following the staff meeting there was a reported increase in staff confidence and a raised awareness of the value of structured play. Monitoring the progress of EAL children was an outcome of the staff discussions. It was decided collaboratively that this could be most effectively carried out in the nursery where targeted children are tracked using the target/child method of observation. This would identify where children talk and what conditions are necessary to ensure the talk is of a high quality, promoting progress. Subsequently, work has developed within the project involving myself, a teacher inexperienced in teaching children under five and the nursery teacher involved in the original project. This focuses on the triggers to the development of English in children with no English on entry to the nursery. The aim, from the school's viewpoint, is to authenticate or otherwise the baseline assessments which are now underway in the nursery, and to assist nursery staff in improving the quality of their teaching to support EAL children and help to raise standards in speaking and listening throughout the school.

Appendix to Chapter 10: Tracking sheet

Issues to consider in tracking children to gather evidence on their use of language in a variety of classroom contexts

• Reassurance to staff that this is not an exercise to check on them.
• How is the information to be used to raise the quality of language use?
• How is this information going to be reported back to staff?
• Who is going to carry out the tracking?
• How many children should be 'tracked' to ensure valid conclusions?
• Should this activity be carried out along with others? e.g. videoing, classroom observation, views of teachers and others involved regularly with the children?

The following questions are a first attempt at identifying the kinds of information to be gathered by tracking:

1 Where do the children talk?
2 What is the effect of teacher instruction on the quality of talk which takes place?
3 What is the effect of teacher involvement on the quality of talk?
4 What effect does the structured play area have on the quality of talk?
5 Who do the children talk to?
6 Which activities appear to create opportunities for talking?
7 What do the children talk about?
8 How does the Section 11 support language development?

Adapted from Hopkins, D. (ed.) (1994) *Schools Make a Difference: Practical Strategies for School Improvement.*

11

Monitoring students' work to raise attainment and investigate the problem of underachievement

Karen Hanks

Schools are about more than just good examination results. If one is part of a successful school, one will sense a vibrancy and liveliness which is apparent in the relationships between the students and staff who work together there. How this atmosphere is created comes, in part, from the quality and vision of the school leadership and those who have been appointed to manage the various sections or departments. It is, therefore, part of my role as head of the faculty of Humanities in an 11–16 high school, to ensure that the best managed procedures are in place and that these provide a strong framework for the teachers in my team to work from, as they endeavour to deliver high quality lessons. The composition of my faculty is unusual with ten staff (all at various stages in their careers) teaching in five different subject areas, not all of which sit naturally side by side. I wanted to use my research as a means of uniting this team and involving them in a process which would not only be a means of providing personal and professional development but would also be of positive benefit to us all and bring about an improvement in our existing practices.

As both a teacher and a manager, two problems had been causing me concern for some time. The first of these was the whole school problem of underachievement and the sense that we were not achieving the results in GCSE public examinations that we could, with the calibre of students we had. Although this matter had been discussed at meetings at all levels, there did not exist at that time any strategies for its resolution, nor were there sufficient hard statistics on which to base or confirm these perceptions. It was not until September 1995 that we could say that we had a broad collection of data describing our new intake as we had a combination of their Key Stage 2 Standard Assessment Task (SAT) results, and the scores from their reading and cognitive ability tests which they sit in their first term.

Secondly, I had been dissatisfied with the way I was carrying out one of my delegated managerial responsibilities, the monitoring of the work of the students and teachers in my faculty subjects. Prior to commencing my research, the system I had used was to examine samples of student work from the classes taught by individuals in my team. I was, however, concerned that I was merely policing policies and procedures – such as the setting and marking of homework – and that this hierarchical 'surveillance' approach did nothing to assess the quality of work produced, nor to raise standards. Furthermore, while this system gave me a broad picture of what was happening across the faculty, unless I fed back my findings in a very thorough manner, I was the only one privy to the information.

The national emphasis on accountability of performance and the raising of student attainment was ample justification of why I should investigate these problems. I was, however, left with the problem of finding the best means to do this. I decided to turn the monitoring of student work into a collaborative exercise in which the faculty team would examine samples of work from classes taught by each other using sets of criteria which we felt manifested quality of learning in our subjects. I intended that this system would enable the team to examine their own teaching styles and share their success with others thus becoming agents of change and improvement. The impact would be on both a personal and professional level. First, the collaborative process would create a climate in which the team were able to ask, and go some way in answering, a series of questions concerning our current practice. Secondly, there would be an examination of the quality of teaching and learning with the purpose of enhancing our understanding of underachievement and raising attainment.

Action research seemed an ideal vehicle as it has the dual purpose of involvement and improvement and offers both a social and curricular approach to the improvement of practice. The social element would come through the fact that the whole faculty team would be involved as a critical community, not only offering me a critique of the way I conducted my research and the final results from it, but also working together as experienced practitioners, sharing strategies and, I hoped, openly admitting to problems and supporting each other through sharing experiences during the course of the inquiry. I was aware that not all teachers would want to admit to problems. This admission can be seen as a challenge to professional competence and both the questioning nature of action research, which probes long-held assumptions and the process of reflecting on and questioning one's aims, can be threatening. One may be quite clear about one's values and intentions as a professional, but when attempts are made to articulate them and prove that one lives out these beliefs in practice, then tensions arise.

I hoped, however, that the value of raising self-awareness and self-esteem through participation in a project which involves listening to others and being listened to, observing and being observed, valuing others and feeling valued oneself, would more than offset these problems. I wanted to create a supportive setting in which morale would be raised and change effected. If a discussion on methodology was central to all our meetings, then the team would develop their own theories on educational practice and find a means of articulating their thoughts and opinions which was above the purely anecdotal. Furthermore, since it is a long-held wisdom that teachers learn 'on the job', I hoped that through the creation of a reflective and self-critical community, the newly and recently qualified staff on the team could draw on, and benefit from, the skills, knowledge and experience of the longer-serving teachers.

It was important that my inquiry methodology matched the context of the school, for schools are social places with many differing and pressing needs and priorities. If one is to embark upon a sustained period of investigation, the methodology must not only be appropriate to the school but the school must have a climate which is conducive to critical, probing investigation. While I am given a great deal of freedom to research my own establishment, I knew that whole school change is slow to take place and that I would have more chance of achieving my aims if I worked within my own faculty. I also had to ensure that there was a high degree of trust and self-esteem among my faculty members before any challenge to accepted values could be broached. Their collaboration was vital for if my inquiry became an exercise in reporting back my findings then it was not action research, merely a form of in-service training. I found, however, that as the research progressed, the faculty team became more interested in evaluating their actions. As staff raised questions about what did or did not work in the classroom, the discussion would often move from the technical level of how to carry out an action to the ethical consideration of why it was appropriate. While the team was using monitoring to control and improve student learning, I was pleased that they were directing the flow of events and that they have improved on a school procedure and adapted it to suit their needs.

Beginning the research

The bulk of the research was carried out at regular faculty meetings and with the students whose work was being monitored. Members of my Year 10 tutor group also completed questionnaires and inventories. I began by introducing my inquiry proposal to my staff at one of our regular meetings. I explained the principles of collaborative monitoring in which we would examine, as a team, examples of student work from each of the subjects in the faculty, using criteria which we had devised to show quality of learning. The staff gave unanimous support for this new procedure, believing it to be a viable means of raising attainment. They felt that it was a fair and equal system which was more dignified than a top-down approach and also wanted to see how other subject areas within the faculty were operating and succeeding.

Developmental stages in the inquiry: our first three faculty meetings

In order to examine whether there was a pattern of underachievement throughout the school I had written to fellow heads of faculty explaining what I was doing with my team and asked them to try the same process at their next meeting. I had two reasons for doing this. First, I needed to validate my findings by comparing our data with that of other faculties and secondly, I wanted to compare our performance with other faculties in the school and find out where they believed themselves to be succeeding. I was motivated in doing this through my reading of Rutter *et al.* (1979) who state that, 'The differences in attainment between children within any one school are much greater than any differences in average attainment between schools' (p. 7).

While the feedback I received was poor in terms of response, the results were interesting. Several faculties presented lists of names which we felt were low achievers, but who were not underachievers. This was confirmed when we checked the Special Educational Needs (SEN) register. When asked to justify their selections, the Heads of Faculty cited poor attendance, poor performance in internal tests and failure to complete or present homework as their criteria. When I presented this information to my faculty team at our second meeting, they became concerned by two factors. First, how little whole school awareness there was of the workings of each faculty, for while one faculty might have highly efficient systems in place, this good practice was not being shared across the school. Secondly, there appeared to be a poor understanding of SEN. Since it is now the responsibility of the classroom teacher to be aware of the students who are on the various levels of the SEN register and provide appropriate work for them, there should be better communication of what these particular needs are and how they can be addressed.

This second meeting continued with a discussion, and drawing up, of a list of criteria which described and defined underachievement. We felt that these needed to be brief but all-encompassing, for deciding that an individual is underachieving is a subjective matter; everyone taking part in the discussion has different perceptions and standards and a large list of subjective opinions does not make for an objective decision. I asked the faculty to offer suggestions and descriptions which reflected personal experience. One expression appeared many times – professional judgement. When asked to describe occasions when they had used their professional judgement, staff mentioned occasions when:

- the student had presented an exceptional piece of work but had never (or rarely) achieved this standard since;
- staff had overheard other colleagues discussing the work of a student and noted that s/he does not perform as well for them in their lessons;
- the student's oral work is often thoughtful, provoking and articulate but written work rarely matches this standard.

A further factor mentioned was that while the teacher may have set expected standards of achievement and the rest of the class are striving to meet these, the underachiever pays only lip service to this and does only what is necessary to meet the minimum requirement. This involves a sense of rejection on the part of the underachiever for the subject, the methodology and perhaps the culture of the school.

I was becoming increasingly aware that the previous monitoring system I had used had not presented a picture of what was happening in our classrooms. Unless I regularly observed my colleagues teaching I was not aware of whether properly differentiated materials were being prepared, whether the pace of the lessons matched the ability of the students, or if the work was sufficiently demanding with high teacher and student expectations. At this early stage in the inquiry process I did not wish to begin a debate on teaching and learning styles as I felt that this would evolve as the group became more confident in describing successful methodology. Yet the concern I felt over linking the process of resolving what we meant by underachievement and the raising of attainment, through addressing the matter of teaching and learning styles, was so important. While most members of the team were willing to examine their teaching and attempt to resolve any perceived weaknesses, some did show reluctance to link the problem to methodology. For them the problem was related to discipline which, in fairness, was an issue of whole school concern at that time.

Prior to our third faculty meeting, the team had time to reflect on the criteria describing underachievement we had drawn up. We decided that these criteria were satisfactory but that in future we would need to combine them with quantitative indicators of performance such as results of internal school tests and cognitive ability test scores. We did, however, re-examine our list of underachieving students and identified a small, manageable target group. The main aim of this third meeting had been the finalization of a set of common, agreed criteria which showed quality of learning in each of the subject areas in the faculty. These would be used at the next meeting as the standards against which we would examine student work. Prior to this meeting I had worked with each head of department in the faculty on the development of two lists, one showing the core skills inherent in their particular subject, the other listing criteria which we believed mani-fested quality there.

Our early attempts at defining the core skills and examples of quality in our subjects were thoughtful and all-encompassing though they did prove to be overly wordy and subject-specific. I do feel, however, that the exercise in drawing up these 'definitions' was invaluable. One of the strongest recom-mendations I can make based on our experience, is that teachers are given the time to examine, in detail, the skills which they believe to be central to their subjects and which they expect their students to learn. This will give teachers a set of standards which they can communicate to students through their teaching, assessment and feedback. We have now revised and simpli-fied these early descriptions and linked them to advice on how to improve work. Two of my departments now display lists of their subject-specific skills in their classrooms and refer to them as part of the reviewing process prior to termly assessments. Also the standard of our marking has improved as we are clearer in our minds as to what constitutes quality of learning in our subjects. Departments now have marking schemes which not only give grade descriptions but also give information on how to improve the quality of their work.

Our fourth meeting: beginning the monitoring process

Already I felt that the team had progressed in four distinct areas:

1 discussing what constitutes underachievement and finding reasons for its existence;
2 examining our methodology and sharing ideas and techniques for suc-cessful teaching;
3 devising definitions of quality of learning in each of our subject areas;
4 forward planning for SEN and for how we would implement a new school initiative: the use of cognitive ability test results and increasingly soph-isticated and detailed analysis of GCSE examination results.

As part of my pre-meeting planning I had prepared a grid listing the names, dates of birth, reading ages and standard scores on entry to school, of each of the target students. These were to be consulted alongside the criteria showing quality of learning as the work from each student was examined in turn. I had several reasons for doing this. First, I wanted to be sure that we had been correct in our assumptions about who was under-achieving. Secondly, I wanted to give the staff the opportunity to have a thorough discussion, with the chance to scrutinize all the examples of work from each student, compare it across the subjects and come to some con-clusion about how to deal with the individual.

As we examined the student's work, no clear pattern of underachievement emerged. For example, we could not state that it was due to low self-esteem as we seemed to have students from both ends of the confidence spectrum. Nor did it link in with my reading about the disparity in achievement between summer and winter born children (Mortimore *et al.* 1988). Three distinct categories did emerge, however, and we decided to call them the 'Coaster', the 'Refuser' and the 'Lazy Student'. We decided to tell the students which category we believed they came under, state why and ask them if they agreed with us. While we did not come up with any startlingly new ideas and indeed only confirmed our suspicions about underachievement, the fact was that we arrived at our conclusions as a group and had used our meeting to discuss the raising of attainment, through both the establishing of efficient school procedures and the sharing of good practice. Also, a list of questions concerning the procedures of both our faculty and the school emerged. Indeed, this became a feature of each meeting as we became absorbed in discussing our research findings. We felt able to prioritize and set about remedying some problems such as making explicit our demand for better quality work by publishing our criteria in our classrooms, and asking for work which did not meet these to be redone.

While the focus on underachievement will become a regular part of the faculty's monitoring system, we intend to be more systematic and objective in our future identification of students and gather a greater bulk of evidence beforehand. Furthermore, our early attempts at collaborative monitoring were marked by slow progress as our criteria were somewhat vague in their wording. The way forward involved a system which was easy to organize but not so simple that it was meaningless. We have adapted four simple but universal criteria devised by Shropshire LEA's RAISE project team (1996) which can be used by all subjects in the faculty:

1 the quality of literacy demonstrated by the student;
2 the amount of work completed on time;
3 the sense of commitment or pleasure suggested by the work;
4 the level of understanding demonstrated by the work. (p. 42)

The system of monitoring we now use is based on a calendar with the focus for each term being on two different year groups depending on key points in the school year. For example, Year 9 will be scrutinized in the first half of term two, prior to choosing GCSE options. The procedure has five clear steps:

1 a list of the names of students that staff believe to be underachieving is drawn up at a faculty meeting;
2 the head of faculty gathers information on these students (e.g. reading ages, SAT scores). The SEN and appropriate year coordinators are consulted about any specific learning or pastoral problem the child may have;
3 the examples of student work are examined at a faculty meeting. Comments on the teachers' findings are written in the students' books and folders;

4 work is returned to the students, who have the opportunity to discuss the feedback with their teachers. Initially, we tried to give both verbal and written feedback but found this time consuming and only of benefit to the minority. Now we ask students to set their own targets for improvement, based on our feedback;
5 following the termly school tests, staff focus on the results of the targeted students. If there is no evidence of improvement, they are referred to the head of faculty.

Asking the students

Up to this stage my inquiry interaction had been with my faculty team. The students, however, were well aware that their work was being scrutinized and knew the reasons for this. Being identified as underachievers provoked a variety of responses from the students and certainly the 'sharper' ones knew they were under the microscope. I had anecdotal evidence from both staff and students that for some, particularly the most able, the mere fact of being singled out for scrutiny was enough to change their work rate and behaviour. I found that the students were more than willing to talk to me about their learning and about reasons for their underachievement. I believed that they had the right to speak and describe their feelings on being identified as underachievers. Also, if I am trying to create a forum for debate within my faculty then I must improve the relationships we have with our students and show them respect by valuing their opinions and offering them the same opportunities. Finally, the students are the ones who know daily what is happening in our classrooms and after more than ten years of compulsory education they are in the best position to assess effective teaching and learning.

They did not, however, like the idea of teachers from other subject areas examining and commenting on their work. One Year 10 student said, 'I don't mind Miss B. showing you my French book because you're head of department and you'll know what she's on about . . . but having a geography or history teacher looking at my French book . . . well, what can they do or say?' This was supported by a Year 11 student who said, 'It's alright for you to show my book to another teacher like Mrs D. (her English teacher) if you're just talking about me in general and saying "isn't . . . (her name) doing well", but for a teacher of a different subject or one who might not even teach me to be looking at my books no . . . no . . . that's not on at all.' Another Year 10 student queried why we were spending our time at meetings doing this kind of activity, stating, 'You go on about how you have all these meetings and how much time they take up but why don't you use that time to talk about us and the work you're giving us and plan your deadlines better?'

When asked to give their opinions on what helps them learn and in which areas they felt they achieved the most, the students put good relations above everything, closely followed by good teaching. Oddly enough, while the quality of relationships was the key to working hard for all the students interviewed, they showed a high degree of tolerance for certain teachers whom they actively disliked but were prepared to work for because these teachers were well organized, gave regular feedback on work, explained teaching and learning aims clearly and appeared to know exactly what they wanted to teach. Confusion arose when describing a good working atmosphere as all students wanted to be 'left to get on with things' but at the same time wanted a lively teacher who 'performed' in class.

My faculty team reacted unsympathetically to these comments. Several members of staff felt that minor matters of indiscipline in class, particularly talking out of turn, interfered with both teaching and the forming of good relationships. Another issue of concern for us was our belief that many students have unrealistic expectations of methodology, expecting it always to be lively and interactive. The perception was that our students cannot cope with the frustration of what they felt was boring, even though staff maintained that sometimes when transmitting certain types of knowledge, the methodology is by its nature boring.

I felt concerned by this conflict of views and by the fact that some of our students seemed unable to 'take the lumps' and get on with work which may not be entertaining but which must be done. This problem was one we failed to resolve or reach agreement on how we would approach it. While some members of the team felt that the students should learn how to accept that not all learning is easy or fun, others decided that as part of their target setting at the start of the lesson they would make explicit the different teaching styles they were going to use and whenever possible explain why they were teaching in a certain way.

The nature of underachievement

It became apparent that the reasons for underachievement were far-reaching and unpredictable. Throughout the inquiry process there was disagreement among staff over which students were underachieving and it was evident that some were performing quite differently in the subjects across our faculty. When the students were asked why this should be so, a small but significant number requested an examination of the advice given at option time, particularly regarding the nature and type of study skills required for different subjects. They felt that if they had been better informed, they would not have made certain choices. The faculty was able to respond to this and has decided that from June 1997, students in Key Stage 3 will follow induction courses prior to beginning their GCSEs. Time will be spent looking at examples of coursework and preparing a piece of work (at GCSE standard) for presentation at the end of term.

Unfortunately, the reasons put forward by boys showed that while they placed as much emphasis as girls did on the quality of their relationships with teachers, they did not feel the same need to receive rewards for their work. They also felt more able to complete work at home in their own time while girls stated that they felt the need for support and encouragement in class. This feeling was most evident among the more able boys in Years 10 and 11 who told me that they were aware of their abilities and did not need extrinsic forms of recognition. Rather they needed to see a purpose and end target to their studies such as a place at a further education college.

Outcomes and recommendations

While my research had been engrossing, I felt that it was time to let the system 'settle in' and spend time with the staff on reviewing, evaluating and improving our process. One unforeseen benefit was that the staff had gained confidence from working together and were not only happy with the system we had devised but wanted to move forward and explore other aspects of learning such as the contrast between the top and bottom ends of achievement. The outcomes of the inquiry proved to have implications for the management of both the faculty and the school. In evaluating my research, the first place I looked for evidence of change was among the target group of students themselves. Most had been pleased at being the focus of attention, even if it was for something negative like underachievement. They proved to be honest about their work rate and open when describing the teaching methods which helped them progress.

The monitoring process we used, however, proved to be more informative for the staff involved than for the students. The benefits for them came through informed feedback following the sessions, especially when the criteria used to examine their work were explained to them. A further step in raising attainment proved to be the development of marking schemes arising from the initial criteria. Through these, the students were given information on the core skills relating to a particular subject, a description of the standard of work required to attain a specific grade and advice on how to improve and progress. This resulted in the students being better informed about their progress, more aware of the school's expectations of their potential achievement and, I believe, more able to prepare in Key Stage 3 for the very different demands of Key Stage 4. Their use also opened up a dialogue on improvement between students and teachers, providing a framework and vocabulary which could be used to talk about learning.

An evaluation of the inquiry and the collaborative approach

Any long-term benefits from this inquiry have yet to be evaluated. While improvement may be relatively easy to achieve in the short term, it needs to be sustained over a period of time for any change to be proved to be effective. I believe that we will succeed as our procedure shows quality and improvement in both the process and the end product. Having a set, agreed procedure means that we are now working as a team with a shared vision of the way forward. Our students have been alerted to the fact that we are not only monitoring and measuring their progress but are guiding them into a means of improving their study skills and enabling them to take on more responsibility for their progress.

Our monitoring approach combined both quantitative indicators of success (e.g. assessment results) with qualitative indicators, such as the results of interviews and observation of student behaviour and work rate in class. Each complements the other but makes it difficult to evaluate whether the improvement shown was due to the good features of the system or to the extra attention given. Certainly, the intensity of focus had proved beneficial but only in the short term. The reasons for this were two-fold. First, the constraints of time meant that staff could not devote too much time to the target group as they still had their other students to consider. Secondly, the target group may have resented any sustained pressure once they had shown improvement of performance.

I presented a report based on my research to my senior management team, two governors and my fellow heads of faculty. I felt it important that I share my findings with them and that we learn from each other. While the latter have their own system in place, they were interested in reading about an alternative system which combined the statistical evidence we gather on our students with valued, professional judgement. All groups were happy to see that the opinions of the students had been valued as this is an important part of our school's ethos and mission. I also asked each individual in the faculty team to describe their feelings and opinions at the end of the inquiry process. The team focused on the improvement in the running of meetings, the interaction, and the sense of purpose and enjoyment which had come from collaboration, rather than realizing the specific aim of identifying underachievement and improving a school system related to raising attainment. From a social angle the inquiry process had been very successful. Through working together, the team developed a sense of unity and purpose and when talking about teaching or related methods of organization would describe doing things 'our faculty way'.

As a manager perhaps I had not fully succeeded in my purpose of emphasizing the importance of an efficient monitoring system in raising performance and leading to improvement. Yet a supportive climate had been created in which staff not only celebrated success through sharing expertise and examples of good practice, but also felt sufficiently confident to discuss problems in an open forum and help each other find solutions. Collaborative monitoring has now become a part of every meeting be it full faculty or individual departments. The team feel confident that they have honed the skills of being able to identify different learning styles and through sharing expertise and knowledge gained 'on the job', can resolve the blockages which prevent progress.

12

Developing literacy

Jill Richford with Tim Whitwell

Upon my appointment as Special Needs Coordinator to Wright Robinson High School, Manchester in April 1995, I was given the specific task by its headteacher, Neville Beischer, to raise standards of literacy within the school. Thus, an action research project entitled 'Improving levels of Literacy amongst Year 7 Students' was embarked upon in July 1995. This was in association with the North West Consortium for the Study of Effectiveness in Urban Schools. The project centred around the Learning Support faculty. As a team, we tried to address our beliefs that:

- self-esteem and reading ability are intrinsically linked;
- children needed greater access to books of their choice and required structured opportunities to fulfil their reading potential;
- poor social and economic backgrounds may deprive children of reading materials and thus they should be given the opportunity to access reading materials;
- an acceptable reading culture among students had to be created using influences that they may relate to.

In our attempts to raise standards of literacy we initially concentrated on the three main features outlined below.

The reading club

In September 1995 Tim Whitwell, Learning Support teacher, advertised and actively marketed a lunchtime reading club to all new Year 7 students. A competition was run for best reading club poster and prizes were given out during assembly in order to publicise the event. The head emphasized the importance of reading during Year 7 assemblies in order to give it credibility and status. Form tutors were asked to encourage children to join the club. The clientele tended to be from Years 7 and 8 but older students, especially those with learning difficulties themselves, were asked to help listen to less able children read. Initially, the reading club was perceived as being only for those with 'reading problems'. There was thus a deliberate move to get away from this reputation. Through advertisements and assemblies we ensured that the message got across that all students were welcome. Some were discreetly encouraged to come, many came because they wanted to. No-one was ever directed!

The students were informally surveyed about why they attended the club on a regular basis. Several reasons were given – to improve reading skills, they enjoyed reading, they wanted to be with friends, they did not like playing outside. Indeed, for some children the club offered peace and quiet and provided a safe environment. With five members of staff actively involved in the club, bullying was never an issue. The atmosphere of the club was essentially less formal than that of the library. One member of staff sat and read his newspaper, other staff often listened to children read. The head made regular visits and remarked on how impressed he was with students' reading. This was valued because we believed that the children should receive praise for attending, and that they should recognize that the school valued the importance of the club.

Initially, we believed that either the staff or the children would get fed up with coming to the club every lunchtime. This, however, was not the case. There was never any 'hassle' from the students. They were there by choice and if anyone behaved inappropriately, they were asked to leave. The club became one of privilege and not of right; students who were asked to leave because of poor behaviour had to earn their place back. The children themselves were in fact quick to complain about any individual spoiling the atmosphere. I believed that the faculty staff would get fed up with each other but this did not happen. If anything, it brought what was a very new faculty team closer together and we even, dare I say it, enjoyed each others' company and that of the children. However, there were certain problems, as outlined below.

Lack of resources

The head donated £200 to purchase books in addition to capitation money used to resource the club. Cost effectiveness of books was, however, a prime consideration when purchasing new materials. With 40–50 children coming to the club every lunchtime there was a high turnover of books. Also, we were unable to purchase non-fiction titles because of their expense. Books were not allowed to be taken home but could be kept aside on request. All books belonging to the faculty are displayed but the thirst for new books has not fully been resolved. More capitation is required to purchase the books children want to read as demand is beginning to outweigh supply. Requests to the head for additional funding are usually granted, reluctantly perhaps, but only because of budget inadequacies. It has been interesting to see what the children enjoy. Certain books, including plays and short stories, are exceptionally popular. There is a wealth of excellent teenage books with low reading ages at present. It has been a pleasure to watch children read real books with enjoyment, especially seeing their surprise when they open attractive titles and realize they can actually access them.

Logistics

The major difficulty we have experienced is with getting the children in at lunchtime. We have had to negotiate closely with the lunchtime organizers to allow students with passes to come to our room. As a lunchtime pass means an early lunch any abuse of the system had to be dealt with firmly.

Senior management

At times we felt that our efforts to run a reading club were being checked upon. With so many students with lunchtime passes (senior management are on permanent lunchtime duty), it appeared that senior management did not believe that they all come to the club. Regular checks were made by some senior teachers which were not always welcome. However, we were soon left alone on the evidence of two classrooms full of children actively engaged in reading.

Advertising the club through assemblies, posters around school and so on has been, and continues to be, an important aspect of the club's success. It was particularly pleasing when a local football manager, in response to a request for his support for the club, donated certificates to those who had improved their reading skills or had helped others with reading. The manager also donated twenty free places to tour his football stadium. Needless to say, membership soared! The time and commitment of staff at every lunchtime is commendable and allows the club to run each and every day. Students want to read; that has been made very clear. Books, however, are expensive but without adequate resources how can one continue to meet demand? Fortunately, we have had financial and moral backing from the head but with budget restraints, sponsorship is perhaps the way forward.

Specific reading groups

In September 1995 all 320 new intake students were screened using the London Reading test. Thirty had a standardized score of below 75 (the national average being 100) and with comparable non-verbal and mathematical scores were considered to have general learning difficulties. There were 128 children who achieved scores which indicated a reading difficulty and were thus targeted for a reading recovery programme (reading for meaning lessons).

The Learning Support faculty made provision for six reading groups to undertake intensive one-hour reading for meaning lessons on a weekly basis for one term, whereupon the children were retested. The groups, with 21–2 students in each, were established according to individual test performance. We informed the parent or guardian about their child's reading score and described the lessons s/he would subsequently receive and the expectations that we had, emphasizing the school–home partnership. The head of Year 7 and form tutors were given the test scores, as were senior management. Students were subsequently withdrawn from lessons with subject teachers being informed. Heads of faculties had been informed of the scheme at a previous consultative curriculum meeting. The reading for meaning lessons covered essential reading skills, including cloze procedures, deduction, prediction, sequencing, comprehension, and so on. Reading for enjoyment was central to our work. All children were expected to read out loud to an adult at least ten minutes a night, five days a week – monitored throughout by the use of a diary signed by the parent or guardian. Merit rewards were given to those completing set targets. Additionally, curriculum spellings relating to maths, English, science and technology were given as part of their homework. Several difficulties were encountered, as follows.

Students missing curriculum lessons

To timetable six withdrawal groups within our own timetable commitments was difficult and not always appreciated. We did not want to withdraw children from lessons they had only once a week, for example music and information technology, as this would deny them their national curriculum entitlement. Thus, we were limited as to when to withdraw them. To counter any criticism arising whenever it was decided to withdraw children, we emphasized the importance of being able to read with understanding in all subject areas. We also emphasized the long-term benefits of raising levels of literacy. Moreover, we promised to rotate the groups every ten weeks. Ultimately, persistent critics were told to speak to the head or our senior management link person. It was essential that the scheme had such backing. Our actions were vindicated upon retesting students in December 1995. With improved test scores, shown to relevant pastoral and curriculum staff, we encountered little further criticism.

Parent/guardian anxiety: my child can read

We received several telephone calls from concerned parents questioning why their child was being placed in a reading group. We were careful to explain the reading course fully and emphasized the importance of being able to read for meaning. By November 1995 at the new intake parents' evening much praise was in fact given to this scheme.

Students did not always want to attend the reading for meaning sessions

We explained that unless children brought a note from their parent or guardian they had no option but to attend the sessions. However, we ensured that the lessons were exceptionally informative and enjoyable. The first class reader we used was especially interesting. We also ensured that the children fully understood what we were wanting to achieve. The importance of raising their self-esteem and telling the children that half of Year 7 were involved in the scheme was essential to its success.

Reading diaries lost

If reading diaries were not handed in, a standard letter with an accompanying diary was sent by post direct to the parent or guardian. Record keeping was, and remains, important and pressure was put on those children not reading at home. Telephone calls home generally remedied particular problems and those students with genuine reasons for not being able to read at home were offered the opportunity to have a member of staff listen to them read at lunchtime. As with any diary, some children forged signatures. They were told regularly that if they cheated then they were only cheating themselves.

Student attitudes

Children not turning up to their lessons were instantly 'tracked down' through the advantageous internal telephone system within the school. They always knew when they had to attend as reminders were placed in registers on the day for which the lesson had been arranged. We found that regular termly testing supplemented by individual reading analysis gave us a wealth of knowledge about the difficulties some students experienced, which we were able to address accordingly. Furthermore, intensive support through well-resourced lessons enabled many children to succeed where they had failed previously. The raised self-esteem once reading scores improved was for some students readily apparent. Certainly, getting the children to want to achieve was imperative to the success of the scheme. Keeping the momentum going and ensuring resources were relevant and interesting was hard at times. However, the reading groups gradually decreased in size due to the scheme's success. By Easter 1996 we only had to run two groups. We decided to have a boys group and a girls group as we felt that, by this stage, different teaching and learning styles were required for students to progress further. The children approved of this and different styles and resources were used with comparable and ultimate success.

Paired reading

The North West Consortium gave us a wider perspective in our attempt to raise standards of literacy. Much research into recovery and extension on reading had already gone into the formation of the Manchester Kick Start Literacy programme. The Consortium was able to discuss with our faculty some of the background research evidence and its relevance to the objectives that we in fact had, and was able to point us in the direction of several opportunities. Thus, my faculty colleague Tim Whitwell was able to undertake training in Kick Start and in Reading PALS (a paired reading scheme). The skills acquired were cascaded through inservice work (INSET) to all faculty members (three other full time teachers and two classroom assistants) as well as to eight very bright Year 9 students. The INSET, which took place during school time, allowed us all to learn, refresh and heighten our awareness of children's reading difficulties. The INSET, in fact, served to help unify a recently formed faculty (five out of six staff all appointed from Easter 1995 onwards) and gave us a common cause and collective strength.

The skills acquired were put into action during registration and lunchtime in the form of paired reading. All those involved in the scheme were given a less able reader to devise a reading programme for. Initially, the paired reading was very successful but towards the end of the summer term 1995 it was difficult to keep the momentum going. Special assemblies, time needed for Records of Achievement activity and other events made it difficult to get those participating in PALS together. However, a sound basis had been set and a paired reading scheme with internal certification has grown into a particular strength of the school. Through experience, trial and error the paired reading scheme has evolved into a highly structured and carefully organized tutorial activity which has the maximum effect in relation to extending students' literacy skills. It has become successful for a variety of reasons. The organization is effective and efficient. Children targeted are those who attend regularly and have shown a commitment to the scheme. Form tutors who are supportive are prioritized, both in terms of providing the listeners and the readers. Furthermore, I have not been allocated a form tutor group, nor am I taken to cover for absent form tutors, so my time can be devoted to running this scheme. Again, the support of the head in keeping me free during registration has been instrumental in its success. On reflection, the prescribed scheme has been adapted to meet the inherent specific needs and nature of the school environment. The paired reading scheme has evolved to respond to the inherent systems, structures and make-up of the school itself.

Outcomes

All of the strategies have had positive outcomes. The success of reading for meaning lessons is perhaps the easiest to measure due to the children being tested termly and scores recorded. In September 1995, 128 were considered to have specific reading difficulties, and another 30 were considered to have more general learning difficulties. By July 1996 only 40 children entered Year 8 with literacy problems. Of those, 14 have specific reading difficulties and 26 are still considered to have more general learning difficulties. In fact, out of the original 128 students, only 12 continue to require support. However, to date, the success of the reading club and paired reading schemes is evident in student attendance only!

Why the success?

The school itself has accepted the work developed within the faculty and support at varying levels, pastoral and curriculum, has been forthcoming if only at times on an individual level. There are several specific reasons and factors, however, that have contributed to the success of this project:

- The head's commitment to raising standards of literacy has been of paramount significance. Indeed, the initial impetus stemmed from Mr Beischer's vision and focus relating to improving levels of achievement. His concerns regarding poor levels of literacy and, indeed numeracy, were also brought to the attention of our primary-secondary school cluster group and ultimately paved the way for a more corporate and collaborative approach in raising standards of literacy which culminated with his conference 'Raising Standards in East Manchester' in January 1996.
- The active support and involvement of the head has been essential. Furthermore, the incorporation of raising literacy standards within the school development plan has been highly relevant. It has provided us with a basis upon which we could argue our case; its prioritization has given us opportunities to capitalize on, and take advantage of, a solid structure upon which to develop.
- Regular visits by Bill Rogers, our North West Consortium consultant have been of crucial importance. He has had the ability to get the faculty to think reflectively about the project, to encourage our efforts and generally inspire us with new ideas. The Consortium action research process certainly enabled us to set manageable objectives. It also helped us to reflect, evaluate and progress further with regard to our objectives.

- We were always able to rely on our consultant's support when problems were apparent and he gave us direction and confidence to extend our perimeters of literacy development. The role of the Consortium cannot be emphasized enough. In particular, the encouragement and practical advice, the generation of ideas and the 'feel good factor' after visits were all important. The Consortium helped us significantly in keeping the momentum going with purposeful direction. It also provided us with an independent overview and fresh perspective. Moreover, the Consortium gave us opportunities to grasp, and often unlocked doors in order to help us extend our development.

- Tim Whitwell, my Learning Support colleague, was throughout the year 1995–6 undertaking a Diploma course with reference to special educational needs and reading difficulties. Information was cascaded to faculty members; he had a knack of inspiring our team with his newly acquired knowledge and specific expertise. Teachers can always learn from such courses. The wealth of knowledge gained from this particular course was put to great use by the faculty. The stimulation resulting from the course is not measurable but I would certainly recommend that other faculty members undertake similar training annually.

- Keeping the momentum going and basically keeping on top of things. We have consistently made our corridor displays specifically reader friendly. We rigorously continue in our efforts to develop a culture among all children that reading is acceptable: for example, posters with footballers advocating the importance of literacy and teenage role models advertising books are constantly advertised. We also highlight reading in assemblies, and generally make every effort to make literacy high profile within the school. Finally, the support of the children and their parents in our efforts to improve levels of literacy have been vital.

The year has been hard work but the faculty has worked well together within a wider, whole school context. We have a platform from which we can extend our work in the knowledge that the school will be supportive. If raising standards of literacy is valued by the school then the project will flourish to the benefit of the children in attendance at Wright Robinson High School and, ultimately, to that of the wider community in this area of East Manchester.

Part 3

Teacher research,
professionalism and
teacher development

13

The case studies discussed

Rob Halsall

It is one thing for research to be undertaken but quite another for it to have an impact. My own sense is that the case studies which form Part 2 of this book generated a wide range of outcomes. I do not intend to identify each and every specific one but, rather, to summarize the most significant, broad types of outcome, albeit with reference to some specific examples.

School level policies, priorities and practices

Various school level policies, priorities and practices have been revised or developed as a result of the raised awareness and debates that came out of the research activity. For example, in Chapter 8 we can note the revision of MCARE policies and the introduction of an anti-bullying policy. The school in Chapter 9 introduced the planning of more opportunities for reflection and evaluation at all levels in the school as a new priority; included achievement as well as effort grades in reports to parents and, more generally, improved the information that went to parents; and, as was also the case for the schools in Chapters 10 and 11, improved the monitoring of achievement system.

Classroom practice

The classroom practice of class teachers and form tutors has changed. For example, the Scottish schools introduced MCARE and bullying as foci within personal and social development lessons. The school in Chapter 9 moved towards more consistent implementation of practice on the part of subject teachers and form tutors, relating to records of achievement, progress reviews and the marking of work. In Hanks's faculty (Chapter 11), teachers now use their lists of subject specific skills and their assessment criteria with the students in order to better inform their work and as part of the progress review process; they make explicit to students the teaching styles they will be using in lessons, and the reasons for their adoption, and subject induction courses have been introduced to help students make a more informed choice of GCSE options. The paired reading scheme at Wright Robinson has been 'institutionalized' as a regular, organized form tutorial activity, and in the infant school new ways of using structured play are being implemented to promote oracy.

Culture

An impact has been made on cultural norms within some of the schools. There do seem to have been differences between the schools as regards the 'cultural conditions' being 'in place' for teacher research to 'take off'. Where these were possibly less firm one can sense the role of the activity in helping to shift the culture. For example, Hanks made a deliberate decision to focus on her own faculty rather than the school at large: 'the school must have a climate conducive to critical, probing investigation ... I knew ... that I would have more chance of achieving my aims if I worked within my own faculty'. And within the faculty, she conducted the research exercise in the way she did in order to foster collaboration among her staff. At Wright Robinson, too, through the action taken, the inservice provision related to this and the research brief itself, a recently formed faculty was given 'a common cause and collective strength'. A similar outcome to this can also be observed in Rodger's chapter where the research promoted 'team building and team work, and development of a common purpose and a shared language'.

Learning

Perhaps most significant of all, the work has helped to develop, or further develop, the schools as learning organizations. It has also pointed to some important research issues. Through identifying different perceptions of problems and issues as they applied in the specific context of their own school, staff learnt more about the nature of these and especially about their complexity. As a result they were often able to produce informed strategies for action which avoided the pursuit of simplistic solutions. Chapters 6 and 7 are particularly compelling in the way they demonstrate that where issues are complex, it is important to see them from different perspectives. It is important to understand the nature of the problem and, here, as Cockett and Brain argue in Chapter 6, reliance 'on one source of evidence ... could lead at best to a great waste of time and at worst to serious damage in the very area one wishes to improve'. What we learn, then, is not to assume that we know what the problem is; often it is only research which will tell us this. The 'rational' model of school improvement – specify a problem, identify a cause, produce a solution – often falls at the first hurdle, and if the problem is not specified accurately the ensuing identification of cause and solutions will take us down cul-de-sacs.

In most of the schools there was at least widespread recognition that there was a problem. This was not the case in the Scottish schools. Here, there were multicultural welcome signs and multicultural curricula content and materials. There were also MCARE policies in place and deputy heads with responsibility for MCARE. All seemed well. It was only through the set of research exercises, especially talking to children, parents and ancillary staff, that 'the problem emerged': not only was it the case that 'the school had not yet touched anti-racist behaviour', but there was denial or lack of awareness of the problem.

In reflecting on their research described in Chapter 8, Donald *et al.* acknowledge that they had not created any new knowledge of racial prejudice. They accept that they had reinvented the wheel, but argue that the work had generated 'personal knowledge (to which commitment could be bound) and local knowledge (from which undeniability could be extracted)'. This takes us back to Cockett and Brain's work in Chapter 6. The fact is that research can rarely provide generalizations. Often, problems are so context specific that the wheel does need to be reinvented; they have to be grounded in the context of the particular school.

The above represents, I think, an impressive set of outcomes and it does not capture everything that came out of the case studies. For example, roles have been reformulated in order to address the issues raised by the research, as in the school in Chapter 7 where the student interviewing strategy initially undertaken by the attendance project coordinator has been integrated into the work of all assistant year heads and many form tutors. Teacher-researchers and other staff involved in the research became more active participants in school debates on the issues (Chapters 9–11 in particular). And in some cases further research ambitions have already been generated; for example, in Hanks's faculty 'the staff . . . were not only happy with the system we had devised but wanted to move forward and explore other aspects of learning'.

Before concluding this section, however, two points do need to be made. First, a key issue identified in Chapter 4 was whether there is, in a school, a willingness to act on research findings. Clearly, much *has* been acted on in the case study schools, but we should note that there were occasions when staff were reluctant to act even if they recognized the problem. As Cockett *et al.* relate in Chapter 7, 'there is still a reluctance to face some of the issues which have emerged', and in the first of the Scottish case studies, although 'Policies were revised, and awareness had risen . . . the school was little different in its response to racist incidents and remained reluctant to try an anti racist approach.' Why is this? A major reason is to do with the culture of the school. It is this which facilitates action to take place but also for it not to take place, or to do so only within certain bounds. Cockett *et al.* point out that:

> Staff ... agree that students should be reintegrated and yet find it difficult to take positive action to achieve this. One reason is that such action arouses cultural sensitivities about the fairness of spending time on the matter and about apparently rewarding rather than punishing deviant behaviour.
>
> (p. 131)

Secondly, there is an issue about whether we can always 'tell' whether what we have done has had an impact. Care needs to be taken in arguing that a particular action taken, including the research activity itself, has generated a particular outcome. As Cockett *et al.* suggest in Chapter 7, 'The figures for the attendance rates ... are not proof of the success or failure of the school's strategies because we cannot be sure that [they] were not produced by some other factors.' Also, as Hanks implies in Chapter 11, it might not have been the particular approach to monitoring achievement that impacted on students: 'I had anecdotal evidence ... that for some ... the mere fact of being singled out for scrutiny was enough to change their work rate and behaviour.'

Contributory factors

In reviewing the case studies, a number of factors can be seen to have contributed to the outcomes explored above. Most of these can be tied back to the questions and issues regarding teacher research and school improvement that were discussed by Carter and Halsall in Chapter 4. Yet others can be seen, in retrospect, to warrant a place in that discussion.

Culture and structure

Was the culture, were the cultural norms, in the schools supportive of teacher research? If so, in what ways? It is not easy to answer these questions but there are clear indications in the research accounts of the existence of supportive cultures.

A belief that teachers can make a difference
In a number of the schools there is a sense that a body of staff really do feel that students can make progress and that teachers can make a difference

– partly as a result of how teacher research can inform their decisions and actions. Thus, Hanks and her staff (Chapter 11) were convinced that 'we were not achieving the results . . . that we could, with the calibre of students we had'. In the chapters on bullying, attendance, language development and literacy, what comes across strongly is the belief that progress on these issues can, indeed should, be made in spite of the counterveiling pressures that were beyond the school's control. Moreover, in the first two of these chapters one sees most clearly the reluctance to adopt strategies which are not based on research into the nature of the issues, on the basis of the fact that not only might these not lead to improvement but could have adverse effects.

A commitment to teacher development

A commitment to teacher development figures strongly across most of the schools. In one sense, of course, a belief in the importance of continuing learning is evidenced by the very fact of the research activity itself! Beyond this, though, there is a strong impression of a realization of the need for even experienced teachers to learn more. For example, Chapters 10 and 11 point to continuing professional development through regular discussions and the sharing of practice and ideas; in the former, about how to improve the quality of children's talk, and in the latter about the meaning of under-achievement and of the quality of learning in subject areas. In Chapter 12, Richford and her colleagues accessed the NWCSEUS for guidance on research evidence to do with reading recovery and extension; Whitwell underwent training through the LEA's Kick Start programme and a paired reading scheme, in addition to being enrolled on an award bearing course; these, in turn, were cascaded to all staff in the faculty. Furthermore, apart from teacher development activity which took place to do with the focus area of the research (and there are other examples of this; the whole staff inservice work on bullying mentioned in Chapter 6, and on able students and underachievement in Chapter 9), there are examples of substantial teacher development activity to do with acquiring research skills and under-standing of research issues.

Openness

The importance of openness and trust as cultural norms can be pointed to in different ways in several of the schools. For example, there was open-ness to external collaborators by way of allowing, indeed welcoming, them to elicit responses from students on some very sensitive topics which were certain to touch on, or raise issues about, individual teachers or groups of staff. Here, Chapters 6, 7 and 11 in particular come to mind. There was openness, too, where teachers sat down with one another to share practice, as in Hanks's and Richford's faculties; where one group of teachers will-ingly provided data about their practice to data gathering colleagues, as in

Chapter 9; and where teachers allowed their classroom practice to be videoed, as in Chapter 10. All of this, of course, reflects on openness on the part of heads, but especially so where teachers and/or external collaborators invest-igated issues that, at the end of the day, were clearly the head's 'provenance'. Here, the interviewing of parents, in Chapter 9, on the ways in which, and the success with which, the school communicated their children's progress to them is especially pertinent.

Senior management's support and whole school priorities

This brings us to the role of senior management support for teacher research. In most of the schools, it was not just the case that their support was forth-coming, but they were actually prime movers. This was closely related to the fact that the areas investigated were to do with their own priorities for school development and about issues to which they had a deep, personal commitment. This is conveyed no more so than in Richford's discussion of her head's determination that literacy levels be raised at Wright Robinson High School. We can also point to the fact that the research described in Chapter 6 was undertaken at the school's specific request; that the school in Chapter 7 put forward a funding bid, played 'the game' by advancing *the* strategy it would pursue in order to solve a problem, but then invested most effort in researching what the problem actually was; and that the heads of the school in Chapters 9 and 10 did not merely view research as a useful way forward but were full and active members of the research teams.

Wider support

Furthermore, it is clear that in some cases middle managers were prime movers behind the research and actively involved in it: Hanks and Richford (Chapters 11 and 12) and a member of staff responsible for assessment (Chapter 9). However, in pointing to the role of managers it is important not to lose sight of the fact that in most cases the priorities, and research activities, were endorsed by a much wider group of staff. Thus, in Chapter 6, the issue of bullying was part of a wider concern about the extent of violent and abusive behaviour which was making many staff anxious, while the focus on underachievement in two of the studies and on language development and literacy in two others reflected a general concern to raise levels of attainment.

Classroom or school level focus?

In Chapter 4 it was suggested that, in keeping with school improvement being about, ultimately, impacting at the classroom level, but also to do with working on school-level internal conditions and the school's capacity for managing change, then teacher research could, and should, focus on both classroom and more 'management-oriented' school-level matters. The majority of the case studies in this book have, in fact, been concerned with the latter. Possibly, this is because of the 'presence' of the heads, but it is also likely that it reflects a shared understanding among staff that certain internal conditions did require attention in the first instance. The debate about classroom or school-level research can be sterile and, ultimately, rather meaningless. The more interesting and possibly more informative matter that arises out of this set of case studies is that, at whatever level the research focused on, there was often a clear impact at, or implications for, another level.

Thus, the classroom level research in case 3 of the set of Scottish studies on MCARE (Chapter 8) led to a realization, not just that racist abuse existed but that it needed to be tackled by addressing the wider school issue of bullying. The work provoked whole school debate on the issues and to revised policies. Indeed, the set of studies as a whole had a region wide impact, for example by way of regional inservice provision. As noted earlier in this chapter, at Wright Robinson, the paired reading scheme has 'evolved into a highly structured and carefully organized tutorial activity' across the school, and in Hanks's school other faculty heads are taking note of the monitoring system introduced by her faculty.

Similarly, the research outcomes of school level studies are having an influence in subject teachers' and form tutors' classrooms. In the school discussed in Chapter 6, staff are moving towards a more shared 'definition' of bullying and, as a result, there are fewer disparities concerning the sorts of behaviour treated as such (and, consequently, less resentment or frustration on the part of students). In the school discussed in Chapter 7 neither the cessation of external funding nor the secondment of the project coordinator prevented project continuance. In fact, as indicated in the preceding section, her work has been undertaken by a wider group of staff. A final example comes from the study described in Chapter 9. Here, the research led to a realization, or confirmation, that certain strategies were being implemented in ways that were leading to very different outcomes in terms of teachers and students being aware of how well they were progressing, and the reasons for this. As a result, attention was focused on reducing the disparities, especially in relation to how form tutors conducted progress reviews, and how subject teachers engaged with records of achievement and the marking of students' work.

Methodology

The case studies point to the particular strengths of the use of qualitative methods, sometimes singly and sometimes in combination with one another, for school-based research – not least when this is for the purposes of school improvement. They have proved to be particularly powerful in 'getting at' people's perceptions in order to further understanding about the *nature* of an issue or problem. This is demonstrated most clearly in Chapters 6–10, and the reason for its importance in school improvement is explained succinctly by Cockett and Brain in Chapter 6: 'it is out of this sort of . . . investigation that appropriate models for action can be developed'.

The strongest message of all that comes out of the case studies, linked to the above, is the importance of talking with the children themselves. In Chapter 7, Cockett *et al.* suggest that 'interviewing students is a starting point open to all schools', and Hanks reminds us in Chapter 11 that 'the students are the ones who know daily what is happening in our classrooms . . . they are in the best position to assess effective teaching and learning'. This message is totally in line with the work of Rudduck *et al.* (1995) who recognize students' capacity for constructive analysis of their school experience and emphasize the contribution this can make to school improvement.

Here, I offer just three examples of the students' role from the case studies. In Chapter 6, Cockett and Brain conclude that 'it is neither the teachers' perceptions nor the abstracted survey definition which gives the clearest guide in identifying bullying . . . but rather the responses of the students themselves'. In the following chapter they argue that 'the simple decision . . . to interview students' is what led to an understanding of the complexities surrounding attendance and, consequently, to the realization that 'simple' strategies could not successfully address the issue. And in Chapter 8 we see that it was largely as a result of discussions with the children that 'the problem [of racism] emerges'.

Collaboration

In Chapter 4, Carter and Halsall suggest several ways in which both internal and external collaboration might contribute to successful teacher research for school improvement. The case studies exemplify some of these.

Internal

Mention has already been made of the way in which the involvement of a group of teachers in a number of the research initiatives appeared to help foster a more collaborative culture within the schools, especially by way of developing a keener sense of shared purpose and commitment. It also seemed to help sustain the research effort itself, through the mutual support that existed, and through the fact that the team effort had the result of sharing the research load. This meant that there were fewer demands, timewise, on any individual and this helped to prevent the occurrence of any demotivating 'sense of time misspent' (Chapter 9). The involvement of several people also generated greater confidence on their part to engage more actively than was usually the case for some of them, in debates about the nature of the problem they were focusing on, and about possible ways forward. This seemed to be very much the situation in the schools discussed in Chapters 9–11.

External
The involvement of external partners clearly helped in spreading the research load, most notably seen in Chapter 9. Here, Halsall drafted the research design, the interview schedules and the final report, as well as taking an equal share of the interviewing load. An even greater contribution was forthcoming for the research described in Chapter 6. Illness to a key member of the school staff meant that the fairly large-scale study which was intended to take place in the wake of the school's inservice work on bullying was only made possible through the participation of the 'outsiders' who had dedicated time available. Indeed, this study can only be viewed as teacher research at all by using a very loose notion of the term; the initiative came from the school and the focus was determined by the school.

Elsewhere, university partners helped schools to clarify their focus or to shift direction, and played a major role in suggesting what research methods might be most appropriate and manageable. Additionally, they sometimes provided training to do with the acquisition of research skills or deepening understanding of research issues. This is most evident in Chapter 9, but it also comes across strongly in Chapter 10. Less evident in the research account, but important to the success of their work, was Stronach's role as mentor to the Central Region's MCARE group. To this can be added the example of an LEA providing access to freely given training to do with the research focus: Wright Robinson's involvement in Manchester's Kick Start and Reading PALS schemes. We can also note that school's support from the NWCSEUS concerning the research literature on literacy, and the benefit reaped by the school in Chapter 10 from its attendance at a NWCSEUS workshop on value added approaches (where it decided, on the basis of this, not to proceed with their initial research idea involving such an approach!). Finally, an important contribution was made by the 'outsiders' in that they were possibly more able at times to elicit more frank and honest responses from this or that person or group. As Cockett and Brain suggest in Chapter 6, it was 'possible that some of this information [on bullying] could only have been gathered by an outsider'.

The support provided by the various external critical friends in the research endeavours described in the case studies did not involve a transference of monies to them from the schools. In one case, the LEA funded the project. In another, the University of Stirling and the Central Region contributed funds. NWCSEUS support for two of the projects came out of its general cash and free consultancy contributions that have been made by, largely, Manchester and Salford LEAs and the Manchester Metropolitan University (MMU) and external support for the work described in Chapter 9 was based solely on free 'consultancy' time.

This account takes us back to a question put by Carter and Halsall in Chapter 4: 'How, though, does a school obtain such support?' In these case studies one can detect the *quid pro quo* motive. For example, one of the reasons why I agreed to be involved in the research of which I have given an account (Chapter 9) was because 'the school was very active in university–school partnership work in initial teacher training'. The same reason applies to Rodger's collaboration with the school in Chapter 10. However, a more common factor, though this can overlap with the *quid pro quo* motive, is that the schools and the 'outsiders' shared a common agenda. Thus, both the Central Region and Stronach himself have a commitment to MCARE issues; the LEAs in the NWCSEUS have their own school improvement agendas (and have adopted action research as one strategy for school improvement); and, as a final example, Brain had been employed by the MMU as a research assistant working in the general area of student disaffection with schooling. It is important, however, not to lose sight of the role of personal contacts and networking in all of this. For example, I have known the head of the school in Chapter 9 for many years and I am also a member of the governing body, while Cockett is a former LEA inspector and TVEI coordinator, and has longstanding relationships with the schools he collaborated with.

Concluding comments

These, then, appear to be the main factors contributing to the successes of the different research initiatives. Is there a danger, though, that they will represent one-off ventures? How can we ensure that teacher research for school improvement will continue? This is the maintenance issue. The argument must be, as it has been throughout this book, that if the culture of the school is 'right' and, in particular, if it is a learning organization within which there is an acknowledgement that teacher research has a key role, then the research orientation *will* be maintained. However, it has to be recognized that time is a real issue even if the culture *is* 'right' (the mind is willing but the flesh is weak!).

I would suggest that of all the possible developments that would support schools that are committed to teacher research for school improvement, the key one is that argued for in Chapter 4, the role of which across the case studies in this book I have acknowledged above. Research partnerships need to be the norm rather than occasional forays. Somehow they need to be 'institutionalized', just as initial teacher training partnerships in the UK have been, though not, necessarily nor hopefully, in the same way. I am not sure how a start could be made on this, and such a discussion lies outside this book's scope. There is much to commend in studying the work taking place in what are presently scattered examples of both internal and external collaborations. It would also make sense to explore further some of the ideas put forward by David Hargreaves regarding the funding of educational research in the UK (1996). In turn, this prompts the suggestion that close scrutiny of the Teacher Training Agency's initiative in promoting school-based education research consortia might have much to offer, though I cannot endorse their predilections for specifying *their* focus areas and for advancing timescales for research activity that can encourage short termism and a search for simple solutions.

Certainly, any moves towards 'institutionalization' of research collaboration involving schools would not make much sense unless they engaged with the sorts of cultural imperatives explored in this book. Nor would they make any sense unless they recognized the importance and value of such matters as teacher autonomy, teacher empowerment and teacher judgement. It is to such notions we now turn in the final chapter by Green.

14

Teacher professionalism, teacher development and school improvement

Jan Green

A major theme of this book has been the need for teachers themselves to contribute to school effectiveness knowledge and school improvement strategies. This has raised a number of issues, for example teacher autonomy, teacher empowerment and teacher judgement. What runs through all of this is the notion of professionalism. This chapter concerns itself with teachers' own sense of professionalism and explores the range of justifications that can be made for professional status for teachers. In the context of government reforms and the fast-changing social environment, emergent professional types are considered in terms of their usefulness in helping teachers improve schooling, and professional development is identified as a major professionalizing influence. Hargreaves and Goodson's (1996) principles of postmodern professionalism are used to identify approaches and forms of professional development likely to foster the sorts of professionalism within teachers that will enable them to take the lead in school improvement.

Teacher professionalism

What teacher professionalism means and whether it should be encouraged is an important and contested question. Hargreaves and Goodson (1996: 1) point out that 'Collectively and individually teachers themselves have often seemed ambivalent about whether their identity is that of professionals or cultural workers.' It is not only this ambiguity among teachers but resistance by government that has hampered any agreed sense of professionalism becoming established. The implied increase in self-regulation and autonomy would pose a threat to continued centralization of control over teachers' work, in which teachers have been cast in the role of technical operatives, implementing a centrally determined curriculum in increasingly pre-determined ways.

Seemingly in contradiction to this are recent moves in some countries to identify and apply 'professional standards' for teachers through such bodies as The National Board of Professional Teaching Standards in the US and the proposed General Teaching Council for England and Wales, while the idea of advanced teaching qualifications for teachers has caught on in areas of Australia and in England and Wales. The contradiction is significantly lessened, however, when it is recognized that the standards policies themselves are mandated by government and passed on for implementation and management, within increasingly limited resources, by teacher bodies who are clearly not self-regulating but largely instrumental in nature.

In Chapter 4, Carter and Halsall have argued that school effectiveness and improvement research can only manifest themselves as useful if controlled by teachers in their own contexts. If autonomy and control are so central to whether teachers can take hold of the research and make it their own in the struggle for school improvement, then the issue of professionalism becomes of prime concern. It is within professional identity, its construction and perpetuation, that much of teachers' capacity to take control of school improvement is rooted. A great deal hangs on whether teachers accept (under pressure) the role of technical operative or whether they fight to hold on to, rediscover and further develop their role as change agents for improvement.

As Carter points out in Chapter 1, the teacher's role has been extended to include a broader range of tasks, mostly managerial and administrative in nature. Hargreaves and Goodson (1996) refer to this shift as 'reprofessionalization'. Alongside this they claim that other aspects of teachers' work are being 'deprofessionalized', in that there is more pragmatic training, reduced discretion over goals and purposes, and an increased dependence on detailed, prescribed learning outcomes. It is when viewed in tandem that the impact is most disempowering. The role extension has resulted in an unprecedented busyness in teachers' lives that does much to preclude them from undertaking the sort of autonomous intellectual work needed to resist deprofessionalization and take the lead in school improvement.

What we need to do is identify models of teacher professionalism that are more readily applicable to school improvement, but first it is worth considering the dangers of professionalism and professionalization. Hargreaves and Goodson (1996) point out that what they call the 'project of professionalization', the self-interested pursuit of status and resources, can be damaging to the provision of service. The sorts of professionalism resulting from such projects can be self-protective, creating a monopoly of service and a dependency amongst those served. So the question presents itself: what should teacher professionalization be like if it is to support, rather than undercut, a professionalism that is about commitment to improving education? To enable teachers to engage as key players in school improvement their sense of professionalism and the process of professionalization must, first, incorporate a clear recognition of the moral nature of teaching. This manifests itself most readily in teachers as a commonly felt duty of care and concern for social justice, along with a sensitivity to the highly contextual nature of learning. This professionalism must also be able to be shaped by, exist within and respond to the condition of postmodernity (as explored in Chapters 1 and 3). Hargreaves and Goodson go on to identify the sorts of new definitions of teacher professionalism that they claim are emerging. They categorize these as flexible, practical, extended, and complex professionalism. In order to relate these to school improvement it is necessary to summarize the key principles and concerns of each.

Emerging definitions of professionalism

'Flexible professionalism' arises through teacher dialogue on the improvement of teaching and learning in local professional communities (teams, departments, schools). It can be a vigorous and positively professionalizing force but can equally restrict itself to more trivial concerns. Such groups can be 'colonized' for managerial and bureaucratic purposes creating a 'false collegiality'. There is also the possibility of the shared interest base resulting in insulation, separation and fragmentation from the wider concerns of the community and society.

'Practical professionalism' arises from teachers reflecting on their own experience and that of others. They exercise judgement over the uncertainties in their work and represent their interpretations of these actions to themselves and others for scrutiny with a view to improvement. The dangers are that teachers' existing assumptions may not necessarily be beneficial; they may in themselves restrict progress and connection with wider concerns. The elevation of teacher experience for its own sake can be taken to extremes resulting in parochialism and the shunning of outside sources of understanding.

'Extended professionalism' recognizes that government reforms have resulted in wider demands being made of teachers. Some argue (Hargreaves 1994) that this has produced increased collaboration, with whole school perspectives being developed around commonly agreed priorities. Others insist that teachers have been effectively confined within their subjects and have been given extra administrative and managerial duties resulting in a great deal of 'busywork' that precludes real engagement with purposes and goals. Control is seen as the province of government with a consequent decline in teacher autonomy, confidence and morale. This model has been described

as 'distended professionalism', indicating the excessive workload and stress involved.

'Complex professionalism' rests on the belief that professionalism should be defined by the complexity of work itself. It can be claimed that school work itself is becoming ever more complex as higher order skills are being introduced in response to the accelerating demands of society on education. Also, some of teachers' extended roles are increasingly complex. However, any sense of increased professionalism is paid for in teachers' health, well being and staying power. It is not difficult to associate this type of professionalism with teacher exploitation.

Each of these emergent models of professionalism has aspects that are potentially empowering and others that may trap or exploit teachers. What is clear in reviewing them is that teacher professionalism must transcend the sorts of subject and technical competence currently being proselytized via organizations such as, in the UK, the Teacher Training Agency (TTA). If a sense of professionalism is to assist teachers in continually improving schooling it must encapsulate the moral and social purposes of teaching, not confine itself to the acquisition of, and identification with, craft or technical skills. 'Professional standards' must be about much more than subject knowledge and technique. They must be created and recreated by teachers in both their immediate and wider social, economic and political context with a clear connection to care for students and the moral purpose of teaching. Anything other is likely to result in either the deprofessionalization of teachers or their reprofessionalization in directions unlikely to lead to sustained school improvement. Hargreaves and Goodson (1996: 20) identify seven principles of postmodern professionalism:

1 increased opportunity and responsibility to exercise *discretionary judgement* over the issues of teaching curriculum and care that affects one's students;
2 opportunities and expectations to engage in the *moral and social purposes* and value of what teachers teach, along with major curriculum and assessment matters in which these purposes are embedded;
3 commitment to working with colleagues in *collaborative cultures* of help and support as a way of using shared expertise to solve the ongoing problems of professional practice, rather than engaging in joint work as a motivational device to implement the external mandates of others;
4 occupational *heteronomy* rather than self-protective *autonomy*, where teachers work authoritatively yet openly and collaboratively with other partners in the wider community;
5 a commitment to active *care* and not just anodyne *service* for students. Professionalism must in this sense acknowledge and embrace the emotional as well as the cognitive dimensions of teaching, and also recognize the skills and dispositions that are essential to committed and effective caring;

6 a self-directed search and struggle for *continuous learning* related to one's own expertise and standards of practice, rather than compliance with the enervating obligations of *endless change* demands by others (often under the guise of continuous learning or improvement);

7 the creation and recognition of high task *complexity*, with levels of status and reward appropriate to that complexity.

It is teachers themselves who are best placed to determine whether educational edicts will further exploit and deprofessionalize or whether they might empower them in leading school improvement. Teacher control of the debate surrounding professionalism and professionalization is crucial to the future of school improvement. It could well be through continuously attempting to define their own professionalism in the turbulent context of education, that teachers will be able to take ownership and lead school improvement work.

MacLure (1992) points out that an important part of the context of education is what she calls 'the teacher's own biographical project . . . the network of personal concerns, values and aspirations against which events are judged and decisions made'. She raises the difficulties teachers have in sustaining meaningful biographical projects in the face of reforms and the resultant alienation. She concludes that a wider range 'of culturally endorsed professional identities' should be available to teachers if their professional development needs are to be met. It is generally accepted that professional development holds within it the intention of the professionalization of teachers. However, because professionalization can result in negative forms of professionalism it is necessary to examine the usefulness of various approaches to professional development. I do this guided by the seven principles of postmodern professionalism which incorporate features more likely to support the sorts of professionalism conducive to sustained school improvement. The professionalizing influences of various approaches to professional development will be examined in the context of the following: purposes of professional development; career-long learning; and forms of professional development activity.

The purposes of professional development

In implementing the National Curriculum and its associated reforms the government have seized control over the purposes and outcomes of education. Teachers have been left to see through the necessary technical implementation and refinement. This radical centralization has been achieved in the name of raising standards and the market principle of choice and diversity. Elliott (1993) points out that there is no longer any choice or diversity of educational vision. The educational 'product' is pre-determined by government. It is for schools to package and market it in a way that provides the semblance of choice to parents. In this way the energy and efforts of teachers and heads are largely diverted into matters of implementation and competition.

Where the prime purpose of professional development is the implementation of central policy for its own sake, then an extended professionalism of the distended type is likely to occur. The danger here is that improvement efforts may be limited by an over-emphasis on the devising and effective implementation of systems concerned with relatively easily measured performance indicators. In simply accepting an external mandate for implementation, teachers and parents become disenfranchised in determining the educational process. Education is, in effect, reduced to a commodity which parents can buy and for which teachers are accountable. As Elliott states, 'The use of the market metaphor in education implies a divorce between power and responsibility. What gets decentralised is not power but responsibility for making the system work and accountability for what goes wrong' (1993: 27). However, where the purposes of professional development transcend issues of implementation, where the moral and social purposes of education and principles of care for students are incorporated, education is not a commodity but a process to be engaged in. This creates opportunities to ask broader and deeper questions about teaching and learning in its context. It provides the opportunity for genuinely collaborative cultures to grow, identify, and tackle the complex questions associated with far reaching school improvement.

In the UK, initial teacher education (ITE) provides a good illustration of the contrast described above. There has been an attempt by government to establish centrally specified standards in this first intensive phase of the professional development of teachers. These

> make little mention of theory . . . require no philosophical insights . . . demand no understanding of how children are motivated . . . attach little importance to the social context in which the school functions . . . attach no significance to historical insight into the present . . . have no place for the ethical formation of those who embark on this, the most important of all moral undertakings.
>
> (Pring 1992: 17)

Pring sees current ITE arrangements as an attack on educational theory and its role in professional development. He traces it back to what has been, at times, the use of theory in isolation from practice which was sometimes of doubtful value. The effects of this were to generate cynicism evident in references to discredited theories and a consequent tendency to over-rely on commonsense craft knowledge. However, the argument that theory is a necessary and vital part of every teacher's professionalism is well put by Carr:

[Teaching] is a consciously performed activity that can only be made intelligible by reference to the quite complex ways of thinking in terms of which teachers understand what they are doing ... And it is this 'way of thinking' that provides the theoretical background against which teachers explain and justify their actions, make decisions and resolve problems. Anybody engaged in teaching then must already possess some 'theory' which guides their practices and makes them intelligible.

(1995: 53)

The usefulness of educational theory and how it might be constructed and used to improve teaching and learning has, in fact, become a central concern in both ITE and continuing professional development (CPD) courses for teachers. Interest in the interaction and integration of theory and practice has persisted and grown. There are, then, clear attempts to resist developing parochial models of professionalism that are likely to isolate and fragment teachers from wider concerns. In particular, and as much of this book shows, wider alliances have been set up in the form of school, LEA and higher education partnerships with their considerable potential for developing greater insights into teaching and learning through new kinds of professional development opportunity.

Career-long learning

A major theme of this book is that the pace of social change requires schools to be learning organizations. The National Commission on Education (1993) underlines the importance of a professional continuum of learning from ITE through newly qualified teacher status (NQT) and on into career-long CPD, and Sammons *et al.* (1995) cite a learning organization as one of their eleven characteristics of effective schools, by which they mean that *all* teachers and managers continue to be learners rather than limiting this to some individuals. Indeed, the TTA have made moves towards the introduction of a career entry profile as a basis for NQT development and beyond. Although the instrumental nature of the pilot was not well received, the idea of a form of profile that offers teachers more influence over their professional development and casts them in the role of self-investors has much to commend it.

The TTA are now attempting to establish national standards for teachers and qualifications for advanced teachers. Indications are that these are likely to follow a performance-based competency model with little place for the development and use of theory. If teachers are not involved in making explicit their theoretical knowledge as it relates to their practice it is unlikely that such standards will support sustained school improvement through professional development. There is an opportunity here for teachers to play a key role in developing professional standards in the context of their practice and the care of students. Indeed, in his annual lecture to the TTA, David Hargreaves (1996) argued that teaching should be a research-based profession. Such a move could provide the sort of self-directing environment where teachers could further develop their discretionary judgement and take responsibility for its outcomes. It is through such involvements that teachers could establish useful and effective professional standards. Elliott (1993) suggests that action research in particular may have a lot to offer in relation to the development of professionalism, though he warns against its possible hijacking by policy makers for the purposes of better implementation of central policy – perhaps a prescient warning in the light of the prescriptive nature of the TTA's initiative of 'teaching as a research-based profession'.

A consistent message in this book is that the success of any such development in schools would benefit greatly from collaborative endeavours. As noted earlier, Hargreaves and Goodson (1996) stress the importance of what they call 'heteronomy', by which they mean open, democratic working with all those involved in education who have a commitment to school improvement. Already evident are examples such as ITE partnerships between schools and universities; the work of Rudduck (1995) and others on involving children in school improvement; school, LEA and university consortia for school improvement and for the design and provision of inservice experience. It is in these open contexts that teachers are more likely to be able to engage with the moral and social purposes of teaching as they relate to the immediate problems of practice.

Forms of professional development activity

At its most powerful, professional development activity can assist teachers to develop practice while evolving their sense of professionalism in keeping with changing contexts. Here, I consider briefly some commonly experienced forms of professional development with a view to the support they offer to the sorts of professionalism consistent with school improvement.

Hopkins *et al.* (1994) identify two main forms of professional development as having dominated for the last thirty years. First, short courses and workshops and secondly, school-based development. The latter shifted the emphasis from optional 'add-on' experiences for individual teachers, to professional development as a professional right and responsibility connected to whole school and individual needs. Many innovations were taken on via these means but they were not necessarily followed through to the point of improvement. Teachers were encouraged to believe in research findings and implement them, rather than use them as a starting point for their own investigations, thus creating a sense of dependency.

These approaches cast schools as rational, predictable organizations where problem solving can be accomplished with a regular 'drip-feed' of well-conceived inservice education for teachers (INSET). In reality there is little evidence of far-reaching change being achieved, especially in terms of class-room effectiveness (Burgess *et al.* 1993). Her Majesty's Inspectors point out:

> neither good management, a good course, or the motivation of its participants is, in isolation, sufficient condition for INSET to have an impact. There is evidence that highly motivated teachers can take back something valuable from an indifferent course just as there are very stimulating courses which leave certain participants quite uninvolved.
> (DES 1991: 14)

This draws clear attention to the tremendous difficulty of providing courses that achieve their aims and the importance of teacher readiness and will-ingness to engage. The problem has been compounded, as suggested in Chapter 2, by a tendency to use staff development to find 'quick fix' solu-tions, driven by the pressure to implement and be accountable for central policy. The identification of problems rather than solutions and longer term learning have been pushed into the back seat.

Further to this, Andy Hargreaves (1994) claims that the fast pace of social change has introduced a great deal of unpredictability into teachers' lives. The frequency and pace of decision making has accelerated resulting in the need for more decision makers. Consequences have been the loss of cer-tainty and a demand for greater flexibility and responsiveness. More tasks have to be done more quickly, teachers experience guilt for not meeting these excessive expectations, and then become more resistant to change as a coping strategy. This sort of intensification combined with the extending of teachers' duties has created stress and 'burn-out'. This perspective in many ways outlines the context that alternative forms of professional develop-ment activity are attempting to emerge within.

These emergent forms of professional development are more clearly rooted in teachers' perceptions of the nature of their work. They offer teachers a greater degree of command over their content, form and use of time. They are underpinned by the sort of paradigm change that involves teachers in developing a sense of personal biography. This is a beginning to helping teachers overcome alienation, lack of confidence and any inertia or unwillingness to question where particular teaching practices come from: to be aware that teaching actions are not 'natural' or 'common sense' and unquestionable, but social constructs susceptible to change. They offer a sort of professional emancipation, a belief that there is still 'a lot to play for'. Professional development needs, then, to offer opportunities for teachers to:

- integrate the development of teaching and learning with their own professional growth;
- digest information and ideas to the point where they are subject to their professional judgement;
- independently prioritize the sorts of activities that occupy their working lives, helping them to balance and ameliorate the damaging effects of role extension and intensification, in favour of activity more likely to result in improvement.

Some forms of development activity already offer teachers the chance to develop useful forms of professionalism. These include participation in teacher networks and associations, mentoring in ITE partnerships and among colleagues within and between institutions, and involvement in teacher research, including participation in extended courses at higher levels and in research consortia. My focus here is on teacher research.

First, long courses such as diploma and masters courses are often built around principles of reflection and the research of one's own practice. They include constructively critical relationships across sectors and institutions, and course providers increasingly offer involvement of participants in course development so that they are tailored to the needs of individuals or groups. Such provision, however, is under threat as the TTA squeezes the funding of CPD provided by universities. Any decline in these award-bearing courses would constitute a serious blow to teacher research, as most teachers who undertake research activity do so as a result of their present, and indeed past, involvement in them.

Secondly, as this book has illustrated, consortia for school effectiveness and improvement are drawing on research and seeking to make sense and use of it in the context of practice. These partnerships are resulting in the redefining of roles. Teachers are taking front-line responsibility for researching and improving practice with university and LEA staff assisting them with their research skills, providing them with information, making connections between colleagues with similar interests, and helping to disseminate their work. Within some of these consortia the potentially powerful approach of teacher research has been identified as the central development process. Teacher development and professionalization occur within systematic attempts at improving aspects of schooling, and within an ethos that teacher research is not done to teachers and managers. Nor is it done instead of, or after, teaching and management, but is an integral part of these activities. It encourages self-directed development among teachers and groups of teachers, through systematically examining practice, one's own and that of others. Ideas are tested out and questioned in the context of wider knowledge and collected information, leading to an increased capacity to make effective professional judgements about future practice in changing contexts.

Such forms of professional activity demand a high degree of involvement and a significant degree of self-direction from teachers. They provide opportunities to exercise professional judgement and develop confidence in relation to work and professional growth. They involve open collaborative cultures where the theory underlying practice can be made explicit and be discussed from various perspectives, making it more likely that broader moral and social concerns will be engaged with. Problem identification and framing has a high profile, creating a greater sense of ownership and control. Research approaches offer teachers fresh ways in which to explore practice and test out the findings of others more reliably. The complexity of teachers' work can be acknowledged and explored within these sorts of frameworks and the powerfully motivating duty of care that teachers feel for students can be accorded due influence in developments. To conclude, it may well be through the pursuit of professionalism through these kinds of professional development activities that teachers will recover their lead in school improvement and establish sustainable ways forward.

References

Ahmad, Y. and Smith, P.K. (1990) Behavioural measures: bullying in schools, *Newsletter of the Association for Child Psychology and Psychiatry*, 12: 26–7.

Ahmad, Y., Whitney, I. and Smith, P.K. (1991) A survey for schools on bully/victim problems, in P.K. Smith and D. Thompson (eds) *Practical Approaches to Bullying*. London: David Fulton.

Barber, M. (1995) From characteristics to strategy, school effectiveness, *Times Educational Supplement*, 6 October.

Barber, M., Hillman, J., Mortimore, P. and Stoll, L. (1995) *Governing Bodies and Effective Schools*. London: Department for Education/Ofsted.

Barnard, C. (1938) *The Functions of the Executive*. Cambridge, Mass.: Harvard University Press.

Barth, R. (1990) *Improving Schools from Within: Teachers, Parents and Principals Can Make a Difference*. San Francisco: Jossey Bass.

Bassey, M. (1995) *Creating Education through Research*. Kirklington: Kirklington Moor Press/British Educational Research Association.

Beare, H., Caldwell, D. and Millikan, R.H. (1989) *Creating an Excellent School – Some New Management Techniques*. London: Routledge.

Berlin. J. (1990) The teacher as researcher: democracy, dialogue and power, in D. Daiker and M. Morenberg (eds) *The Writing Teacher as Researcher*. Portsmouth, New Hamp.: Boynton/Cook Publishers.

Berman, P. and McLaughlin, M. (1976) Implementation of educational innovation, *Educational Forum*, 40: 345–70.

Bernstein, B. (1971) On the classification and framing of knowledge, in M.F.D. Young *Knowledge and Control: New Directions for the Sociology of Education*. London: Collier-Macmillan.

Besag, V. (1989) *Bullies and Victims in Schools*. Milton Keynes: Open University Press.

Black, P., Harrison, G., Hill, A. and Murray, R. (1988) *The Technology Education Project, 1985–1988: Report*. London: Technology Education Project.

Black, P. and Harrison, G. (1985) *In Place of Confusion: Technology and Science in the School Curriculum*. London: Nuffield, Chelsea Curriculum Trust.

Boje, D.M. and Dennehy, R.F. (1993) *Managing in the Post Modern World, America's Revolution Against Exploitation*. Dubuque, Iowa: Kendall/Hunt Publishing.

Brighouse, T. (1994) Magicians of the inner city, *Times Educational Supplement*, 22 April.

Brown, S., Duffield, J. and Riddell, S. (1995) School effectiveness research: the policy makers' tool for school improvement, *The European Educational Research Association Bulletin*, pp. 6–15.

Burgess, R., Connor, J., Galloway, S., Morrison, M. and Newton, M. (1993) *Implementing In-Service Education and Training*. London: Falmer Press.

Burrell, G. (1994) Foreword, in H. Tsoukas *New Thinking In Organizational Behaviour*. Oxford: Butterworth-Heinemann.

Carlen, P., Gleeson, D. and Wardhaugh, J. (1992) *Truancy: The Politics of Compulsory Schooling*. Buckingham: Open University Press.

Carr, W. (1995) *For Education: Towards Critical Educational Inquiry*. Buckingham: Open University Press.

Carr, W. and Kemmis, S. (1991) *Becoming Critical: Education Knowledge and Action Research*. Lewes: Falmer.

Carroll, H.C.M. (1977) *Absenteeism in South Wales: Studies of Pupils, their Homes and their Secondary Schools*. Swansea: Faculty of Education, University College Swansea.

Central Regional Council (1990) *Multicultural and anti-racist education. Guidelines for all educational establishments and services*. Stirling: Central Regional Council.

Chrispeels, J. (1996) Effective schools and home-school-community partnership roles: a framework for parental involvement, *School Effectiveness and School Improvement*, 7(4): 297–323.

Coleman, J.S., Campbell, E.Q., Hobson, C.J. *et al.* (eds) (1996) *Equality of Educational Opportunity (the Coleman Report)*. Washington, DC: Government Printing Office.

Creemers, B. (1994) Effective instruction: an empirical basis for a theory of educational effectiveness, in D. Reynolds, B. Creemers, S. Stringfield, C. Teddlie, E. Schaffer and P. Nesselrodt (eds) *Advances in School Effectiveness Research and Practice*. Oxford: Pergamon.

Dadds, M. (1996) Supporting practitioner research: a challenge. Paper presented to the Supporting Practitioner Research Conference, University of Cambridge Institute of Education in collaboration with San Jose State University, California and University of Sydney, Australia, July.

Day, C., Whitaker, P. and Johnston, D. (1990) *Managing Primary Schools in the 1990s*. London: Paul Chapman.

Dearing, R. (1996) *Review of Qualifications for 16–19 Year Olds*. London: SCAA.

Deming, W.E. (1986) *Out of the Crisis*. Cambridge, Mass.: MIT Centre for Advanced Engineering Study.

Denny, P.J. (1992) *Indicators of Quality Performance*. Hampshire: Inspection and Advisory Service.

DES (1963) *Half Our Future*. A report of the Central Advisory Council for Education (England). London: HMSO.

DES (1989a) *Discipline in Schools*. A report of the Committee of Inquiry chaired by Lord Elton. London: HMSO.

DES (1989b) *Attendance at School: Education Observed*. London: Department of Education and Science.

DES (1991) *Report on the Second Year of LEATAGS*. London: DES.

Donald, P. (1993a) *Friendships in a Primary Class*. Stirling: Central Regional Council/University of Stirling, Department of Education.

Donald, P. (1993b) *Beth's Story – the Party.* Stirling: Central Regional Council/University of Stirling, Department of Education.

Elliott, J. (1991) *Action Research For Educational Change.* Buckingham: Open University Press.

Elliott, J. (1993) Professional development in a land of choice and diversity: the future challenge for action research, in D. Bridges and T. Kelly (eds) *Developing Teachers Professionally.* London: Routledge.

Elliott, J. (1996) School effectiveness research and its critics: alternative visions of schooling, *Cambridge Journal of Education,* 26(2): 199–224.

Elliott, J. and Ebbutt, D. (eds) (1986) *Case Studies in Teaching for Understanding.* Cambridge: Cambridge Institute for Education.

Epstein, J. (1995) School/family/partnerships: caring for the children we share, *Phi Delta Kappan,* 76(a): 701–12.

Epstein, J., Herrick, S. and Coates, L. (1996) Effects of summer home learning packets on student achievement in language arts in the middle grades, *School Effectiveness and School Improvement,* 7(4): 383–410.

Everard, K.B. (1988) *Developing Management in Schools.* Oxford: Basil Blackwell.

Everard, K.B. and Morris, G. (1990) *Effective School Management.* London: Paul Chapman.

Fitz-Gibbon, C. (1996) Monitoring school effectiveness: simplicity and complexity, in J. Gray, D. Reynolds, C. Fitz-Gibbon and D. Jesson (eds) *Merging Traditions: The Future of Research on School Effectiveness and School Improvement.* London: Cassell.

Fletcher, C. (1993) *Appraisal: Routes to Improved Performance.* London: Institute of Personnel Management.

Frisby, C. (1987) The role of the subject co-ordinator, in I. Craig (ed.) *Primary School Management in Action.* Harlow: Longman.

Fullan, M. (1993) *Change Forces: Probing the Depths of Educational Reform.* London: Falmer Press.

Fullan, M. (1995) Change a very moral purpose, school effectiveness, *Times Educational Supplement,* 6 October.

Fullan, M., Bennett, B. and Rolheiser Bennett, C. (1990) Linking classroom and school improvement, *Educational Leadership,* 47(8): 13–19.

Galloway, D. (1976) Size of school, socio-economic hardship, suspension rates and persistent unjustified absence from school, *British Journal of Educational Psychology,* 46: 40–7.

Galloway, D. (1985) *Schools and Persistent Absentees.* London: Pergamon Press.

Gleeson, D. (1994) Wagging, bobbing and bunking off: an alternative view, *Educational Review,* 46(1): 15–19.

Gleick, J. (1987) *Chaos: Making a New Science.* London: Cardinal.

Glover, D. (1995) *Issues in School Effectiveness and School Improvement.* London: Ofsted.

Gosling, S. (1993) *Multicultural and Anti-racist Education: Research into Policy and Practice.* Stirling: Central Regional Council/University of Stirling, Department of Education.

Gray, J., Jesson, D. and Reynolds, D. (1996) The challenges of school improvement: preparing for the long haul, in J. Gray, D. Reynolds, C. Fitz-Gibbon and D. Jesson (eds) *Merging Traditions: The Future of Research on School Effectiveness and School Improvement.* London: Cassell.

Groundwater-Smith, S. (1996) Putting teacher professional judgement to work. Paper presented to the Supporting Practitioner Research Conference, University of Cambridge Institute of Education in collaboration with San Jose State University, California and University of Sydney, Australia, July.

Gurney, M. (1989) *Implementer or Innovator?: a Teacher's Challenge to the Restrictive Paradigm of Traditional Research*, BERA Dialogues No. 1. Clevedon: Multilingual Matters Ltd.

Haggarty, L. and Postlethwaite, K. (1995) Working as consultants on school-based teacher-identified problems, *Educational Action Research*, 3(2): 169–81.

Hamilton, J. (1993a) *Not the Same as Us!* Stirling: Central Regional Council/University of Stirling, Department of Education.

Hamilton, J. (1993b) *Black Children are Fair Game for the School Bullies*. Stirling: Central Regional Council/University of Stirling, Department of Education.

Hargreaves, A.(1994) *Changing Teachers, Changing Times: Teachers' Work and Culture in the Post-modern Age*. London: Cassell.

Hargreaves, A. and Goodson, I. (1996) Teachers' professional lives: aspirations and actualities, in I. Goodson and A. Hargreaves (eds) *Teachers' Professional Lives*. London: Falmer Press.

Hargreaves, D. (1990) Accountability and school improvement in the work of LEA inspectorates: the rhetoric and beyond, *Journal of Education Policy*, 5(3): 230–9.

Hargreaves, D. (1994) The New Professionalism: the synthesis of professional and institutional development, *Teaching and Teacher Education*, 10(4): 423–38.

Hargreaves, D.(1996) Teaching as a research based profession: possibilities and prospects, Annual Lecture for The Teacher Training Agency, April.

Hargreaves, D. and Hopkins, D. (1991) *The Empowered School*. London: Cassell.

Hargreaves, D. and Hopkins, D. (1993) School effectiveness, school improvement and development planning, in M. Preedy (ed.) *Managing the Effective School*. London: Paul Chapman Publishing.

Harradine, J. (1996) *The Role of Research in the Work of the National Schools Network*. Ryde, NSW, Australia: National Schools Network.

Hewton, E. and West, N. (1992) *Appraising Primary Headteachers*. Buckingham: Open University Press.

Hopkins, D. (1989) *Evaluation for School Development*. Milton Keynes: Open University Press.

Hopkins, D. (1993) *A Teacher's Guide to Classroom Research*, 2nd edn. Buckingham: Open University Press.

Hopkins, D. (ed.) (1994) *Schools Make a Difference: Practical Strategies for School Improvement*. London: Resource Base/LWT.

Hopkins, D. (1995) Successful school improvement: what works and why. Inaugural Conference of the North West Consortium for the Study of Effectiveness in Urban Schools, Wigan, July.

Hopkins, D. (1996) Towards a theory for school improvement, in J. Gray, D. Reynolds, C. Fitz-Gibbon and D. Jesson (eds) *Merging Traditions: The Future of Research on School Effectiveness and School Improvement*. London: Cassell.

Hopkins, D., Ainscow, M. and West, M. (1994) *School Improvement in an Era of Change*. London: Cassell.

Hoskin, K. (1990) Foucault under examination: the crypto-educationalist unmasked, in J. Ball (ed.) *Foucault and Education: Disciplines and Knowledge*. London: Routledge.

Hustler, D., Milroy, E. and Cockett, M. (1991) *Learning Environments for the Whole Curriculum: 'It's not like normal lessons'*. London: Unwin Hyman.

Jenks, C. (1972) *Inequality: An Assessment of the Effect of Family and Schooling in America*. New York: Basic Books.

Joyce, B. (1992) Cooperative learning and staff development, *Cooperative Learning and Staff Development*, 12(2): 10–13.

Joyce, B., Wolf, J., and Calhoun, E. (1993) *The Self Renewing School*. Alexandria, Va.: ASCD.

Levine, D.U. and Lezotte, L.W. (1990) *Unusually Effective Schools: A Review and Analysis of Research and Practice*. Madison, Wis.: National Center for Effective Schools Research and Development.

Lopinska, E. (1991) *Report of a national education conference, 'Race equality in education in Scotland' (November)*. Edinburgh: Scottish Council for Research in Education.

Lortie, D. (1975) *School Teacher: A Sociological Study*. Chicago: University of Chicago Press.

Louis, K.S. and Miles, M. (1992) *Improving the Urban High School*. London: Cassell.

MacGilchrist, B., Mortimore, P., Savage, J. and Beresford, C. (1995) *Planning Matters: The Impact of Development Planning in Primary Schools*. London: Paul Chapman.

MacLure, M. (1992) Arguing for yourself: identity as an organising principle in teachers' jobs and lives. Mimeo, Norwich Centre for Applied Research in Education, University of East Anglia.

Maden, M. and Hillman, J. (1996) Lessons in success, in National Commission on Education *Success Against the Odds*. London: Routledge.

May, J.B. (1975) *Growing Up in the City*. Liverpool: Liverpool University Press.

McLaughlin, M. (1990) The Rand change agent study: macro perspectives and micro realities, *Educational Researcher*, 19(9): 11–15.

Meadows, S. (1988) *Helping Children Learn*. London: David Fulton.

Menter, I., Muschamp, Y., Ozga, J., with Nicholls, P., and Pollard, A. (1995) Public collusion, private trouble: the discursive practices of managerialism and their impact on primary teachers. Draft conference paper, ECER, Bath.

Merttens, R. (1996) The IMPACT project: parental involvement in the curriculum, *School Effectiveness and School Improvement*, 7(4): 411–26.

Mintzberg, Y. and Mintzberg, H. (1988) Strategy making as craft, in K. Urabe and J. Child (eds) *Innovation and Management: Its International Comparison*. New York: De Gruyter.

Moore, J. (1988) Guidelines concerning adult learning, *The Journal of Staff Development*, 9(3): 2–5.

Mortimore, P. (1995) Mappers of the best way forward, *Times Educational Supplement*, 6 October.

Mortimore, P., Sammons, P., Stoll, L., Lewis, D. and Ecob, R. (1988) *School Matters: The Junior Years*. Wells: Open Books.

Myers, K. (1996) *School Improvement in Practice: Schools Make a Difference Project*. London: Falmer Press.

National Commission on Education (1993) *Learning to Succeed*. London: Heinemann.

NCC (National Curriculum Council) (1989) *Design and Technology for All Ages*. London: HMSO.

NWCSEUS (North West Consortium for the Study of Effectiveness in Urban Schools) (1995) *Action Based Research Projects – A Handbook For Schools and Research Teams*. Manchester: NWCSEUS.

O'Keefe, D.J. (1994) *Truancy in English Secondary Schools*. London: HMSO.

Ofsted (1993) *Technology*. London: HMSO.

Ofsted (1995) *Guidance on the Inspection of Secondary Schools*. London: HMSO.

Olweus, D. (1989) Prevalence and incidence in the study of anti social behaviour: definitions and measurement, in M. Klein (ed.) *Cross-national Research in Self-reported Crime and Delinquency*. Dordrecht: Kluwer Press.

Olweus, D. (1993) *Bullying at School*. Oxford: Blackwell.

Pack, D.C. (1977) *Truancy and Indiscipline in Schools in Scotland: The Pack Report*, Report of a committee of inquiry appointed by the Secretary of State for Scotland. Edinburgh: HMSO.

Popkewitz, T. (1991) *A Political Sociology of Educational Reform: Power/Knowledge in Teaching, Teacher Education and Research*. New York: Teachers College Press.

Pring, R. (1989). Fifty years on, *British Journal of Educational Studies*, 37(1): 17–29.

Pring, R. (1992) Academic respectability and professional relevance, inaugural lecture delivered before the University of Oxford. Oxford: Clarendon.

Purkey, W. and Novak, J. (1990) *Inviting School Success*. Belmont, USA: Wadsworth.

Raab, C. (1991) Education policy and management: contemporary changes in Britain, paper to International Institute of Administrative Sciences, Copenhagen, July.

Ramsay, P. (1983) Fresh perspectives on school transformation – reproduction debate: a response to Anyon from the Antipodes, *Curriculum Enquiry*, 13.

Reid, K. (1986) Truancy and school absenteeism: the state of the art, *Maladjusted and Therapeutic Education*, 4(7): 4–17.

Reynolds, D. (1992) School effectiveness and school improvement: an updated review of the British literature, in D. Reynolds and P. Cuttance (eds.) *School Effectiveness Research, Policy and Practice*. London: Cassell.

Reynolds, D. (1996) The problem of the ineffective school: some evidence and some speculations, in J. Gray, D. Reynolds, C. Fitz-Gibbon and D. Jesson (eds) *Merging Traditions: The Future of Research on School Effectiveness and School Improvement*. London: Cassell.

Reynolds, D. and Packer, A. (1992) School effectiveness and school improvement in the 1990s, in D. Reynolds and P. Cuttance (eds) *School Effectiveness Research, Policy and Practice*. London: Cassell.

Rodger, R. (ed.) (1995) *An Identification of Factors Contributing to Quality Educare for Children Under Five*. Manchester: the Manchester Metropolitan University Papers in Education, No. 4.

Rogers, G. and Badham, L. (1992) *Evaluation in Schools*. London: Routledge.

Rosenholtz, S.J. (1989) *Teachers' Workplace: The Social Organisation of Schools*. London: Longman.

Rudduck, J. (1985) in Gurney, M. (1989) *Implementer or Innovator: A Teacher's Challenge to the Restrictive Paradigm of Traditional Research*. BERA Dialogues, No. 1. Clevedon: Multilingual Matters Ltd.

Rudduck, J., Chaplain, R. and Wallace, G. (eds) (1995) *School Improvement: What Can Pupils Tell Us?* London: David Fulton Publishers.

Rutter, M., Maughan, B., Mortimore, P. and Ouston, J. (1979) *Fifteen Thousand Hours: Secondary Schools and their Effects on Children*. London: Open Books.

Sachs, J. (1996) Reinventing teacher professionalism through innovative links. Paper presented to the Supporting Practitioner Research Conference, Cambridge University, July.

Sammons, P., Hillman, J. and Mortimore, P. (1995) *Key Characteristics of Effective Schools.* London: Ofsted.

Sammons, P., Thomas, S., Mortimore, P., Owen, C., Pennell, H. and Hillman, J. (1994) *Assessing School Effectiveness.* London: Ofsted.

SCAA (School Curriculum and Assessment Authority) (1995) *Key Stage 3. Design and Technology: The New Requirements.* London: SCAA.

SCAA (School Curriculum and Assessment Authority) (1996a) *Teaching English as an Additional Language: A Framework for Policy.* London: SCAA.

SCAA (1996b) *Desirable Outcomes for Children's Learning.* London: SCAA.

Schaffer, E.C., Nesselrodt, P.S. and Stringfield, S. (1994) The contributions of classroom observations to school effectiveness research, in D. Reynolds, B. Creemers, S. Stringfield, C. Teddlie, E. Schaffer and P. Nesselrodt (eds) *Advances in School Effectiveness Research and Practice.* Oxford: Pergamon.

Scheerens, J. (1992) *Effective Schooling: Research, Theory and Practice.* London: Cassell.

Schroeder, M. (1991) *Fractals, Chaos, Power Laws: Minutes from an Infinite Paradise.* New York: Freeman.

Scottish Education Department (1990) *English Language 5–14, Working Paper No. 2.* Edinburgh: Scottish Education Department.

Shearn, D., Broadbent, J., Laughlin, R. and Willig-Atherton, H. (1993) Headteachers, governors and local management of schools. Paper presented to the British Educational Research Association Annual Conference, Liverpool, September.

Shropshire LEA RAISE Project (1996) Voices to be heard, *Managing Schools Today,* 5(5): 41–5.

Sian, G., Callaghan, M., Glissov, D., Lockhart, R. and Rawson, L. (1993) Who gets bullied? The effects of schools, gender and ethnic group, *Educational Research,* 36(2): 123–33.

Skelton, M. Reeves, G. and Playfoot, D. (1991) *Development Planning for Primary Schools.* Windsor: NFER-Nelson.

Smith, P.K. and Sharp, S. (eds) (1994) *School Bullying: Insights and Perspectives.* London: Routledge.

Stacey, R.D. (1996) *Strategic Management and Organisational Dynamics.* London: Pitman.

Steedman, J. and Fogelman, K. (1980) Secondary schooling: findings from the National Child Development Study, *Concern,* Summer, 5–33.

Stenhouse, L. (1984) Artistry and teaching: the teacher as focus of research and development, in D. Hopkins and M. Wideen (eds) *Alternative Perspectives on School Improvement.* Lewes: Falmer Press.

Stoll, L. (1996) Linking school effectiveness and school improvement: issues and possibilities, in J. Gray, D. Reynolds, C. Fitz-Gibbon and D. Jesson (eds) *Merging Traditions: the Future of Research on School Effectiveness and School Improvement.* London: Cassell.

Stoll, L. and Fink, D. (1996) *Changing Our Schools.* Buckingham: Open University Press.

Stoll, L. and Thomson, M. (1996) Moving together: a partnership approach to improvement, in P. Earley, B. Fidler and J. Ouston (eds) *Improvement Through Inspection?* London: David Fulton.

Stronach, I. (1992) The Howie Report: a glossary and a commentary, or 'Watch out Europe. Here comes the lad o'pairts', *Scottish Educational Review,* 24: 93–104.

Svyantek, D.J. and DeShon, R.P. (1993) Organisational attractors: chaos theory explanation of why cultural change efforts often fail, *Public Administration Quarterly*, Fall: 339–55.

TES (1996) Stigma may force end of special needs label. Report by Nicholas Pyke of a presentation by Professor Ron Davie at the North of England Conference, *Times Educational Supplement*, 5 January.

Tobin, J.J. (1989) Visual anthropology and multivocal ethnography: a dialogical approach to Japanese preschool class size, *Dialectical Anthropology*, 13: 173–87.

Tsoukas, H. (1994) *New Thinking in Organizational Behaviour*. Oxford: Butterworth-Heinemann.

Tyerman, M. (ed.) (1968) *Truancy*. London: University of London Press.

Van Velzen, W., Miles, M., Eckholm, M., Hameyer, U. and Robin, D. (1985) *Making School Improvement Work*. Leuven, Belgium: ACCO.

Webb, R. (1994) *After the Deluge*. London: Association of Teachers and Lecturers.

Weik, K. (1988) Educational organisations as loosely coupled systems, in A. Westoby (ed.) *Culture and Power in Educational Organisations*. Milton Keynes: Open University Press.

Westoby, A. (ed.) (1988) *Culture and Power in Educational Organisations*. Milton Keynes: Open University Press.

Willis, P. (1977) *Learning to Labour: How Working Class Kids Get Working Class Jobs*. Farnborough: Saxon House.

Yoshihara, H. (1988) Dynamic synergy and top management leadership: strategic innovation in Japanese companies, in K. Urabe, J. Child and T. Kagono (eds) *Innovation and Management: International Comparisons*. New York: De Gruyter.

Index

CHANGING OUR SCHOOLS
Linking school effectiveness and school improvement

Louise Stoll and Dean Fink

Many of our schools are good schools – if this were 1965. Processes and structures designed for a time that has passed are no longer appropriate in a rapidly changing society. Throughout the world a great deal of effort and money has been expended in the name of educational change. Much of it has been misdirected and some of it wasteful. This book assists people inside and outside schools to bring about positive change by helping them to define the purposes behind change, the processes needed to achieve change and the results which they should expect. By linking the **why**, **what** and **how** of change, the authors provide both a theoretical critique and practical advice to assist all those committed to changing and improving schools.

Very few books on school reform contain so many ideas and insights while managing to construct a coherent and comprehensive message. Stoll and Fink have written an invaluable resource which is rich both conceptually and practically. This is a book that can be read in part or whole with great profit.

Michael Fullan

Contents
Good schools if this were 1965: the context of change – The Halton Effective Schools Project: a story of change – School effectiveness can inform school improvement – The possibilities and challenges of school improvement – School development planning: a path to change – The power of school culture – Invitational leadership – Changing concepts of teaching and learning – The need for partnerships – Learning for all: building the learning community – Evaluate what you value – Changing our schools: linking school effectiveness and school improvement – References – Index.

240pp   0 336 19290 4 (paperback)   0 335 19291 2 (hardback)